Inside

Microsoft®

Windows NT®

Internet
Development

Ronan Sorensen

PUBLISHED BY
Microsoft Press
A Division of Microsoft Corporation
One Microsoft Way
Redmond, Washington 98052-6399

Library of Congress Cataloging-in-Publication Data
Sorensen, Ronan, 1963-
    Inside Microsoft Windows NT Internet Development / Ronan Sorensen.
       p.   cm.
    Includes index.
    ISBN 1-57231-852-X
    1. Microsoft Windows NT.   2. Operating systems (Computers)
  I. Title.
QA76.76.O63S6546 1998
005.4'469--dc21   98-29431
                                      CIP

Printed and bound in the United States of America.

1 2 3 4 5 6 7 8 9 MLML 3 2 1 0 9 8

Distributed in Canada by ITP Nelson, a division of Thomson Canada Limited.

A CIP catalogue record for this book is available from the British Library.

Microsoft Press books are available through booksellers and distributors worldwide. For further
information about international editions, contact your local Microsoft Corporation office or
contact Microsoft Press International directly at fax (425) 936-7329. Visit our Web site at
mspress.microsoft.com.

Acquisitions Editor: Eric Stroo
Project Editor: Victoria Thulman
Manuscript Editor: Ina Chang
Technical Editor: Jim Fuchs

To my wife, Irene,
and my parents, James and Catherine

CONTENTS

PART II: THE NT SERVER PLATFORM

CHAPTER THREE

CHAPTER SEVEN

Microsoft Message Queuing 249

CHAPTER EIGHT

Microsoft Cluster Server   **249**

PREFACE

Why did I write this book? I have asked myself this question on numerous occasions. While the answers have changed many times, a common theme has permeated them all: something special about the Internet captures the imagination. The Internet is really just a TCP/IP network, not unlike any other. So it's not the technical composition that makes the Internet special; it's the Internet's relationship to society. The Internet is revolutionary in that it transforms the computer from a machine that performs calculations to an exceptionally powerful communications tool.

Over the next 50 years, the Internet will have a profound effect on our world, both good and bad. One could dedicate an entire book to critiquing its potential influence on humanity—a fascinating topic, but not the subject of this book. This book focuses on the challenge the Internet poses to the software development community. The software development process needs to evolve in dramatic ways if it is to realize the potential of the Internet. The first chapter of this book suggests a people-oriented programming paradigm that could move us forward. Unlike the object-oriented programming paradigm, this new paradigm does not focus on the reuse capabilities of a programming language, but rather on leveraging the sophisticated services in the Microsoft Windows NT operating system. The many millions of lines of code in Windows NT exceed any class library that is currently used in object-oriented programming. The ability to reuse the rich services of Windows NT in building Internet systems through COM offers much more potential than the inherent capabilities of languages like C++ or Java.

As Windows NT evolves, many of its services could be provided in other operating systems. However, I feel that Windows NT will likely dominate the operating system infrastructure of the Internet for many years. Therefore, in this book I focus on its specific capabilities for implementing a people-oriented programming paradigm, which will ultimately help us meet the Internet challenge.

Acknowledgments

Writing this book has been a great challenge. I am indebted to my wife, Irene, and my two daughters, Mary and Catherine, for tolerating my physical and mental absence for many weekends and evenings.

I am grateful to all my colleagues at Micro Modeling Associates with whom I have had the privilege of sharing the joys and sorrows of building Windows NT–based Internet systems.

I would also like to thank many people at Microsoft: Dave Reed, Robert Barnes, and Jim Gray, for assisting me in some of the more ambitious Windows NT–based software development projects that I have undertaken; Greg Hope, who first suggested the idea of writing a book on Transaction Server and for putting me in contact with Microsoft Press; Nat Brown, Dale Rogerson, Mary Kirkland, Mark Anders, Henry Sanders, and Keith Moore, who were kind enough to review chapters and offer suggestions for improving the material in this book; the Microsoft Press team of Victoria Thulman, Jim Fuchs, Ina Chang, Barb Runyan, Shanna Brown, Michael Victor, Devon Musgrave, and Teri Kieffer for their fabulous work; and Eric Stroo, acquisitions manager at Microsoft Press, for his continued support and confidence in me.

Contact Information

There will no doubt be some updates required or inaccuracies discovered in this book. The web site *http://Fast.to/NT* will list these additions or corrections as they become available. If you happen to discover any errors or have suggestions for improvements, you can report them at this web site or send me an e-mail at v-ronans@microsoft.com.

PART I

THE PEOPLE-ORIENTED PROGRAMMING PARADIGM

CHAPTER ONE

The Internet Challenge

What is the purpose of software? The answer to this general question is somewhat elusive: software is an artificial entity that has no end in itself. Purely a tool for human objectives, software is oriented toward what people choose for it, and thus its purpose changes as society changes. Perhaps, then, the more cogent and compelling question to ask is "What will the purpose of software be in the future?" The answer shapes our Internet challenge.

The Internet Revolution

The term "revolution" implies a quick, radical, and pervasive change in the process of doing things, and today we are in the midst of one—the "Internet revolution"—an era of widespread social and economic changes resulting from radically new modes of communication and a burgeoning global community. The seeds for this revolution were sown with the widespread use of personal computers, particularly as vehicles for communication. But this era is most appropriately called the Internet revolution (rather than the "Computer revolution") because the Internet has the potential to profoundly affect every aspect of society.

We can understand better why the Internet is revolutionary by reflecting on our human nature. People are social beings. Computers have long enhanced our ability to compute or to calculate, but the Internet is touching the much more profound human quality of social interaction. We have already witnessed the tremendous impact of other communication mechanisms, such as the printing press, radio, and television. The Internet has the potential to be more powerful than any of these, as it can easily have global reach, have a greater abundance of content, and can also be less expensive. Even more important, the Internet introduces a new radical element to mass communication—personal interaction.

For the first time in the history of civilization, we have a mass communication mechanism that allows many people to interact rather than just be passive recipients of information. Television, radio, and newspapers do not allow for broad, active participation; consequently, they tend to serve as gatekeepers for the flow of information about many things that affect people's lives, including politics, religion, the economy, and culture. The Internet offers much greater freedom of expression, allowing any person to participate in many dynamic and active ways. It fosters a wider exchange of ideas, stimulating people's creative capacity for the operation of our society.

The purpose of the Internet is seldom technological in nature. Consider how it will affect the following areas by dramatically increasing the exchange of information:

- *Education* Whether a student is studying medicine, law, theology, or any other academic discipline, the Internet is a mine of information that can assist with in-depth learning opportunities.

- *Advertising* More than other mediums, the Internet gives businesses an opportunity to present a full picture of their products and services. Consumers can more easily attain the information they need to make informed decisions.

- *Law* Through email and group meeting technology, the Internet greatly facilitates the collaboration required in the drafting of legal contracts.

- *Physical sciences* Astronomers, geologists, meteorologists, oceanographers, and physicists are in fields where new information is constantly being discovered. The Internet can create global communities for these people, enabling them to exchange their discoveries more immediately.

- *Finances* The Internet will standardize electronic commerce, making it easy to perform financial transactions with individuals or institutions all over the world. Much of this activity will consist of business-to-business transactions, but the Internet will also have a huge impact on retailing.

- *Tourism and hospitality*   Making reservations for flights and car rentals will be easily accomplished on line. Tourists can use the Internet to quickly research upcoming local events and explore places to wine and dine at their vacation spots.

- *Entertainment*   The entertainment industry is already taking advantage of the Internet, with most major television networks supporting an Internet site. People can now get current information about a news story when they want it, without having to wait for a network broadcast.

- *Politics*   The principle of freedom of speech is greatly safeguarded through the Internet, particularly in countries where other communication media are highly regulated.

The Internet is in its infancy today, but over the next fifty years it will evolve into a much more powerful broadband global network that will have significant effects on the way society is organized politically, socially, economically, and culturally. It is not the purpose of this book to critique these changes; such a critique is a complex topic that will no doubt be the subject of many other books. Rather, this book addresses what is required of the software developer to meet the challenges of this Internet era.

People-Oriented Programming

The Internet revolution represents a dramatic shift in the way society conducts itself, and so it necessarily represents a dramatic shift in the purpose of software—a paradigm shift from technologies focused on individual computing tasks to technologies focused on social interaction, cultural expression, and information exchange. Essentially, software designed for the Internet will be responsible for building a global community. It will focus on improving the ordinary circumstances of living, enabling people to more effectively accomplish day-to-day activities. Thus, you could aptly call this new paradigm *people-oriented programming*. A natural development from the concepts of structured programming, object-oriented programming, and distributed computing, people-oriented programming technologies offer software developers an opportunity to focus on meeting basic human needs, transforming a computing device into a spectacular interactive medium.

Toward People-Oriented Technologies: Paradigm Shifts in Software Development

Briefly reviewing the significant paradigm shifts in software development provides some context for understanding the technologies available now for creating powerful Internet solutions, solutions that will help us meet the Internet challenge.

The First Paradigm Shift: Structured Programming

Before the 1950s, programming languages were largely dependent on the hardware. It was not until the mid 1950s that a third generation of languages were introduced, moving us away from binary languages to structured programming languages. Called "high-level," these languages, such as FORTRAN, COBOL, BASIC, and C, were designed to solve particular types of problems in a way that was largely independent of the hardware. They facilitated the first paradigm shift in software development, the shift to structured programming.

Modularity

In a way, structured programming is to computers what language is to humankind. When you communicate with a child who has not yet learned how to comprehend words, you need to attach an action to a word each time you want the child to behave in a certain way. Eventually, the child can associate each word with an action (or a collection of actions) and can perform the desired behavior when given a single command. A computer, in an analogous way, associates a series of instructions with a function name.

The concept at the basis of structured programming is modularity. You can accomplish complicated tasks by breaking them down into many smaller, simpler tasks. For example, if you wanted to instruct a computer to print a result, you could code a function called "print." This print function might consist of 50 lines of code, yet it could be used many times throughout your program by simply writing the word *print*. It could also be used in other applications or put in a library and shared with other users.

Structured programming allowed a programmer to develop a new vocabulary that could be used to instruct the computer to do increasingly more sophisticated and complicated things. This vocabulary could be shared with other developers, greatly increasing their overall productivity. High-level programming languages, then, moved the focus of software development away from controlling hardware toward creating and implementing a vocabulary that could be shared and expanded, and thus used to implement more global solutions.

The Second Paradigm Shift: Object-Oriented Programming

Structured programming, however, was still very procedural-oriented. The new vocabulary could represent many types of actions but could not describe things or objects. The second paradigm shift in the computer industry addressed this problem with the introduction of object-oriented programming.

Classes and Subclasses

The key principle of object-oriented programming is basing software development on objects rather than on procedures, which introduces the concepts of classes and subclasses. We can relate the way in which object-oriented programming works to the way human beings comprehend and interpret the world. We perceive the world as being made up of things or objects. These objects have properties and perform actions. For example, a plane has properties like height, weight, and shape, and performs actions like flying, landing, and taking off. To "code a plane" by using object-oriented programming, we would do the following:

- Create a class with member variables to represent the properties of the plane

- Create member functions for the class to represent the actions that a plane can perform

Each of the classes can be extended further through a technique called inheritance, enabling software developers to program at increasingly higher levels of abstraction. This ability to encapsulate functions and related properties into a single object results in software that has a more meaningful representation of reality.

The most widely used object-oriented language today is C++, which was developed in the mid 1980s. C++ extends the highly efficient C structured programming language with object-oriented capabilities. Because it is a hybrid of structured and object-oriented programming, C++ supports both programming paradigms. For this reason, it was quickly adopted by the large base of existing C users and it greatly facilitated the move of the software industry to object-oriented programming.

The Third Paradigm Shift: Distributed Computing

Most of the programs developed using structured programming and object-oriented programming ran on a single computer and within one memory address space on that computer. The computer languages predominantly used made it very difficult to do otherwise, as they provided no natural way to communicate across memory address space boundaries or across physical network boundaries.

Two-tier client server computing was the first step in breaking down those boundaries. In this model, the data resides on a server computer and many client computers can access it over a network. To access data from the database, programmers generally use SQL, a relational database interface developed in the late 1970s. SQL is a nonprocedural programming language that operates by allowing us to specify what data we want to access but not how to access it. This has the great advantage of hiding our database implementation from the client, allowing us to modify our database or even to port it to another platform. SQL, however, was not designed to be an application programming language and does not have some fundamental programming features, let alone object-oriented capabilities.

Multitier distributed computing was the natural progression from the two-tier model, as it allowed greater separation of business logic and data storage on the server. As SQL was not sufficient to access anything other than the data layer, new technologies like ActiveX and Java emerged to fulfill the more sophisticated requirements of multitier distributed computing.

The introduction of inexpensive personal computers connected together through a network has made the need for distributed computing pervasive throughout most organizations and has spurred on the development of the ultimate network: the Internet.

World Wide Web

The World Wide Web (WWW) is a distributed system, where the data on the server is on web pages in the two-tier model or is accessed through gateway programs in the multitier model. Created for the Internet quite recently, the WWW has made the Internet a household term. The Internet itself dates back to 1969 with ARPAnet, a network set up by the U.S. government's Department of Defense to link military sites, defense contractors, and universities. The most important military feature of ARPAnet was that it was decentralized, allowing it to continue functioning even if some of the computers on the network were down. This decentralized nature is still a key feature of the Internet today.

No one group owns the Internet, because it is both global and decentralized. We could say that the Internet belongs to the world or to all the people in the world who use it. It has grown from just four host computers in 1969 to more than 642,000 hosts today, connecting over 25 million people. Estimates for the number of Internet users by the turn of the century have ranged from 30 million to 800 million. Despite a wide difference of opinion regarding these estimates, the trend is clearly showing a rapid expansion in the use of the Internet.

Technologies of the Third Paradigm Shift: Java and ActiveX

The World Wide Web has largely contributed to the growth of the Internet because of its ease of use and attractive graphical qualities. The desire to move the WWW from delivering static information-based Web pages to active distributed applications has resulted in the emergence of new technologies like Java and ActiveX, which are designed for creating components that can be integrated to provide robust, scalable, and widely distributed software solutions.

Java

Today some people are proposing the Java programming language as a new way forward for the Internet. Java was originally created to produce applications for small computing devices like personal digital assistants, but has since been revamped to target the burgeoning Internet market. The Java language is like a simpler version of C++ and is ideal for developing small, platform-independent applets that can run in an Internet browser.

A key feature of Java is that it generates bytecode rather than machine code. The bytecode is platform independent and operates by running on a platform-specific Java virtual machine. This design promises programmers who code an application for the Java virtual machine that their applications will automatically run on any platform without requiring any code changes.

ActiveX

ActiveX is an even more intriguing approach because it allows the creation of language-independent software components. ActiveX can be implemented in Java, and therefore it subsumes its benefits, but it also proposes many important additional features.

First, it is based on the Microsoft component object model (COM), which was designed with the purpose of enabling powerful software integration and is a very widely used industry standard today. COM allows software developers to easily leverage the work of other programmers without requiring any coordination from them. This will be a great advantage in managing the complexity of building multitier distributed Internet systems.

Second, through the services of distributed COM (DCOM), ActiveX is location-transparent, allowing components to reside on the same PC or to be distributed across the Internet, without any changes to code. This is an essential requirement for building flexible, scalable Internet systems.

Internet Development Today: Microsoft Windows NT Technologies

While both ActiveX and Java make valuable contributions to Internet development, they are insufficient by themselves to meet the needs of the Internet era. To rapidly build reliable, scalable, distributed software solutions, we need to take ActiveX and Java and embed them in Internet-enabling systems. This is what the Windows NT server platform technologies provide.

Windows NT and Microsoft Windows Distributed interNet Applications Architecture (Windows DNA) provide the tools for implementing people-oriented programming. Their components hide technological complexity and make software easier to develop and easier to use, enabling many more people to participate in this mass exchange of information and social networking we are calling the Internet revolution. Users of computers can focus their efforts on the disciplines I listed at the beginning of this chapter and thus on creating solutions.

Internet Information Server (IIS), Common Gateway Interface (CGI), Internet Server Application Programming Interface (ISAPI), Active Server Pages, Transaction Server Development with ATL, and Message Queuing are all included with the Windows NT operating system and constitute the software layer required for developing reliable Internet systems with ActiveX and Java technology. These components bring the operating systems to a more sophisticated level of operation. Instead of focusing on the generic physical control of the different pieces of hardware, the NT server components concentrate on the software plumbing required to enable the computer to interact with people over the Internet—that is, to perform reliable transactions and send asynchronous messages. This book will examine Windows NT technologies in detail and demonstrate why they represent the new, people-oriented programming paradigm for the Internet.

CHAPTER TWO

The Backbone of People-Oriented Software: COM

Building software systems using the people-oriented programming paradigm we examined in Chapter One is an exciting task. The challenge is to build Internet systems that focus on areas such as healthcare, insurance, banking, tourism, and culture without implementing the many required system-level programming components, such as transaction processing, message queueing, multithreading, multimedia, and network programming. Building these types of systems enables developers to concentrate more directly on the human end of their Internet applications.

The key element in Microsoft's strategy for enhancing the developer's efficiency, quality, and productivity when designing code is the Component Object Model (COM) technology. COM enables the technologies we examine later in the book to satisfy the requirements for supporting the principles of the people-oriented paradigm. Specifically, COM is the backbone of the following technologies:

- ■ **_Microsoft Internet Information Server_ (IIS)** provides World Wide Web, FTP, and Gopher services that are fully integrated into the Microsoft Windows NT operating system. This makes IIS a very fast, secure, and easily administered system. Active Server Pages (ASP) within IIS is a server-side execution environment that runs ActiveX scripts and ActiveX server components. It is pivotal to transforming the World Wide Web into a platform for dynamic, powerful, Internet-based applications.

▪ *Microsoft Transaction Server* (**MTS**) is a component-based transaction processing system for developing, deploying, and maintaining high-performance, scalable, and reliable distributed applications.

▪ *Microsoft Message Queuing* (**MSMQ**) is the component within Windows NT that concentrates on enabling asynchronous communications between applications.

▪ *Microsoft Cluster Server* (**MSCS**) is a built-in feature of the Enterprise Edition of Windows NT Server that is designed to provide greater system scalability and availability.

COM is an open industry standard designed to enable software interoperability for components no matter what programming language is used or which vendors developed the components. The design of COM allows these components to be integrated via the distributed version of COM—that is, Distributed COM, or DCOM—even if these components reside on different machines that use diverse operating systems. One of the most important features of COM is that it provides a way for components to evolve and change over time without breaking the software applications to which they belong, thus solving the versioning problem.

COM applies its object-oriented principles in the context of a running system. Its encapsulation, polymorphism, and reusability are achieved through binary integration rather than through source code integration. This allows new components to be added to a running system in a way that immediately extends the services offered to applications without requiring the system to be restarted. COM's binary standard makes COM language-independent, because any programming language can communicate through a binary format.

COM is far too broad a topic to examine comprehensively in this book, so in this chapter I will cover the following fundamentals: objects and interfaces, COM applications, COM clients and servers, and location transparency. A review of these topics will give you a deeper understanding of COM, which is a basis for many emerging technologies.

NOTE Many good books on COM are available if you want to explore the topic further. Some especially good ones are *Essential COM* by Don Box (Addison Wesley, 1998); *Inside COM* by Dale Rogerson (Microsoft Press, 1997); *Understanding ActiveX and OLE* by David Chappell (Microsoft Press, 1997); and *Inside OLE2* by Kraig Brockschmidt (Microsoft Press, 1995).

COM Objects and Interfaces

COM interfaces are immutable contracts between components. When a COM object publishes that it supports a particular interface, all components are assured of the ability to communicate with the object through that interface. An interface consists of a collection of methods that follow a binary standard, which enables the methods to be invoked across process and machine boundaries.

IUnknown, AddRef, and Release

IUnknown is the base interface for every COM interface, and all COM objects must support it. The *IUnknown* interface is defined as follows:

```
interface IUnknown
    {
    public:
        virtual HRESULT STDMETHODCALLTYPE QueryInterface(
            /* [in] */ REFIID riid,
            /* [iid_is][out] */ void RPC_FAR *_RPC_FAR *ppvObject) = 0;

        virtual ULONG STDMETHODCALLTYPE AddRef(void) = 0;

        virtual ULONG STDMETHODCALLTYPE Release(void) = 0;
};
```

The *AddRef* and *Release* members implement a reference-counting mechanism that controls the object during its lifetime. Essentially, this reference-counting mechanism requires that the COM component destroy itself when it is no longer needed. Let's take a look at why this is important.

When an application creates a variable, it has to allocate memory for it. If the application no longer needs this variable, it releases this memory back to the rest of the system. Similarly, when an application requires the creation of a new COM component, memory needs to be allocated for it. This memory also needs to be released when the COM component is no longer required.

However, implementing memory allocation and release is more complicated for a COM component than it is for a variable because of the way applications typically interact with operating system memory management and networks. An application can easily allocate additional memory for a variable because the variable is within its own process space, which the operating system permits. But a COM component might reside in a different process space on the same machine, or it might reside on another machine on the other side of the globe, connected through the Internet. Operating systems do not allow applications to directly access memory structures in other address spaces.

Another complication to memory allocation for COM objects involves clients using the same COM component. Suppose that both client "A" and client "B" are using a COM component. If clients were responsible for memory allocation, one client potentially could destroy the component while the other client still required it.

To handle these problems, COM implements the *AddRef* and *Release* reference-counting mechanism mentioned earlier. Whenever a client creates a COM component or calls a function that returns an interface pointer to that component, the *AddRef* function is invoked, incrementing by 1 a 32-bit counter. When the client is finished with the component, it calls the *Release* function, which decrements the counter by 1. Because the counter is a 32-bit value, the COM component can theoretically support up to about 4 billion clients. When the counter is reduced to 0, the COM component realizes that it has no clients to support and terminates its own existence to free up resources. This Reference counting mechanism essentially gives the component control over its own lifetime.

QueryInterface

The other member function of the *IUnknown* interface is named *QueryInterface*. A COM component can support any number of interfaces, and the *QueryInterface* function provides a navigation mechanism that allows clients to determine which interfaces the component supports. Although *QueryInterface* is a simple idea, it is an exceptionally powerful mechanism for software integration because it solves the versioning problem.

Let's take a look at how it works. *QueryInterface* enables a client to request a pointer to a desired interface so that it can call all the functions of that interface. An input parameter to *QueryInterface* specifies the interface ID of the desired interface, and if the object supports this interface, the output parameter *ppvObject* will contain a pointer to that interface. If the object does not support the interface, the *QueryInterface* method returns the value E_NOINTERFACE in its HRESULT return parameter and *ppvObject* should be set to NULL.

The following example illustrates how *QueryInterface* provides an easy mechanism for managing component evolution within applications and avoids the need to maintain different versions of those components. Suppose that a company called StockShop has created a stock ticker component that implements the *IStock* interface over the Internet and that many software companies have decided to use this stock ticker component to avoid writing such a component for their own Internet applications. Suppose also that StockShop wants to release a more advanced interface for its stock ticker component. Thousands of clients are connected to the old component interface. Without COM, StockShop would have to create and maintain a separate component for each version of the stock ticker and the software companies using the original component would have to deal with the added complexity of interacting with two stock ticker components. With COM's *QueryInterface* function, however, Stock-Shop can create an updated stock ticker component that supports the original interface, *IStock*, in addition to a new, more advanced interface, perhaps named *IStock2*. All existing clients can work seamlessly with the updated component by using the *IStock* interface, and new clients can take advantage of the component's new functionality by querying for the *IStock2* interface. Also, the *IStock2* interface can be derived from *IStock*, so both interfaces are supported with little code duplicated within the component.

COM Applications

To function correctly, COM applications have a few requirements:

- COM applications must be initialized with a thread concurrency model.
- COM applications must allocate and pass around chunks of memory by using the *CoGetMalloc* function.

In the next two sections, we'll examine these requirements in more detail.

COM Initialization

The COM library is initialized by calling the following function:

```
HRESULT CoInitializeEx(
    void * pvReserved,    //Reserved
    DWORD dwCoInit        //COINIT value
);
```

This function must be called before any additional COM functions can be used, with the exception of the *CoGetMalloc* function and memory allocation calls. The second parameter dwCoInit specifies the thread concurrency model for any COM objects created by the thread that initialized COM, and can be either COINIT_MULTITHREADED or COINIT_APARTMENTTHREADED. These flags designate how incoming calls to the COM objects are handled. If the COINIT_MULTITHREADED flag is used, the objects must be able to receive method calls from other threads at any time. You would typically use Win32 synchronization primitives such as critical sections, semaphores, or mutexes to protect the object's data from concurrent access by multiple threads. If the default COINIT_APARTMENTTHREADED flag is used, incoming calls to the objects from other threads are serialized through a message queue. The thread that created the object uses the queue to make calls on behalf of the other threads that called the object. *CoInitializeEx* needs to be called only once by the thread that wants to use the COM library; any subsequent calls return S_FALSE because the library is already initialized. In the case of a multithread apartment, one call to *CoInitializeEx* is sufficient for all threads in the apartment.

To close the library gracefully, all successful calls to *CoInitializeEx*, including those that return S_FALSE, require a corresponding call to its companion helper function, *CoUninitialize*:

```
void CoUninitialize();
```

The *CoUninitialize* function is the last call made to the COM library after the application hides its main windows; it falls through its main message loop when the application shuts down. This frees the resources maintained by the COM library and forces all Remote Procedure Call (RPC) connections to close.

Managing Memory by Using *CoGetMalloc*

COM applications also have responsibilities in the way they allocate and pass around chunks of memory. They do this with the *CoGetMalloc* function, which is a COM function that can be called before *CoInitialize*. This function retrieves a pointer to the default COM task memory allocator, enabling applications to manage memory.

We have already seen that object memory management in COM is handled through a reference-counting mechanism that determines when an object should be destroyed. However, this mechanism requires dealing with interface pointers that expose the *Release* member function. If you are dealing with non-by-value parameters for types such as strings or pointers to data structures, the reference-counting mechanism cannot be used. A universal memory allocation and deallocation policy for these kinds of parameters is required. This is the purpose of the *CoGetMalloc* function, shown here:

```
HRESULT CoGetMalloc(DWORD dwMemContext, LPMALLOC * ppMalloc);
```

The *dwMemContext* in parameter indicates whether memory is private or shared, and the *ppMalloc* out parameter is an indirect pointer to the COM allocator, which is an implementation of the *IMalloc* interface. The COM allocator must be used to allocate memory whenever ownership of a memory chunk is passed through a COM interface or between a client and the COM library. If memory is allocated internally within an object, any allocation scheme can be used; however, the COM allocator is efficient and thread-safe and is therefore a desirable scheme to use internally as well. The *IMalloc* interface is defined as follows:

```
interface IMalloc : public IUnknown
    {
    public:
        virtual void __RPC_FAR *STDMETHODCALLTYPE Alloc(
            /* [in] */ ULONG cb) = 0;

        virtual void __RPC_FAR *STDMETHODCALLTYPE Realloc(
            /* [in] */ void __RPC_FAR *pv,
            /* [in] */ ULONG cb) = 0;

        virtual void STDMETHODCALLTYPE Free(
            /* [in] */ void __RPC_FAR *pv) = 0;

        virtual ULONG STDMETHODCALLTYPE GetSize(
            /* [in] */ void __RPC_FAR *pv) = 0;

        virtual int STDMETHODCALLTYPE DidAlloc(
            void __RPC_FAR *pv) = 0;

        virtual void STDMETHODCALLTYPE HeapMinimize( void) = 0;

    };
```

The *Alloc* function allocates a block of memory, and the *Free* function frees a previously allocated block of memory. The *GetSize* function returns the size (in bytes) of a previously allocated block of memory, whereas *Realloc* changes the size of a previously allocated block of memory. The *DidAlloc* function determines whether this instance of *IMalloc* was used to allocate the specified block of memory. Finally, the *HeapMinimize* function minimizes the heap by releasing unused memory to the operating system.

Remember that the lifetime of pointers to interfaces is always managed through the *AddRef* and *Release* methods of the *IUnknown* interface. All other parameters of interface methods that are not passed by value, including the return value, must adhere to the following rules:

- The in parameters must be allocated and freed by the caller.
- The out parameters must be allocated by the method called and freed by the caller by using the COM memory allocator.
- The in-out parameters are initially allocated by the caller and then freed and reallocated by the method called, if necessary.

If a function fails, the caller has no way to clean up the out or in-out parameters that are returned. Therefore, if a function returns a failure status code, the out parameters must always be reliably set to a value that will be cleaned up without any action on the caller's part. In addition, all out pointer parameters must be explicitly set to NULL when an error occurs. An in-out parameter must either be left alone by the code called so that the parameter remains unchanged or be explicitly set, as in the out parameter error case.

COM Clients and Servers

What are COM clients and servers, and how do they interact? A COM client is any piece of code that has an interface pointer to a COM server. A COM server is any piece of code that implements an interface through an object, which the COM library can locate with a class identifier (called a CLSID). Because a COM client and server can be in the same process space, in different process spaces, or on different computers connected through a network, COM provides a mechanism that enables clients to locate servers they can communicate with.

How does a COM client find its server and connect to it? Every COM server is identified by a unique 128-bit CLSID to prevent object names from colliding. This CLSID is not issued by any central authority but is instead generated by a program that uses an algorithm specified by the Open Software Foundation's Distributed Computing Environment. The algorithm ensures a CLSID's global uniqueness by using a combination of elements, such as the current date and time, the network card address in the computer the program runs on (if the computer has a network card), and incremented counters.

COM maintains a registration database that maps all CLSIDs on the system to the specific location of the DLL or EXE that houses the server. Whenever a client instantiates a server object by passing a CLSID to COM, COM invokes the Service Control Manager (SCM) to locate the server. SCM is the system element of COM that is responsible for locating the code for a CLSID. If the

COM service is not a DLL or an EXE on that computer, the SCM can try to locate it on the network to which the local machine is connected.

This architecture is essential to COM's location transparency, which we examine in detail a little later in the chapter. The client code does not have to concern itself with the location of the server object because it needs only the CLSID to locate it. In fact, the location of the server is mobile and can be moved to another machine to improve the scalability of the application. Irrespective of the type of server used (in-process, local, or remote), a client can request that COM instantiate the object just by passing in the CLSID to the COM function *CoCreateInstance*. This helper function encapsulates a call to *CoGetClassObject* to retrieve a pointer to the *IClassFactory* interface, which creates the object as follows:

```
CoGetClassObject(rclsid, dwClsContext, NULL, IID_IClassFactory, &pCF);
hresult = pCF->CreateInstance(pUnkOuter, riid, ppvObj);
pCF->Release();
```

The class factory object is a special type of COM object that exists only to create another object specified by the CLSID. Every COM server has to implement the *IClassFactory* interface pointer, which is defined as follows:

```
interface IClassFactory : public IUnknown
    {
    public:
        virtual /* [local] */
            HRESULT STDMETHODCALLTYPE CreateInstance(
            /* [unique][in] */ IUnknown __RPC_FAR *pUnkOuter,
            /* [in] */ REFIID riid,
            /* [iid_is][out] */
            void _RPC_FAR *_RPC_FAR *ppvObject) = 0;

        virtual /* [local] */ HRESULT STDMETHODCALLTYPE LockServer(
            /* [in] */ BOOL fLock) = 0;
    };
```

This *IClassFactory* interface has only two methods in addition to the three methods of the *IUnknown* interface it inherits: *LockServer* and *CreateInstance*. The *LockServer* method locks the object's server in memory by incrementing a lock count. In this way, a client forces a server that has not yet created any objects to stay around so that it will be able to create objects more quickly when the client requests them. The client can decrement the lock count with the call *LockServer(FALSE)*.

CreateInstance creates an uninitialized object of the specified CLSID that is associated with the class factory object. Because each instance of a class factory object is associated with only a single CLSID, you do not have to pass a CLSID as a parameter to the *CreateInstance* function. You do pass in a parameter to specify the particular interface from the object that you are interested in and an out parameter to contain that interface pointer.

COM has a reuse mechanism called aggregation, through which an outer object exposes interfaces from the inner object as if they were implemented on the outer object itself. If the new object will be contained within another object by using COM aggregation, you would use the first parameter, *pUnkOuter*, as a pointer to the controlling unknown. (The controlling unknown is the *IUnknown* of the outer component.)

The use of the COM function *CoCreateInstance* is fine if you need to create only a single instance of an object. However, when you are creating multiple instances of an object, you can do so more efficiently by obtaining a pointer to the *IClassFactory* interface of the object's class factory and using its *CreateInstance* method to create each instance.

The second parameter of the *CoGetClassObject* function, *dwClsContext*, specifies the context for the running executable code, and its value is specified using the following enumeration:

```
typedef enum tagCLSCTX
{
    CLSCTX_INPROC_SERVER    = 1,
    CLSCTX_INPROC_HANDLER   = 2,
    CLSCTX_LOCAL_SERVER     = 4
    CLSCTX_REMOTE_SERVER    = 16
} CLSCTX;
```

The following list describes what each identifier specifies:

CLSCTX_INPROC_SERVER specifies that the component code run in the same process as the caller of the function specifying the class context.

CLSCTX_INPROC_HANDLER specifies that the in-process handler DLL for the component run in the client process to implement the client-side structures of the class when instances of the class are accessed remotely.

CLSCTX_LOCAL_SERVER specifies that the EXE code that creates and manages objects of the class load in a separate process space running on the same machine.

CLSCTX_REMOTE_SERVER specifies that the EXE code that creates and manages objects of the class run on a different machine.

The way a server exposes the *IClassFactory* interface to clients through COM differs depending on whether the server is a DLL or an EXE. If the server is a DLL, a client request for the *IClassFactory* interface results in COM loading the DLL into memory by using the *CoLoadLibrary* function. COM then calls the DLL's function *DllGetClassObject*, which all DLL servers must implement and export. *DllGetClassObject* creates the class factory object for the CLSID passed in and returns the requested *IClassFactory* interface pointer.

If the client is requesting an EXE server, things are more complex because COM does not have a way to pass to the EXE the CLSID of the associated class factory. This means that the EXE should instantiate the class factories it supports when it starts up and should register them with COM through the function *CoRegisterClassObject*, which has the following signature:

```
STDAPI CoRegisterClassObject(
    REFCLSID rclsid, //Class identifier (CLSID) to be registered
    IUnknown * pUnk, //Pointer to the class object
    DWORD dwClsContext, //Context for running executable code
    DWORD dwUsage, //How to connect to the class object
    LPDWORD * lpdwRegister //Pointer to the value returned
);
```

The fourth parameter of *CoRegisterClassObject* serves as a flag that specifies whether a single instance of the EXE can support one or more instances of the component. The *REGCLS* enumeration defines the possible values of this flag:

```
typedef enum tagREGCLS
{
    REGCLS_SINGLEUSE        = 0,
    REGCLS_MULTIPLEUSE      = 1,
    REGCLS_MULTI_SEPARATE   = 2,
} REGCLS;
```

If the flag is set to REGCLS_SINGLEUSE, the class factory can be used only once and COM must launch another instance of the EXE to retrieve another instance of the component. This operation is expensive but necessary because more than one instance of a component within an EXE could cause problems.

REGCLS_MULTIPLEUSE allows multiple clients to create components by using the single class factory that was registered when the EXE started up. This results in faster execution because the EXE does not have to be loaded each time, and it also conserves the resources required by different instances of the EXE. If the third parameter of *CoRegisterClassObject* specifies a context of CLSCTX_LOCAL_SERVER, the REGCLS_MULTIPLEUSE flag will append the context of CLSCTX_INPROC_SERVER, which prevents an EXE from launching another instance of itself to use one of its own components. This feature is suppressed by using the REGCLS_MULTI_SEPARATE flag instead of REGCLS_MULTIPLEUSE.

COM also needs to be able to unload servers that it has launched. This is accomplished in different ways for DLL and EXE servers. In the case of DLLs, COM will, from time to time, call the *DllCanUnloadNow* function of a COM server. (A client can also force this by calling the function *CoFreeUnusedLibraries*.) Every COM DLL must implement the *DllCanUnloadNow* function, which takes no parameters and returns an HRESULT that can be S_FALSE or S_OK. If the function returns S_FALSE, COM will not try to unload it. If the function returns S_OK, no locks are on the class, allowing COM to call the *CoFreeLibrary* function to unload the DLL server.

In the case of EXEs, unloading servers is more complicated, especially when the server has a user interface. The EXE is responsible for unloading itself, and to determine when to do so, it uses a zero value for the lock count of the class factory. However, a zero value for the lock count by itself cannot be sufficient to shut down a server, since the lock counter is initially set to zero when the server starts up. It is when the lock count becomes zero through a call to *IClassFactory::LockServer(FALSE)* that the EXE knows that it can terminate itself. The EXE will also terminate itself if the lock count is zero and the last object receives a call to its *IUnknown::Release* method, allowing it to destroy itself. If the EXE server has a user interface, a user might take control of an object that COM started. For example, suppose a COM application starts Microsoft Word to check a document's spelling. Because Word exposes a user interface, the user realizes that Word has been started and decides to open and edit another document. To prevent COM from shutting down the server when the COM application is finished with Word and thereby leave the user who is currently editing a document undisturbed, a user control flag is set to *true*.

Location Transparency

Our analysis of COM so far has explained the purpose of COM interfaces and how COM objects are created and destroyed. We also briefly looked at the COM functions that enable chunks of memory to be transferred between objects that live in different processes or on different machines. This section on location transparency explains how COM abstracts the location of objects so that the programmer doesn't have to be concerned with where they reside.

As mentioned earlier in the chapter, a server can communicate with clients that are in another process space or even on another computer. That's what location transparency *means,* but how does it *work?* The key to understanding location transparency is knowing that a client application and the server application always communicate by using surrogate objects that live in their process space. (This client surrogate object is called a *proxy,* and it communicates with a server surrogate object called a *stub.*) Thus, neither a client nor a server ever needs to be concerned with code outside its process space. For this reason, a crashing server cannot crash the client because the client is calling methods on only its surrogate objects, which are not in the server's memory address space. Both the proxy and the stub need to understand the structure of the remote interface, but they do not need to know how it is implemented.

Marshaling

We have already seen that to create a COM object, the client must obtain a pointer to the server's *IClassFactory* interface and then call the *CreateInstance* method of this interface to instantiate the object. If the server and client are in the same memory address space, passing this interface pointer is easy.

However, if the client and server are in different processes on the same machine or if they are on different machines, the server's *IClassFactory* interface needs to be made visible to the client's process space. You can accomplish this by constructing a proxy of the interface in the client's process space. The client then simply calls the *CreateInstance* method of this proxy, leaving it up to the proxy to relay these calls to the real interface on the server so that the object is created on the server. In this way, out-of-process calls are transparent because the client treats them as if they were in-process calls. The mechanism by which this is accomplished is called *marshaling.* Marshaling an interface involves the following:

- Creating the proxies and stubs for the client and server
- Passing the method calls, with their associated parameters and return values, back and forth

Some parameters are more difficult to marshal than others. For example, marshaling a simple parameter type such as an integer involves copying its value into a message buffer, but marshaling a pointer involves passing all the data to which the pointer is pointing and then reconstructing that data on the other side. All marshaling is accomplished by some means of interprocess communication.

Custom Marshaling

Custom marshaling allows the developer to fine-tune interprocess communication between the proxy and the stub so that the interface can be constructed and called as efficiently as possible. Custom marshaling can be particularly advantageous if the object has immutable state, since in this case the whole object can be marshaled (often termed *passing-by value*) to eliminate any network round-trips. Standard marshaling is a particular implementation of the custom marshaling architecture that COM provides for free. It uses the RPC run-time library to marshal the standard COM interfaces. Custom interfaces can also leverage standard marshaling through the use of the Microsoft Interface Definition Language (MIDL) compiler, which generates the proxy and stub code for you. Although standard marshaling is by far the most common mechanism used, we will examine custom marshaling because it best explains the marshaling architecture.

We saw earlier that an EXE server calls the *CoRegisterClassObject* function to register all its class factory interfaces with COM. Within this function, COM requests from the object the CLSID of the proxy to be used for marshaling. COM also asks for a marshaling packet, which contains the information required by the proxy to perform interprocess communication. If the object does not return the proxy CLSID and a marshaling packet, COM defaults to using standard marshaling. COM stores the proxy CLSID and marshaling packet in a global table so that other processes can access them.

The marshaling packet in the global table is transferred to the client process through the service control manager. We have already seen that the SCM is responsible for locating the code for a particular CLSID and for launching the server. Given that the SCM has to be aware of the server location and the server's proximity to the client, the SCM is best suited to transfer the marshaling packet to the client. The COM function *CoMarshalInterface* is used to write into a stream the data required to initialize the client proxy object. It has the following signature:

```
STDAPI CoMarshalInterface(
    IStream *pStm, //Pointer to the stream used for marshaling
    REFIID riid, //Reference to the identifier of the interface
    IUnknown *pUnk, //Pointer to the interface to be marshaled
    DWORD dwDestContext, //Destination context
    void *pvDestContext, //Reserved for future use
    DWORD mshlflags //Reason for marshaling
);
```

The *dwDestContext* parameter is the destination context where the interface specified in the *riid* parameter will be unmarshaled. Its value can be taken from the *MSHCTX* enumeration:

```
typedef enum tagMSHCTX
{
    MSHCTX_LOCAL            = 0,
    MSHCTX_NOSHAREDMEM      = 1,
    MSHCTX_DIFFERENTMACHINE = 2,
    MSHCTX_INPROC           = 3
} MSHCTX;
```

Following is a description of each identifier:

> **MSHCTX_LOCAL** means that the interface has shared-memory access with the marshaling process.

> **MSHCTX_NOSHAREDMEM** means that the unmarshaling process does not have shared-memory access with the marshaling process.

> **MSHCTX_DIFFERENTMACHINE** means that the unmarshaling process is on a different machine. The COM specification does not allow the marshaling code to assume that a particular piece of application code is installed on that machine.

> **MSHCTX_INPROC** means that the unmarshaling will be done in another apartment in the same process. In this case, if the object supports multiple threads, a custom marshaler can pass a direct pointer instead of creating a proxy object.

The implementation of the *CoMarshalInterface* function will query the object for a pointer to the *IMarshal* interface, which is defined as follows:

```
interface IMarshal : public IUnknown
    {
    public:
        virtual HRESULT STDMETHODCALLTYPE GetUnmarshalClass(
            /* [in] */ REFIID riid,
            /* [unique][in] */ void __RPC_FAR *pv,
            /* [in] */ DWORD dwDestContext,
            /* [unique][in] */ void __RPC_FAR *pvDestContext,
            /* [in] */ DWORD mshlflags,
            /* [out] */ CLSID __RPC_FAR *pCid) = 0;
```

(continued)

```
virtual HRESULT STDMETHODCALLTYPE GetMarshalSizeMax(
    /* [in] */ REFIID riid,
    /* [unique][in] */ void __RPC_FAR *pv,
    /* [in] */ DWORD dwDestContext,
    /* [unique][in] */ void __RPC_FAR *pvDestContext,
    /* [in] */ DWORD mshlflags,
    /* [out] */ DWORD __RPC_FAR *pSize) = 0;

virtual HRESULT STDMETHODCALLTYPE MarshalInterface(
    /* [unique][in] */ IStream __RPC_FAR *pStm,
    /* [in] */ REFIID riid,
    /* [unique][in] */ void __RPC_FAR *pv,
    /* [in] */ DWORD dwDestContext,
    /* [unique][in] */ void __RPC_FAR *pvDestContext,
    /* [in] */ DWORD mshlflags) = 0;

virtual HRESULT STDMETHODCALLTYPE UnmarshalInterface(
    /* [unique][in] */ IStream __RPC_FAR *pStm,
    /* [in] */ REFIID riid,
    /* [out] */ void __RPC_FAR *__RPC_FAR *ppv) = 0;

virtual HRESULT STDMETHODCALLTYPE ReleaseMarshalData(
    /* [unique][in] */ IStream __RPC_FAR *pStm) = 0;

virtual HRESULT STDMETHODCALLTYPE DisconnectObject(
    /* [in] */ DWORD dwReserved) = 0;

};
```

If the object does not implement this interface, COM defaults to using standard marshaling and its implementation of *IMarshal.* The *CoMarshalInterface* function calls the *IMarshal::GetUnmarshalClass* function to get the CLSID of the object's proxy and then writes the CLSID of the proxy to the stream parameter *pStm.* It then calls the *IMarshal::MarshalInterface* function to marshal the interface pointer.

The implementation of the *IMarshal::MarshalInterface* function must contain all the data needed to initialize the proxy on the client side, such as a handle to a window, a named pipe, or a pointer to an RPC channel. To create a proxy for an object, COM needs to know the amount of data to be written to the marshaling stream. The marshaling stub determines this information by a call to *CoGetMarshalSizeMax,* which in turn calls the *GetMarshalSizeMax* function of the *IMarshal* interface. Because the value returned by this method is guaranteed to be valid only as long as the internal state of the object being marshaled is unchanged, the actual marshaling should be done immediately after the *GetMarshalSizeMax* function returns. If the marshaling stub waits, it runs the risk that the object might require more memory to marshal than it originally indicated due to some change in its state.

After the call to the *CoMarshalInterface* function, COM has a proxy CLSID and a marshaling packet in the stream, which it can use to create and initialize the marshaling proxy in the client's address space. It accomplishes this through a call to *CoUnmarshalInterface*:

```
STDAPI CoUnmarshalInterface(
    IStream * pStm, //Pointer to the stream
    REFIID riid, //Reference to the identifier of the interface
    void ** ppv //Indirect pointer to the unmarshaled interface
);
```

This function reads, from the stream, the CLSID that will be used to create an instance of the proxy. It queries the proxy for a pointer to its *IMarshal* interface, calls the *IMarshal::UnmarshalInterface* method to initialize the newly created proxy, and returns an interface pointer to that proxy.

The last two methods of the *IMarshal* interface have to do with releasing marshaled packets and server disconnects. If an object's marshaled data packet does not get unmarshaled and is no longer needed, the *IMarshal::Release-MarshalData* method can be called to instruct the object to destroy the data packet. This call occurs within the *CoReleaseMarshalData* function. The method *IMarshal::DisconnectObject* enables a server to correctly disconnect all external clients to the object and is typically called in response to a user closing the server application. *IMarshal::DisconnectObject* is called within the *CoDisconnectObject* method to forcibly release all external connections to an object. An object's client would not call *CoDisconnectObject* to disconnect itself from the server because it can use the *IUnknown::Release* method for this purpose.

Standard Marshaling and DCOM

All the complexity of implementing marshaling is eliminated if object interprocess communication is handled through standard marshaling. Standard marshaling is by far the most common way in which COM will be used in a distributed environment, and Microsoft has provided all the marshaling code for standard COM interfaces within the Windows operating system. If a company develops new COM interfaces and does not want to do any custom marshaling for them, the MIDL compiler can quickly churn out the proxy and stub code to allow these new interfaces to be marshaled in a standard way.

Microsoft's standard implementation of marshaling DCOM components includes some additional features, including a system-failure detection protocol that can notify an object when its client machine suffers a catastrophic hardware failure or when the network connection has dropped. Rather than giving each component the responsibility for detecting systems failures, DCOM handles detection on a per-machine basis. This greatly simplifies implementation issues and reduces the network bandwidth consumption that would be required for an individual component to verify that all its clients are alive. For example, if a client machine uses 50 server components, DCOM will send a single keep-alive message at periodic intervals to verify that clients and network connections are alive. The keep-alive message consists of pinging the client machine a few times to see if it will respond. This procedure has been optimized to reduce the size of ping messages and also to piggyback them onto regular messages to avoid unnecessary network round-trips.

DCOM provides security transparency in addition to location transparency. We have seen that location transparency allows administrators to distribute integrated components to different machines at will, without requiring any code changes to these components. Similarly, administrators can configure the security rights for different components without any support from developers. All objects within the Windows NT operating system are integrated into the Windows NT security model. Every time access to an object such as a file, thread, event, or semaphore is requested, Windows NT performs a check against its security database to determine whether sufficient rights exist. DCOM security runs on top of this architecture so that administrators can assign different types of rights to the users within a Windows NT domain. For example, an administrator can give a user the right to launch a particular component but give only the right to access an existing running instance of a different component.

DCOM applications are not tied to any specific network protocol since the network infrastructure has been abstracted from the application code. DCOM applications can be seamlessly transferred to networks that use different protocols such as TCP/IP, UDP, IPX/SPX, and NETBIOS. DCOM can even be tunneled through the Internet HTTP protocol to avoid complications with firewalls. Since the DCOM wire protocol is based on Distributed Computing Environment Remote Procedure Call (DCE RPC), implementing DCOM on other platforms that support DCE RPC is made considerably more straightforward. DCOM is currently supported on Microsoft Windows NT, Microsoft Windows 95, Apple Macintosh, and on various versions of the UNIX platform. To facilitate easier integration with other platforms, Microsoft has transferred the ActiveX\COM\DCOM standard over to an open group, so it is no longer proprietary.

PART II

THE NT SERVER PLATFORM

Web Servers and IIS Protocols

The Internet revolution began with the use of web servers. In this chapter, we will look at web servers in general and examine the protocols of Microsoft Internet Information Server (IIS). We will not discuss setting up IIS or configuring it for different environments. Rather, we will examine the lower level protocols that operate within IIS and allow it to act as a web server on the Internet. All web servers must fulfill these requirements, which are specified in the various reference documents that we will discuss in this chapter. The chapter will also include an example of building a customized web server from scratch using Microsoft Windows sockets.

The OSI Model

At its most basic level, the Internet is simply a huge computer network using open standards that approximate the Open Systems Interconnected (OSI) network model proposed by the International Organization of Standards (ISO) in 1978. The OSI model consists of the seven layers that abstract the different elements involved in network communication between computers.

In this model, when a computer sends data over a network, header information is added to the data as the data passes through each network layer. The receiving computers strip off the appropriate headers at each layer and pass the data up to the next layer. Because the respective layers in the sending and receiving computers use the same protocol, they can understand the header format. The seven layers are as follows, from lowest to highest:

- *Physical layer*   Deals directly with the physical media. It uses electrical voltages to transmit 1s and 0s over the wire without any knowledge of what the bits represent.

- *Datalink layer*   Detects and corrects errors that occur when bits are transmitted through the physical layer. It groups the bits together into frames, or packets. These frames have fields that hold the address of the sending and receiving nodes as well as errors and control conditions.

■ **Network layer** Provides a mechanism for routing packets to their destinations by using a uniform addressing scheme that can operate with different types of data link implementations. It also prevents congestion by controlling flow.

■ **Transport layer** Responsible for ensuring reliable communication between nodes. It uses the error checking features of the lower layers but augments them to ensure reliable data delivery. This layer must manage many different connections at the same time, and it is the first end-to-end mechanism that can communicate with the remote node across networks.

■ **Session layer** Focuses on the dialog between nodes in a way that is meaningful to the applications running on the sending and receiving computers. It manages the synchronization issues involved in the two-way flow of data between systems.

■ **Presentation layer** Negotiates how data is represented to each system. For example, data can be presented in ASCII or EBCDIC format; this layer manages any conversion required to ensure correct communication.

■ **Application layer** Use is determined by the application services at both ends. It can be responsible for tasks such as file transfer, e-mail, and directory service.

The Internet uses the TCP/IP network protocol, which was developed before the OSI model and does not exactly match its specification. In general, Internet Protocol (IP) fits into the network layer and Transmission Control Protocol (TCP) fits into the transport layer. We'll look at IP first.

Internet Protocol

IP was created for the Department of Defense Advanced Research Project Agency in the 1970s. The latest version of the specification can be found in Request For Comment (RFC) 791. RFC 791 places IP within the protocol hierarchy, as shown in Figure 3-1.

You can see that IP is the layer above the primitive local network protocol and that it must interface with other, higher level protocols in order to facilitate even the simplest of tasks, such as file transfer. IP provides a mechanism that

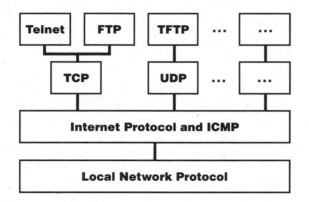

Figure 3-1.
The latest version of the protocol hierarchy.

transfers packages of bits (called *datagrams*) from a source to a destination through interconnected systems of packet-switched computer networks. It does not, however, guarantee the delivery of packets, control flow, or provide any way to ensure that network packets arrive in the order in which they were sent. Its capabilities lie in the areas of fragmentation and addressing.

Internet Modules and Diagram Headers

IP works through Internet modules, which run on every host and gateway. These modules are responsible for fragmenting datagrams into smaller packets and reassembling them, which is necessary when a datagram traverses a network that specifies a packet size smaller than the datagram. The Internet modules are also responsible for routing datagrams to their destinations by mapping the address fields contained in the IP header to either another gateway or a local network address.

Here's how an Internet module works: When an application calls its *send* function, it passes data and the destination address as arguments. If the destination address is in another network, the Internet module determines the appropriate gateway address for it. It adds a datagram header to the data and sends the datagram to the gateway host. An Internet module on the gateway host picks up the datagram and either sends it to another gateway or sends it to a local host if the datagram's final destination is in the adjoining network. After determining the local network address for the datagram, the Internet module calls upon the local network interface to create a network header to which it can attach the datagram and then send it to its destination host.

When the datagram arrives at the destination host, the local network interface strips off the local network header and passes the datagram to the

Internet module residing on that host. This Internet module passes data in the datagram to the appropriate application on the host. Figure 3-2 shows RFC 791's example of an Internet datagram header.

```
 0                   1                   2                   3
 0 1 2 3 4 5 6 7 8 9 0 1 2 3 4 5 6 7 8 9 0 1 2 3 4 5 6 7 8 9 0 1
```

Version	IHL	Type of Service	Total Length
Identification		Flags	Fragment Offset
Time to Live	Protocol		Header Checksum
Source Address			
Destination Address			
Options			Padding

Figure 3-2.
An example of an Internet datagram header.

The following are the fields in the Internet datagram header:

Version

This field is 4 bits and reveals the format of the header.

IHL

IHL, an abbreviation of Internet Header Length, is used to locate the beginning of the data.

Type Of Service

This field is used to request the delay, throughput, and reliability settings for a datagram. Its effectiveness depends on whether networks implement these settings.

Total Length

This field specifies the total length of the data and the header. Although the length of the datagram can be 65,535 octets (an octet is 8 bits), the maximum number of octets that receiving hosts must accept is only 576, so sending a larger datagram is risky. Larger datagrams can be safely sent, of course, if the host can receive them. These sizes are irrespective of whether the datagram arrives whole or in fragments.

Identification, Fragment Offset

If a datagram arrives fragmented, the Identification and Fragment Offset fields are used to reassemble them.

Flags

A datagram that is marked "don't fragment" in the Flags field remains intact and is discarded if the network maximum packet size is smaller than the datagram. This field also specifies whether the host has received the last fragment or whether more fragments will arrive.

Time To Live

The Time To Live field specifies the maximum number of seconds the datagram is allowed to live; the datagram is destroyed if the value in this field reaches *0*.

> **NOTE** Every module that processes a datagram must reduce this value by one, even if the processing time is less than a second.

Protocol

This field is 8 bits and specifies the next level of protocol in the data portion of the datagram. RFC 791 lists possible values for this field; these are shown in Table 3-1 on the following page.

Header Checksum

This field, which is recomputed and verified every time the header is processed, protects against transmission errors. If an error is detected, the Internet Control Message Protocol (ICMP) can be used to report it.

Options

This field might not appear in a datagram. It is used for security, loose or strict source routing, record routing, the stream ID, and the Internet time stamp.

Padding

This field is used to ensure that the header ends on a 32-bit boundary.

Source Address, Destination Address

Both of these fields hold IP addresses, which are represented by 32-bit numbers. A 32-bit number is often represented in dotted decimal notation, where four decimal numbers are separated by periods, as in 192.80.191.56. These addresses can be divided into two parts—a network part and a local address part—as specified in RFC 790. The network part is used to route a datagram to the network containing the host. The local address part is used to specify the particular host within the network receiving the datagram.

The number of bits allocated to the network part and local address part determines the class of the address. In Class A addresses, the first octet specifies the network portion and the remaining three octets identify the host. You can use Class A addresses when you need a small number of networks with a large number of hosts. In Class B addresses, the first two octets specify the network and the last two specify the host. You can use Class B addresses when you need a moderate number of networks with a moderate number of hosts.

With Class C addresses, the first three octets specify the network portion and only one octet specifies the hosts. You use Class C addresses when you have a large number of networks with a small number of hosts. In addition, several addresses are reserved for special purposes. For example, the address 255.255.255.255 is used to broadcast all hosts for current networks.

Values for the Protocol Field

Decimal	Octal	Protocol
0	0	Reserved
1	1	ICMP
2	2	Unassigned
3	3	Gateway-to-Gateway
4	4	CMCC Gateway Monitoring Message
5	5	ST
6	6	TCP
7	7	UCL
8	10	Unassigned
9	11	Secure
10	12	BBN RCC Monitoring
11	13	NVP
12	14	PUP
13	15	Pluribus
14	16	Telenet
15	17	XNET

Table 3-1. *(continued)*

Possible values for the Protocol field in an Internet datagram header.

Table 3-1. *continued*

Decimal	Octal	Protocol
16	20	Chaos
17	21	User Datagram
18	22	Multiplexing
19	23	DCN
20	24	TAC Monitoring
21–62	25–76	Unassigned
63	77	any local network
64	100	SATNET and Backroom EXPAK
65	101	MIT Subnet Support
66–68	102–104	Unassigned
69	105	SATNET Monitoring
70	106	Unassigned
71	107	Internet Packet Core Utility
72–75	110–113	Unassigned
76	114	Backroom SATNET Monitoring
77	115	Unassigned
78	116	WIDEBAND Monitoring
79	117	WIDEBAND EXPAK
80–254	120–376	Unassigned
255	377	Reserved

Transmission Control Protocol

TCP is a highly reliable, host-to-host, connection-oriented protocol. Created by the Department of Defense in the 1970s, TCP gave the military a robust, decentralized, multinetwork communications mechanism for an environment that was often unreliable, especially in terms of availability and congestion. It was designed to fit into a layered hierarchy of protocols that support multinetwork applications. The latest version of the specification is in RFC 793.

TCP assumes that it can use a lower level protocol such as IP to send and receive variable-length datagrams, but it does not assume that the sending and receiving process will be reliable. The services that TCP provides on top of IP are in the areas of basic data transfer, reliability, flow control, multiplexing, connections, precedence, and security.

Reliable Data Transfer

TCP improves basic data transfer because it can send continuous streams of data to a host by packaging the data into IP datagrams and then managing the blocking and forwarding issues involved in their transmissions. It also exposes a push method, which ensures that all data submitted to the TCP is promptly delivered to the receiver. When lower level protocols transmit packets, data can be damaged or lost. Packets can also be sent out of order or sent multiple times. TCP provides reliable data transfer by assigning a sequence to each octet transmitted. The receiver uses these sequence numbers to correct the delivery order and to detect and manage packets that are received more than once. The receiver comparing a checksum value prepared by the sender detects damaged data.

TCP also requires an acknowledgment (ACK) from the receiving TCP for every octet transmitted. It puts a copy of the data into a retransmission queue, starts a timer, and waits for an ACK. If the ACK arrives, the copy of the data in the retransmission queue is deleted. If the timer runs out before the ACK arrives, the data is retransmitted.

Flow Control and Multiplexing

The receiver includes in the ACK a "window" of sequence numbers that can be accepted from the sender. This is used for flow control; it allows the receiver to specify the amount of data the sender can send.

Many applications within a host might want to multiplex the services of TCP. TCP distinguishes different applications on a single host through the use of port numbers concatenated to the IP address. For example, 80 is the default port number for a Web server, and 21 is the default port number for file transfer using FTP. This combination of an IP address and a port number is called a *socket* (according to the TCP specification in RFC 793).

Connections

A unique TCP connection is a communication path identified by a pair of sockets. A pair of sockets maintains status information about the sending, receiving, and acknowledging of packets, and it includes data such as sequence numbers and window sizes. A connection between two processes is established when both TCPs have initialized the required status information. TCP connections are *full duplex,* which means that data can be sent in both directions.

Security and Precedence

The security and precedence of the communication can be indicated in the TCP header information, as shown in Figure 3-3.

The header in Figure 3-3 does not contain destination or source addresses because the IP header already has this information. The TCP header follows the IP header in the datagram, and it must add only information specific to its protocol. These are the fields added by the TCP header:

0										1										2										3	
0	1	2	3	4	5	6	7	8	9	0	1	2	3	4	5	6	7	8	9	0	1	2	3	4	5	6	7	8	9	0	1

Source Port				Destination Port			
Sequence Number							
Acknowledgment Number							
Data Offset	Reserved	URG ACK PSH RST SYN FIN		Window			
Checksum				Urgent Pointer			
Options						Padding	
Data							

Figure 3-3.
An example of the TCP header.

Source Port, Destination Port 16-bit fields that along with the IP addresses define the pair of sockets that identify the connection.

Sequence Number A 32-bit field that helps order the packets received.

Acknowledgment Number A 32-bit field that holds the next sequence number the sender expects to receive.

Window A 16-bit field used for flow control.

Checksum A 16-bit field used to detect corrupted data.

Data Offset A 4-bit field that indicates where the data in the datagram begins.

Reserved A 6-bit field reserved for future use; its value must be *0*.

Options A 24-bit field used to specify the maximum segment size during the establishment of a connection.

There are six control bits, which are defined as follows:

URG

Urgent Pointer field significant

When the URG flag is set, the TCP layer informs the application layer asynchronously that urgent data has arrived.

PSH

Push Function

The PSH flag tells the TCP layer not to aggregate data but to immediately deliver it.

RST

Reset the connection

The RST flag is used to reset the connection. It should be sent only if a packet arrives that is apparently not intended for the current connection.

FIN

No more data from sender

The FIN flag is used to terminate a connection. Both sides must set the FIN flag to 1 before a termination can take place to ensure that data is not lost when one side has closed unilaterally.

ACK

Acknowledgment field significant

The ACK flag indicates whether the Acknowledgment field is significant.

SYN

Synchronize sequence numbers

The SYN flag is used in a process known as the three-way handshake, which prevents confusion when old duplicate connections are initiated during the opening of TCP connections. By matching ACK and SYN numbers, you can prevent the arrival of old packets that confuse the connection process.

The following example of the three-way handshake procedure is from RFC 793. Figure 3-4 illustrates this.

1. TCP A begins by sending a sequence number of 100 without a significant acknowledgment field.

2. TCP B replies with a sequence number of 300 and an acknowledgment number of 101, which acknowledges the previous sequence number of 100 sent by TCP A.

3. TCP A sends the next number in its sequence (101) and acknowledges the TCP B sequence number 300 by sending an acknowledgment number of 301.

4. The connection is established.

5. A TCP connection can progress through a series of states.

TCP A   **TCP B**

1 CLOSED   LISTEN

2 SYN-SENT   ➔<SEQ=100><CTL=SYN>   ➔SYN-RECEIVED

3 ESTABLISHED ◄<SEQ=300><ACK=101><CTL=SYN,ACK>   ◄SYN-RECEIVED

4 ESTABLISHED➔<SEQ=101><ACK=301><CTL=ACK>   ➔ESTABLISHED

5 ESTABLISHED➔<SEQ=101><ACK=301><CTL=ACK><DATA>➔ESTABLISHED

Figure 3-4.
*The three-way handshake procedure prevents confusion during the opening
of TCP connections.*

RFC 793 defines the possible states for a connection as follows:

LISTEN Waiting for a connection request from any remote TCP
   and port.

SYN-SENT Waiting for a matching connection request after sending a
   connection request.

SYN-RECEIVED Waiting for a confirming connection request acknowledgment after both receiving and sending a connection
   request.

ESTABLISHED This is an open connection; data received can be
   delivered to the user. This is the normal state for the data transfer
   phase of the connection.

FIN-WAIT-1 Waiting for a connection termination request from the
   remote TCP, or an acknowledgment of the connection termination request previously sent.

FIN-WAIT-2 Waiting for a connection termination request from the remote TCP.

CLOSE-WAIT Waiting for a connection termination request from the local user.

CLOSING Waiting for a connection termination request acknowledgment from the remote TCP.

LAST-ACK Waiting for an acknowledgment of the connection termination request previously sent to the remote TCP (which includes an acknowledgment of its connection termination request).

TIME-WAIT Waiting for enough time to pass to be sure the remote TCP received the acknowledgment of its connection termination request.

CLOSED Represents no connection state at all.

Events

The activity of the TCP connection in terms of progressing from one state to another is determined by events such as a timeout. Events can occur through user calls, arriving segments, and timeouts. Timeouts can be user timeouts, retransmission timeouts, or time-wait timeouts. Arriving segments (such as segments that contain the SYN, ACK, RST, and FIN flags) can cause events. Six TCP user calls can cause events, and every TCP implementation must have these basic functions to support interprocess communication:

- OPEN
- SEND
- RECEIVE
- CLOSE
- ABORT
- STATUS

Shortly after the TCP protocol was developed, it was incorporated into the kernel of the Berkeley Software Distribution (BSD) UNIX operating system. The functionality of the TCP user calls in RFC 793 were exposed to programmers through the socket routines defined by the Berkeley system. This became the standard application programming interface (API) for developing TCP applications. Windows sockets is based on this standard. This book focuses on the internals of IIS, so our analysis of the TCP user calls will concentrate on how they are implemented in Windows sockets.

Windows Sockets

Windows sockets is not a protocol but rather an open, industry-standard interface for accessing network protocols. Windows sockets 1.1 was used primarily to access the TCP/IP protocol; Windows sockets 2.0 (API) is a protocol-independent interface that is also based on the sockets model that was first popularized by BSD UNIX. We'll look at its Berkeley-style socket routines to gain a deeper understanding of how Web servers work. The operation of sockets is fairly straightforward and usually follows one of two patterns, depending on whether the user is a client or a server. These patterns are described below.

Clients and sockets   The operation of a client begins when a client creates a socket with the *socket* function. The client can call the *bind* function to bind the socket to an address and port number, which the server can use to send data back to the client. If the client specifies port number 0, TCP/IP chooses an unused port in the range 1024 to 5000. Similarly, if the client calls connect on an unbound socket, the socket is bound automatically on an unused port. The client uses the *connect* function to create a connection to a remote server. After the connection is established, the client uses the *send* and *recv* functions to send data to and receive data from the server. Finally the client terminates the connection with a call to *closesocket*. This pattern is shown in Figure 3-5 on the following page.

Servers and sockets   The operation of a server also begins when the server creates a socket with the *socket* function and then calls the *bind* function to bind it to an address and port number. The client uses this address to locate the server; most web servers use port 80. The server calls the *listen* function to create a queue of pending connection requests. The server uses the *accept* function to complete a connection by assigning a new socket to handle communication with the client. The original socket remains in a listening state to accept additional connection requests. The new socket connection uses the *send* and *recv* functions to send data to and receive data from the client. Finally the server terminates the connection with the client by calling *closesocket*. This pattern is shown in Figure 3-6 on the following page.

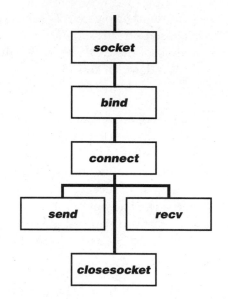

Figure 3-5.
How a client works with a socket.

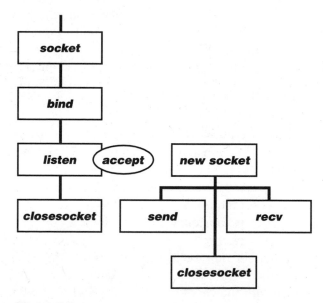

Figure 3-6.
How a server and a socket function.

Routines in the Windows sockets 2.0 specification   The Windows sockets 2.0 specification includes the following Berkeley-style socket routines, which are described later in this chapter:

- socket
- setsockopt
- bind
- listen
- accept
- connect
- send
- sendto
- recv
- recvfrom
- select
- closesocket
- shutdown
- getpeername
- getsockname
- getsockopt
- htonl
- htons
- inet_addr
- inet_ntoa
- ioctlsocket
- ntohl
- ntohs

After we examine the HTTP protocol, we will build a sample web server using Windows sockets.

HTTP

IIS uses various network protocols on top of TCP/IP to provide Internet services. In addition to its Web capabilities, IIS 4.0 ships with e-mail, newsgroup, and file transfer servers, which use the Internet protocols SMPT, NNTP, and FTP, respectively.

IIS uses the Hypertext Transfer Protocol (HTTP). We will mostly concentrate on HTTP version 1.1, which is defined in RFC 2068. This specification improves on HTTP version 1.0, which is defined in RFC 1945.

HTTP is an application-level protocol for distributed, collaborative, hypermedia information systems. Available since 1990, HTTP facilitated the creation of the Web. HTTP is placed in the application layer of the OSI model and thus relies on lower level protocols to implement data transfer and network routing. Although other lower level protocols can be used, HTTP is primarily used with TCP/IP.

The HTTP protocol is transactional in nature: A client sends a request to a server, and a server replies with a response. The request consists of a request method, a universal resource identifier, a protocol version, request modifiers, client information, and possibly body content. The response consists of a status line that indicates the protocol version and a success or error code, followed by a MIME-like message, metainformation, and possibly body content.

Request and response messages use a generic format for transferring entities. An entity consists of metainformation in the form of entity-header fields and content in the form of an entity-body. An entity is usually an HTML file or a graphic image, but it can be many different data types. Request and response messages consist of a start line, one or more header fields, an empty line indicating the end of the header fields, and an optional message-body. The format is as follows:

```
generic-message = start-line
                  *message-header
                  CRLF
                  [ message-body ]
```

Most of the complexity of HTTP lies in the use of message headers. We will examine the four types of header fields: request headers, response headers, general headers, and entity headers. All HTTP header fields use the generic format of a name followed by a colon (:) and the field value. Field names are case insensitive, and the order in which header fields with differing field names are received is not significant.

Request Messages

The operation of HTTP consists of requests from a client to a server and responses from a server to a client. A request message from a client to a server has the following format:

```
Request    = Request-Line
             *( general-header
             | request-header
             | entity-header )
             CRLF
             [ message-body ]
```

Here is an example of a request message sent from an Internet browser to a web server requesting the file default.htm:

```
GET /default.htm HTTP/1.0
Accept: image/gif, image/x-xbitmap, image/jpeg, image/
pjpeg, application/msword, */*
Accept-Language: en
```

```
UA-pixels: 1024x768
UA-color: color8
UA-OS: Windows NT
UA-CPU: x86
If-Modified-Since: Thu, 28 Aug 1997 17:56:10 GMT; length=150
User-Agent: Mozilla/2.0 (compatible; MSIE 3.02; Win32)
Host: 192.168.205.76
Connection: Keep-Alive
```

The start line can be a request line or a status line. In the case of a request message from a client to a server, the first line includes the method to be applied to a resource, the identifier of that resource, and the protocol version in use. General-purpose servers must support the *GET* and *HEAD* methods; all other methods are optional. The HTTP 1.1 specification defines the following methods:

OPTIONS requests the necessary client information to determine the options or requirements or both associated with a resource or to determine the capabilities of a server.

GET retrieves the information identified by a Request-Uniform Resource Identifier (URI). The HTTP specification defines a URI as a formatted string that identifies a resource by name, location, or any other characteristic. If the Request-URI identifies a program that generates data, the URI actually refers to the data produced rather than to the program itself. The *GET* method becomes conditional if any of the following are included in the request message: If-Modified-Since, If-Unmodified-Since, If-Match, If-None-Match, or If-Range header.

HEAD gets the same header information retrieved by the *GET* method, but it does not retrieve the message-body. One reason that the HTTP protocol defines this method is that it is useful for testing hypertext links for validity, accessibility, and recent modification. You can use these modifiers to avoid the downloading of data that is already cached on the client computer.

POST is a uniform method that covers the following functions:

❑ Annotation of existing resources

❑ Posting a message to a bulletin board, newsgroup, mailing list, or similar group of articles

❑ Providing a block of data, such as the result of submitting a form, to a data-handling process

❑ Extending a database through an append operation

However, the actual functionality of the *POST* method is determined by the server. A response of 201 (*Created*) means that a resource has been created on the server. A response of either 200 (*OK*) or 204 (*No Content*) means that the *POST* method did not result in a resource that could be identified by a URI.

PUT requests that the server store the enclosed entity under the supplied Request-URI. A response of 201 (*Created*) means that the server created a new resource identified by the Request-URI. If an existing resource is already identified by the Request-URI, a response of 200 (*OK*) or 204 (*No Content*) means that the resource was modified.

DELETE requests that a server delete the resource specified by the Request-URI. However, even though the server responds with a success code, the delete operation might not have been carried out. According to RFC 2068, a success code means that the server intends to either delete the resource or move it to an inaccessible location.

TRACE is used for testing and diagnostic purposes. It allows the client to see what is being received by the server.

Response Messages

After a server has received and interpreted a request message, it sends back an HTTP response message. Response messages use the following format:

```
Response     = Status-Line
                 *( general-header
                  | response-header
                  | entity-header )
                 CRLF
                 [ message-body ]
```

Here is an example of a response message sent from the web server to the client browser:

```
HTTP/1.0 200 OK
Server: Microsoft-IIS/3.0
Connection: keep-alive
Date: Thu, 28 Aug 1997 18:20:35 GMT
Content-Type: text/html
Accept-Ranges: bytes
Last-Modified: Thu, 28 Aug 1997 18:19:48 GMT
Content-Length: 173
```

```
<HTML>
<HEAD>
<TITLE>Inside Active Server</TITLE>
</HEAD>
<BODY>
<CENTER>
<FONT SIZE=3>This is a test page</FONT>
<IMG SRC="test.gif">
</CENTER>
</BODY>
</HTML>
```

Notice that the HTML file contains the image file test.gif, which prompts the following additional request from the Internet browser to the web server:

```
GET /test.gif HTTP/1.0
Accept: image/gif, image/x-xbitmap, image/jpeg, image/pjpeg, image/x-
jg, */*
Referer: http://192.168.205.76/default.htm
Accept-Language: en
UA-pixels: 1024x768
UA-color: color8
UA-OS: Windows NT
UA-CPU: x86
If-Modified-Since: Fri, 09 Aug 1996 05:30:00 GMT; length=982
User-Agent: Mozilla/2.0 (compatible; MSIE 3.02; Win32)
Host: 192.168.205.76
Connection: Keep-Alive
```

It's possible, however, that the image test.gif is cached locally on the client computer and has not been modified since it was last retrieved. When this happens, the following response message is sent:

```
HTTP/1.0 304 Not Modified
Connection: Keep-Alive
Content-Length: 0
```

The response message begins with a status line, indicating the protocol version and a numeric status code along with its textual interpretation. The numeric status code consists of three digits; the first digit defines the class of response. RFC 2068 lists the following five response categories, along with the individual values of the numeric status codes and their textual interpretations:

```
1xx: Informational - Request received, continuing process
2xx: Success - The action was successfully received, understood,
     and accepted
3xx: Redirection - Further action must be taken in order to
     complete the request
```

(continued)

```
4xx: Client Error - The request contains bad syntax or cannot be
     fulfilled
5xx: Server Error - The server failed to fulfill an apparently
     valid request

Status-Code   = "100"    ; Continue
              | "101"    ; Switching Protocols
              | "200"    ; OK
              | "201"    ; Created
              | "202"    ; Accepted
              | "203"    ; Non-Authoritative Information
              | "204"    ; No Content
              | "205"    ; Reset Content
              | "206"    ; Partial Content
              | "300"    ; Multiple Choices
              | "301"    ; Moved Permanently
              | "302"    ; Moved Temporarily
              | "303"    ; See Other
              | "304"    ; Not Modified
              | "305"    ; Use Proxy
              | "400"    ; Bad Request
              | "401"    ; Unauthorized
              | "402"    ; Payment Required
              | "403"    ; Forbidden
              | "404"    ; Not Found
              | "405"    ; Method Not Allowed
              | "406"    ; Not Acceptable
              | "407"    ; Proxy Authentication Required
              | "408"    ; Request Time-out
              | "409"    ; Conflict
              | "410"    ; Gone
              | "411"    ; Length Required
              | "412"    ; Precondition Failed
              | "413"    ; Request Entity Too Large
              | "414"    ; Request-URI Too Large
              | "415"    ; Unsupported Media Type
              | "500"    ; Internal Server Error
              | "501"    ; Not Implemented
              | "502"    ; Bad Gateway
              | "503"    ; Service Unavailable
              | "504"    ; Gateway Time-out
              | "505"    ; HTTP Version not supported
```

The HTTP 1.1 protocol differs from earlier versions of the HTTP protocol in that persistent connections are the default behavior of the HTTP connection. If persistent connections are not used, a separate TCP is established for each HTTP request. The HTTP 1.1 specification in RFC 2068 lists the following advantages of persistent connections:

- Opening and closing fewer TCP connections saves both CPU time and memory used for TCP protocol control blocks.

- HTTP requests and responses can be pipelined on a connection. Pipelining allows a client to make multiple requests without waiting for individual responses, which enables a single TCP connection to be used much more efficiently without a significant loss of time.

- Network congestion is reduced by minimizing the number of packets caused by TCP connections and allowing TCP sufficient time to determine the congestion state of the network.

- HTTP can evolve more gracefully because errors can be reported without the penalty of closing the TCP connection. In the future, clients using newer versions of HTTP can try a new feature, but if the client is communicating with an older server the client can retry with old semantics after an error is reported.

The example response message on page 47 was obtained using IIS 3.0; it contains the Connection: Keep-Alive header field. The Keep-Alive value is used to implement persistent connections under HTTP 1.0. However, this mechanism does not work correctly when messages are passed through some proxy servers. The HTTP 1.1 persistent connection mechanism was designed to resolve these kinds of difficulties and therefore replaces Keep-Alive.

Request Headers

HTTP 1.1 specifies the following request-header fields to allow the client to pass additional information about the request and the client to the server:

```
request-header = Accept
                | Accept-Charset
                | Accept-Encoding
                | Accept-Language
                | Authorization
                | From
                | Host
                | If-Modified-Since
                | If-Match
                | If-None-Match
                | If-Range
                | If-Unmodified-Since
                | Max-Forwards
                | Proxy-Authorization
                | Range
                | Referer
                | User-Agent
```

These are the request-header fields:

Accept specifies the media types that are acceptable for the response. If the server cannot send a response that is acceptable to the client, it should send a 406 (not acceptable) response.

Accept-Charset is used to indicate character sets that are acceptable responses, such as the ISO-8859-1 character set, which can be assumed to be acceptable to all user agents.

Accept-Encoding specifies the content-coding values that are acceptable in the response.

Accept-Language restricts the set of natural languages that are preferred as a response to the request.

Authorization added to a request allows a user agent to authenticate itself with a server.

From contains the user's Internet e-mail address.

Host specifies the Internet host and port number of the resource being requested.

If-Modified-Since, If-Match, If-None-Match, If-Range, and If-UnModified-Since place conditions on the request so that it will return only the entity if the request was or was not modified by a specified date, or if it does or does not match a specified entity tag. The If-Range header allows a client to complete a partial copy of an entity in its cache by requesting only the missing portion rather than a complete fresh copy from the server.

Max-Forwards is used with the *TRACE* method to limit the number of proxies or gateways that can forward the request to the next inbound server.

Proxy-Authorization contains the user agent's required authentication information to allow the client to identify itself (or its user) to a proxy.

Range is used to request one or more subranges of the entity rather than the entire entity.

Referer informs the server of the address of the resource from which the Request-URI was obtained.

User-Agent contains information about the user agent originating the request.

Response Headers

In the same way that additional information about a request can be passed through request-header fields, response-header fields can give information about the server and about further access to the resource identified by the Request-URI. The HTTP 1.1 specification lists the following response headers:

```
response-header = Age
                | Location
                | Proxy-Authenticate
                | Public
                | Retry-After
                | Server
                | Vary
                | Warning
                | WWW-Authenticate
```

The following are the response header fields:

Age is used to convey age information between caches. Age refers to the sender's estimate of the time elapsed since the response was generated at the originating server. This is the sum of time that the response has been resident in each of the caches along the path from the origin server and the amount of time it has been in transit along network paths.

Location redirects the recipient to a location other than the Request-URI for completion of the request or the identification of a new resource.

Proxy-Authenticate is included as part of a 407 Proxy Authentication Required response.

Public is used to inform the client of the capabilities of a server to which it is directly connected. If a response method has to pass through a proxy, the proxy must replace the header with a method that is appropriate to its capabilities or remove the header field. The specification states that this method is meant only to inform the recipient of unusual methods the server might support.

Retry-After can be used to inform the client how long a service is expected to remain unavailable. (The client has already received a 503 response indicating that the service is unavailable.) This value can be either the number of seconds of delay or a date when the service will be available.

Server conveys information about the web software running on the originating server. Administrators can configure the value of this field to avoid revealing software information to a possible intruder.

Vary is used by the server to notify a client that a particular response entity was selected from different available representations. The field is important for handling the caching of the possible different responses for this entity.

Warning provides additional information about the status of a response. A response message can carry more than one warning header, and any server or cache can add extra warning headers to a response. The HTTP specification provides the following currently defined warning codes with their recommended warning text in English:

Warning Code	Recommended Text
10	Response is stale
11	Revalidation failed
12	Disconnected operation
13	Heuristic expiration
14	Transformation applied
99	Miscellaneous warning

WWW-Authenticate challenges the authorization of a user agent. HTTP provides an authentication mechanism by which a server can challenge a client to provide authentication, and the server includes a WWW-Authenticate header field in its 401 (Unauthorized) response message to challenge the authorization of a user agent. A user agent that wants to authenticate itself with the server must include an Authorization header field that contains the appropriate credentials.

General Headers

In addition to request and response headers, the following headers are applicable to both request and response messages:

```
general-header = Cache-Control
               | Connection
               | Date
               | Pragma
               | Transfer-Encoding
               | Upgrade
               | Via
```

HTTP supports a caching system for storing a successful response as a cache entry. The caching system allows a response to be returned to a client after successful validation or, if it is fresh, to be returned without validation.

Cache-Control

The Cache-Control general-header field allows an origin server to override the default caching of a response. For example, the no-cache directive conveys that all or part of the response message will not be cached anywhere.

Connection

The HTTP 1.1 protocol uses persistent connections by default, but the Connection general-header field can be used to specify various connection options. For example, according to HTTP 1.1, the *close* option specifies that a connection should be closed after a response has been received.

Date

The Date general-header field indicates the date and time at which the message originated. A Date header field is required for evaluating caching behavior, so origin servers must include this in all responses. A Date header field for clients is optional and should be sent only in messages that include an entity-body, as in the case of the *PUT* and *POST* requests.

Pragma

The Pragma general-header field specifies implementation-specific directives that might apply to any recipient along the request/response chain. These directives must be passed through by any proxy or gateway application along the way. From the perspective of the protocol, all pragma directives specify optional behavior, although some systems might require that behavior be consistent with the directives.

Transfer-Encoding

If a message body must be transformed for safe transfer over the network, the Transfer-Encoding general-header field is used to indicate the type of transformation that was applied. For example, *Transfer-Encoding: chunked* indicates that the message body was chunked. The chunked encoding modifies the body of a message in order to transfer it as a series of chunks, which allows the transfer of dynamically produced content.

Upgrade

The Upgrade header field requests the use of another protocol. For example, a client can indicate that it wants to use a newer version of HTTP over the existing transport-layer connection. A client cannot use the Upgrade header field to insist on a protocol change because its acceptance and use by the server is optional.

Via

Gateways and proxies use the Via general-header field to list the intermediate protocols and recipients between the user agent and the server for requests, and between the origin server and the client for responses. This field provides a way to track message forwards, avoid request loops, and identify the protocol capabilities of all senders along the request/response chain.

Entity Headers

The transfer of entities over the Internet is the primary purpose of the HTTP protocol. Entities can be of many types, and both Request and Response messages can transfer them. Entity-header fields define optional meta-information about the entity-body or the resource identified by the request. RFC 2068 lists the following entity headers:

```
entity-header  = Allow
               | Content-Base
               | Content-Encoding
               | Content-Language
               | Content-Length
               | Content-Location
               | Content-MD5
               | Content-Range
               | Content-Type
               | ETag
               | Expires
               | Last-Modified
```

Allow

The Allow entity-header field informs the recipient of the valid methods for the associated resource. For example, if a resource supports the *GET*, *HEAD*, and *PUT* methods, the Allow entity-header field appears as "Allow: GET, HEAD, PUT".

Content-Base

Relative URLs within an entity can be resolved using the base URI contained in the Content-Base entity-header field.

Content-Encoding

The Content-Encoding entity-header field informs the recipient of any additional content coding that has been applied to the entity-body. The recipient uses this information to decode the message to obtain the media-type referenced by the Content-Type header field.

Content-Language

The natural language(s) of the intended audience for the enclosed entity are indicated in the Content-Language entity-header field. The field indicates the size of the message-body. Its value is given in a decimal number of octets.

Content-Length

Content-Length is the size of the message-body.

Content-Location

The resource location of the entity enclosed in the message can be found in the Content-Location entity-header field. This field can be a relative URI, in which case the URI is interpreted relative to the Content-Base URI provided in the response. If no Content-Base header exists, the relative URI is interpreted relative to the Request-URI.

Content-MD5

The Content-MD5 entity-header field is an MD5 digest of the entity-body that can be used to provide an end-to-end message integrity check of the entity-body. This can be helpful in detecting accidental modifications of the entity-body in transit, but it is not intended to safeguard against malicious attacks.

Content-Range

The Content-Range entity-header field indicates where in the full entity-body the partial entity-body should be inserted when a partial body is sent.

Content-Type

The Content-Type entity-header field communicates the media type of the entity-body that is sent to the recipient, as in the following example:

```
Content-Type: text/html; charset=ISO-8859-4
```

ETag

An entity tag for an entity-body is indicated in the ETag entity-header field.

Expires

The Expires entity-header field conveys the date and time that a response should be considered stale. The Expires field is overridden if a response includes a Cache-Control field with the max-age directive.

Last-Modified

The Last-Modified entity-header field informs the recipient of the date and time that the originating server believes the variant was last modified. The calculation of this field might involve checking the file system's last-modified time for server files or the checking the last-update timestamp of the record in a database.

Case Study: InternetJump

The following example builds a customized web server from scratch using Windows sockets. This case study is based on the InternetJump web site, which you can find at *www.internetjump.com*. This web site provides a useful service to people who have long URLs. For example, if your current address is *http://www.teztrisp.com/ourusers/~directories/YourCompany.html*, the InternetJump web site can give you a much shorter URL, such as *http://Fast.to/YourCompany*. This shorter URL will automatically jump users to the longer URL. Try out *http://fast.to/Aristotle* as an example.

Even if your current address is a full domain name, such as *www.Your-Company.com*, you can use the InternetJump service to obtain an additional personal address that will point to a page within your company web site, such as *Fast.to/JamesDean*. If you move your web site to another server, you can update your Jump address to point to the new location. You can also register your Jump address in search engines so that they will always link to your web site, no matter where it is located. In this way, you don't have to explain to users that your web site has moved or change your printed letterhead.

Our case study builds a customized web server to provide this URL forwarding service using Windows sockets and the Active Template Library. We will build a web server that accepts TCP/IP connections from Internet browsers on port 80. When a browser requests a short URI such as Aristotle, we will map it to a long URL such as *http://paul.spu.edu/~hawk/aristotle.html*. You'll recall that in the HTTP specification, the Location field is used to redirect the recipient to a location other than the Request-URI for completion of the request. In the response header that we send back to the browser, we will set the Location field with the value of the long URL. Our response header will also

THREE: Web Servers and IIS Protocols

contain a status value of 302, indicating that the object has moved. The Internet browser will then automatically issue a second request using the long URL.

Only six steps are required to build this application. All of the code is listed here; you can find a list of the Windows Socket calls later in this chapter.

Step 1: Create a Generic Microsoft Windows NT Service

Create a generic Windows NT service called Jump using the ATL application wizard that comes with Microsoft Visual C++ 5.0. Pull up the project settings, and add the Windows socket library ws2_32.lib to the Object/library modules using the Link tab. Then select the Debug Multithreaded option for the run-time library within the code generation setting under the C/C++ tab. You now have a generic Windows NT service project called Jump that is configured for Windows socket programming.

Step 2: Modify the *CServiceModule* Definition

The file StdAfx.h defines a class named *CServiceModule*, which is responsible for implementing all the generic tasks of a Windows NT service. In addition to actually running the service, this class also has code for installing, registering, starting, pausing, and stopping it. We want to add two additional capabilities to the service. First, we want the service to listen on port 80 for TCP/IP connection requests. Second, we want the service to be able establish a new TCP/IP connection for each request. To accomplish this, add these two additional thread routines to the service:

```
static unsigned __stdcall ListenThreadProc(void* p);
static unsigned __stdcall JumpThreadProc(void* p);
```

Step 3: Add Header Files and Defines
to the *CServiceModule* Implementation File

CServiceModule is implemented in a file named Jump.cpp. We will add the following header file required for multithreaded programming, a few defines, and a global event handle that we will use later on:

```
#include <process.h>
#define MAX_PENDING_CONNECTS 400
#define MESSAGE_BUFF_SIZE  500
#define MAX_BUFF_SIZE  9000
#define MAX_URL_SIZE  1000
HANDLE g_hExitEvent = FALSE;
```

Step 4: Modify the *CServiceModule* Run Method

The ATL code generated by the application wizard has an error that we need to fix. In the run method, an assert function is performed on *hr* instead of *hres* after the following line:

```
HRESULT hRes = CoInitialize(NULL);
```

We need to replace the code _ASSERTE(SUCCEEDED(hr)) with the code _ASSERTE(SUCCEEDED(hRes)) after this line. The run method is a good place to start the thread that will create the socket that listens on port 80 for TCP/IP connections. To be able to stop this thread gracefully, we will also create an event handle named g_hExitEvent:

```
g_hExitEvent = CreateEvent(NULL, TRUE, FALSE, NULL);
DWORD hListenThreadID;
HANDLE hListenThread;
hListenThread = (HANDLE) _beginthreadex(NULL, 0, &ListenThreadProc,
    (CServiceModule*) this, 0, (UINT*) &hListenThreadID);
```

After this code is executed, the run method goes into a loop in which it gets and dispatches a message. When it gets a message to terminate, it exits from the loop and executes the following code, which we will now add:

```
SetEvent(g_hExitEvent);
WaitForSingleObject(hListenThread, 15000);
CloseHandle ((HANDLE) hListenThread);
```

This code sets an event using the g_hExitEvent handle, which we will use to notify our thread that it should also terminate. We have given the thread 15 seconds to do this with the call to *WaitForSingleObject*.

Step 5: Add the Implementation for the *CServiceModule ListenThreadProc* Method

The *ListenThreadProc* method is responsible for listening for new TCP/IP connection requests on port 80. It will do so when someone types the IP address or domain name of the computer that the Windows NT service is running on. For example, if you type *http://www.internetjump.com/me* in your Internet browser, the browser will attempt to set up a TCP/IP connection to the Windows NT web service running on that computer over port 80. Incidentally, if you want the browser to connect to the service over a different port—82, for example—you would type *http://www.internetjump.com:82/me*.

In the following code, we create a socket, bind it to an address, and listen for incoming connections.

```
unsigned __stdcall CServiceModule::ListenThreadProc(void* p)
{

    CServiceModule* pThis = (CServiceModule*) p;
    _ASSERT(pThis);

    // WinSock needs initialization
    WSADATA WSAData;
    WSAStartup(MAKEWORD(1,1), &WSAData);

    // Assign address fields and set up to listen on port 80
    SOCKADDR_IN local_sin;
    local_sin.sin_family = AF_INET;
    local_sin.sin_addr.s_addr = INADDR_ANY;
    local_sin.sin_port = htons(80);

    // Create socket
    SOCKET socListen;
    socListen = socket (AF_INET, SOCK_STREAM, 0);
    if(socListen == INVALID_SOCKET)
    {
        ATLTRACE("socket() failed: %d is the error\r\n",
            WSAGetLastError());
        goto cleanup;
    }

    // Bind address to socket
    if (bind( socListen, (struct sockaddr FAR *) &local_sin,
            sizeof(local_sin)) == SOCKET_ERROR)
    {
        ATLTRACE("bind(sock) failed: %d is the error\r\n",
            WSAGetLastError());
        goto cleanup;
    }

    if (listen( socListen, MAX_PENDING_CONNECTS ) ==
        SOCKET_ERROR )
    {
        ATLTRACE("listen(sock) failed: %d is the error\r\n",
            WSAGetLastError());
        goto cleanup;
    }

    ATLTRACE("Accepting connections...\r\n");

    while(1)
    {
```

(continued)

```
            while(1)
            {
                int iu, is;
                struct timeval timeout;
                fd_set setR;
                FD_ZERO(&setR);
                FD_SET(socListen, &setR);

                timeout.tv_sec = 5;
                timeout.tv_usec = 0;

                is = select(iu, &setR, NULL, NULL, &timeout);
                if(is == SOCKET_ERROR)
                {
                    ATLTRACE("select failed: %d is the error\r\n",
                        WSAGetLastError());
                    goto cleanup;
                }
                else if (is != 0 )break;

                // check for termination
                if(WaitForSingleObject(g_hExitEvent, 0) !=
                    WAIT_TIMEOUT)
                {
                    ATLTRACE("Termination Requested\r\n");
                    goto cleanup;
                }

            }

        SOCKADDR_IN acc_sin;
        int acc_sin_len;
        acc_sin_len = sizeof(acc_sin);

        SOCKET* pSocket = new SOCKET;

        *pSocket = accept( socListen,(struct sockaddr FAR *)
            &acc_sin(int FAR *) &acc_sin_len );

        if (*pSocket == INVALID_SOCKET)
        {
            ATLTRACE("accept(sock) failed: %d is the error\n",
                WSAGetLastError());
            goto cleanup;
        }

        DWORD hJumpThreadID;
        HANDLE hJumpThread;
```

```
        hJumpThread = (HANDLE) _beginthreadex(NULL, 0,
            &JumpThreadProc, pSocket, 0, (UINT*) &hJumpThreadID);
        if (hJumpThread != 0) CloseHandle ((HANDLE) hJumpThread);
    }

cleanup:

    closesocket(socListen);
    WSACleanup();

    _endthreadex(S_OK);

    return 0;
}
```

Note that we periodically call the select function to check whether a call to the accept method will block. If it will, we then check whether an application termination request has been made. We can do this by checking whether the event handle *g_hExitEvent* has been set. If it has, we exit the thread so that the service will no longer be listening for incoming connections and can be terminated gracefully.

If a call to the accept method does not block, it means that an incoming connection request is already in the queue waiting to be handled. After we accept the new socket connection, we want to handle its communication on a new thread so that our listening thread can immediately go back to listening for other incoming connections. We do this by creating new threads for each connection request using the *JumpThreadProc* thread procedure. In this way, we can accommodate a large volume of users connecting to our customized web service at the same time. If you expect an even larger number of concurrent users, it is more efficient to create a pool of thread in which each thread handles a number of connections.

Step 6: Add the Implementation for the *CServiceModule JumpThreadProc* Method

Adding the implementation for *JumpThreadProc* is the final step in building our customized web server. This thread is responsible for communication over the socket connection between our web server and the client Internet browser. This thread procedure therefore must understand the HTTP protocol so that it can correctly interpret the data sent from the client browser and respond in a way that the browser will understand. This procedure begins by receiving the data sent from the browser as shown on the following page.

```
unsigned __stdcall CServiceModule::JumpThreadProc(void* p)
{

    SOCKET* pSocket = (SOCKET*) p;

    char szRead[MESSAGE_BUFF_SIZE];
    memset( (void*) szRead, '\0', MESSAGE_BUFF_SIZE );
    char szRequest[MAX_BUFF_SIZE];
    memset((void*) szRequest, '\0', MAX_BUFF_SIZE);
    char szResponse[MAX_BUFF_SIZE];
    memset((void*) szResponse, '\0', MAX_BUFF_SIZE);

    const char * szHeader1 = "HTTP/1.1 302 Object Moved\r\nLocation: ";
    const char * szHeader2 = "\r\nServer: InternetJump/1.0\r\nContent-/
    Type: text/html\r\nContent-Length: ";
    const char * szBody1 =
        "<head><title>Document Moved</title></head>\r\n<body>/
    <h1>Object Moved</h1>This document may be found <a HREF=\"";
    const char * szBody2 = "\">here</a>";

    while (1)
    {

        // Receive request
        int ncount_read = 0;
        ncount_read = recv(*pSocket, (char*) szRead,
            MESSAGE_BUFF_SIZE, 0);
        if (ncount_read == SOCKET_ERROR)
        {
            ATLTRACE("recv(sock) failed: %d is the error\n",
                WSAGetLastError());
            break;
        }
        else if (ncount_read > 0)
        {
            szRead[ncount_read] = '\0';
            strcat(szRequest, szRead);
            // Check to see whether we have received
            // all of the request
              if( strstr( szRequest, "\r\n\r\n" ) != NULL )
            {
                // Check whether the get method has been used
                int isize = strlen( szRequest );
                for( int i = 0; i < isize; i++ )
                {
                    if(islower(szRequest[i])) szRequest[i] =
                        _toupper( szRequest[i]);
                }
```

```
char *pdest1 = strstr( szRequest, "GET" );

// Extract target of a GET request and
// send back response
if( pdest1 != NULL )
{
    char szGet[MAX_URL_SIZE];
    memset( (void*) szGet, '\0', MESSAGE_BUFF_SIZE);
    pdest1 = pdest1+4;
    char *pdest2 = NULL;
    pdest2 = strstr( pdest1, "HTTP" );
    if( pdest2 != NULL )
    {
        strncat( szGet, pdest1+1, pdest2 - pdest1 - 2 );
        // Map GET to forwarding URL and
        // create response string
        char szURL[MAX_URL_SIZE];
        memset( (void*) szURL, '\0', MAX_URL_SIZE);

        if (!strcmp(szGet, "MEET")) strncat(szURL,
            "http://www.InternetJump.com/Meeting",
            MAX_URL_SIZE);
        if (!strcmp(szGet, "CGI")) strncat(szURL,
            "http://hoohoo.ncsa.uiuc.edu/cgi/",
            MAX_URL_SIZE);
        if (!strcmp(szGet, "ARISTOTLE")) strncat(szURL,
            "http://paul.spu.edu/~hawk/aristotle.html",
            MAX_URL_SIZE);
        // Put in a default if no map found.
        if (!strcmp(szURL, "")) strncat(szURL,
            "http://www.internetjump.com/",
            MAX_URL_SIZE);

        // Create response string
        strcat(szResponse, szHeader1);
        strcat(szResponse, szURL);
        strcat(szResponse, szHeader2);
        size_t istrl = strlen(szBody1) +
            strlen(szURL ) + strlen(szBody2 );
        char strsize[20];
        _itoa( istrl, strsize, 10 );
        strcat(szResponse, strsize);
        strcat(szResponse, "\r\n\r\n");
        strcat(szResponse, szBody1);
        strcat(szResponse, szURL);
        strcat(szResponse, szBody2);
        size_t ist1 = strlen(
```

(continued)

```
                        (const char *) szResponse );
                }
                else break;
            }
            else break;

            // Send back response
            int nbytesleft, npoint, nsize, ncount_sent;
            nsize = strlen( (const char *) szResponse );
            npoint = 0;
            nbytesleft = nsize;
            ncount_sent = 0;
            while(nbytesleft > 0)
            {
                ncount_sent = send(*pSocket, szResponse+npoint,
                    MESSAGE_BUFF_SIZE, 0);
                if ( ncount_sent == SOCKET_ERROR)
                {
                    ATLTRACE("send(sock) failed: %d is the error\n",
                        WSAGetLastError());
                    break;
                }
                npoint += ncount_sent;
                nbytesleft -= ncount_sent;
            }
            break;

        }
    }
}

closesocket(*pSocket);

delete pSocket;

_endthreadex(S_OK);
return 0;
}
```

According to the HTTP specification, the request message ends with the characters \r\n\r\n. We therefore continue to receive data on this socket until these characters have been received. After they have been received, we extract the target of the *GET* method sent from the Internet browser. If someone connected to our server over port 80 without using a browser does not use the *GET* method, we can simply close the socket connection and exit the thread. After we extract the target of the *GET* method, we map it to a long URL. I put in only three samples above, but you can add any number here. A default URL is given if no match is found.

Next we need to create a response header and body to send back to the client browser. Following the HTTP specification, we send a response message with the status of 302 indicating that the requested object has been moved. We set the Location field to indicate the new URL. After this response has been sent, we close the socket connection and exit the thread. After the Internet browser has received this response, we automatically issue a new request to the web server specified in the long URL.

Starting the Web Server

After you compile the Jump project, you can register and start the Jump web service. You register it by executing the command *Jump.exe /service.* You start it with the command *C:\> net start Jump.* (Remember to first stop any other web server running on that computer that might be listening for connections over port 80.) You can easily test this by typing *http://localhost/cgi* in an Internet browser on the same computer as the service.

The Jump service returns a response that automatically directs your Internet browser to *http://hoohoo.ncsa.uiuc.edu/cgi/.*

The code files that we modified using the Jump wizard–generated project are listed here and on the following pages:

STDAFX Header File

```
// stdafx.h : include file for standard system include files,
//      or project specific include files that are used frequently,
//      but are changed infrequently

#if !defined(AFX_STDAFX_H__981BF269_D3D8_11D1_9162_0080C7205DC0__/
INCLUDED_)
#define AFX_STDAFX_H__981BF269_D3D8_11D1_9162_0080C7205DC0__INCLUDED_

#if _MSC_VER >= 1000
#pragma once
#endif // _MSC_VER >= 1000

#define STRICT

#define _WIN32_WINNT 0x0400
#define _ATL_APARTMENT_THREADED

#include <atlbase.h>
//You may derive a class from CComModule and use it if you want to
```

(continued)

```
//override something, but do not change the name of _Module

class CServiceModule : public CComModule
{
public:
    HRESULT RegisterServer(BOOL bRegTypeLib, BOOL bService);
    HRESULT UnregisterServer();
    void Init(_ATL_OBJMAP_ENTRY* p, HINSTANCE h, UINT nServiceNameID);
    void Start();
    void ServiceMain(DWORD dwArgc, LPTSTR* lpszArgv);
    void Handler(DWORD dwOpcode);
    void Run();
    BOOL IsInstalled();
    BOOL Install();
    BOOL Uninstall();
    LONG Unlock();
    void LogEvent(LPCTSTR pszFormat, ...);
    void SetServiceStatus(DWORD dwState);
    void SetupAsLocalServer();

//Implementation
private:
    static void WINAPI _ServiceMain(DWORD dwArgc, LPTSTR* lpszArgv);
    static void WINAPI _Handler(DWORD dwOpcode);

    static unsigned __stdcall ListenThreadProc(void* p);
    static unsigned __stdcall JumpThreadProc(void* p);

// Data members
public:
    TCHAR m_szServiceName[256];
    SERVICE_STATUS_HANDLE m_hServiceStatus;
    SERVICE_STATUS m_status;
    DWORD dwThreadID;
    BOOL m_bService;
};

extern CServiceModule _Module;
#include <atlcom.h>

//{{AFX_INSERT_LOCATION}}
// Microsoft Developer Studio will insert additional declarations
// immediately before the previous line

#endif //!defined(AFX_STDAFX_H__981BF269_D3D8_11D1_9162_
       //0080C7205DC0__INCLUDED)
```

Jump Implementation File

```cpp
// Jump.cpp : Implementation of WinMain

// Note: Proxy/Stub Information
//          To build a separate proxy/stub DLL,
//          run nmake -f Jumpps.mk in the project directory

#include "stdafx.h"
#include "resource.h"
#include "initguid.h"
#include "Jump.h"

#include "Jump_i.c"

#include <stdio.h>

#include <process.h>
#define MAX_PENDING_CONNECTS 400
#define MESSAGE_BUFF_SIZE  500
#define MAX_BUFF_SIZE  9000
#define MAX_URL_SIZE  1000
HANDLE g_hExitEvent = FALSE;

CServiceModule _Module;

BEGIN_OBJECT_MAP(ObjectMap)
END_OBJECT_MAP()

LPCTSTR FindOneOf(LPCTSTR p1, LPCTSTR p2)
{
    while (*p1 != NULL)
    {
        LPCTSTR p = p2;
        while (*p != NULL)
        {
            if (*p1 == *p++)
                return p1+1;
        }
        p1++;
    }
    return NULL;
}

// Although some of these functions are big, they are declared inline
// since they are used only once
```

(continued)

```
inline HRESULT CServiceModule::RegisterServer(BOOL bRegTypeLib,
    BOOL bService)
{
    HRESULT hr = CoInitialize(NULL);
    if (FAILED(hr))
        return hr;

    // Remove any previous service since it might point to
    // the incorrect file
    Uninstall();

    // Add service entries
    UpdateRegistryFromResource(IDR_Jump, TRUE);

    // Adjust the AppID for Local Server or Service
    CRegKey keyAppID;
    LONG lRes = keyAppID.Open(HKEY_CLASSES_ROOT, _T("AppID"));
    if (lRes != ERROR_SUCCESS)
        return lRes;

    CRegKey key;
    lRes = key.Open(keyAppID,
        _T("{981BF264-D3D8-11D1-9162-0080C7205DC0}"));
    if (lRes != ERROR_SUCCESS)
        return lRes;
    key.DeleteValue(_T("LocalService"));

    if (bService)
    {
        key.SetValue(_T("Jump"), _T("LocalService"));
        key.SetValue(_T("-Service"), _T("ServiceParameters"));
        // Create service
        Install();
    }

    // Add object entries
    hr = CComModule::RegisterServer(bRegTypeLib);

    CoUninitialize();
    return hr;
}

inline HRESULT CServiceModule::UnregisterServer()
{
    HRESULT hr = CoInitialize(NULL);
    if (FAILED(hr))
        return hr;
```

```
        // Remove service entries
        UpdateRegistryFromResource(IDR_Jump, FALSE);
        // Remove service
        Uninstall();
        // Remove object entries
        CComModule::UnregisterServer();

        CoUninitialize();
        return S_OK;
    }

    inline void CServiceModule::Init(_ATL_OBJMAP_ENTRY* p, HINSTANCE h,
        UINT nServiceNameID)
    {
        CComModule::Init(p, h);

        m_bService = TRUE;

        LoadString(h, nServiceNameID, m_szServiceName,
            sizeof(m_szServiceName) / sizeof(TCHAR));

        // Set up the initial service status
        m_hServiceStatus = NULL;
        m_status.dwServiceType = SERVICE_WIN32_OWN_PROCESS;
        m_status.dwCurrentState = SERVICE_STOPPED;
        m_status.dwControlsAccepted = SERVICE_ACCEPT_STOP;
        m_status.dwWin32ExitCode = 0;
        m_status.dwServiceSpecificExitCode = 0;
        m_status.dwCheckPoint = 0;
        m_status.dwWaitHint = 0;
    }

    LONG CServiceModule::Unlock()
    {
        LONG l = CComModule::Unlock();
        if (l == 0 && !m_bService)
            PostThreadMessage(dwThreadID, WM_QUIT, 0, 0);
        return l;
    }

    BOOL CServiceModule::IsInstalled()
    {
        BOOL bResult = FALSE;

        SC_HANDLE hSCM = ::OpenSCManager(NULL, NULL,
            SC_MANAGER_ALL_ACCESS);
```

(continued)

```
        if (hSCM != NULL)
        {
            SC_HANDLE hService = ::OpenService(hSCM, m_szServiceName,
                SERVICE_QUERY_CONFIG);
            if (hService != NULL)
            {
                bResult = TRUE;
                ::CloseServiceHandle(hService);
            }
            ::CloseServiceHandle(hSCM);
        }
        return bResult;
}

inline BOOL CServiceModule::Install()
{
        if (IsInstalled())
            return TRUE;

        SC_HANDLE hSCM = ::OpenSCManager(NULL, NULL,
            SC_MANAGER_ALL_ACCESS);
        if (hSCM == NULL)
        {
            MessageBox(NULL, _T("Couldn't open service manager"),
                m_szServiceName, MB_OK);
            return FALSE;
        }

        // Get the executable file path
        TCHAR szFilePath[_MAX_PATH];
        ::GetModuleFileName(NULL, szFilePath, _MAX_PATH);

        SC_HANDLE hService = ::CreateService(
            hSCM, m_szServiceName, m_szServiceName,
            SERVICE_ALL_ACCESS, SERVICE_WIN32_OWN_PROCESS,
            SERVICE_DEMAND_START, SERVICE_ERROR_NORMAL,
            szFilePath, NULL, NULL, _T("RPCSS\0"), NULL, NULL);

        if (hService == NULL)
        {
            ::CloseServiceHandle(hSCM);
            MessageBox(NULL, _T("Couldn't create service"),
                m_szServiceName, MB_OK);
            return FALSE;
        }
```

```
        ::CloseServiceHandle(hService);
        ::CloseServiceHandle(hSCM);
        return TRUE;
}

inline BOOL CServiceModule::Uninstall()
{
    if (!IsInstalled())
        return TRUE;

    SC_HANDLE hSCM = ::OpenSCManager(NULL, NULL,
        SC_MANAGER_ALL_ACCESS);

    if (hSCM == NULL)
    {
        MessageBox(NULL, _T("Couldn't open service manager"),
            m_szServiceName, MB_OK);
        return FALSE;
    }

    SC_HANDLE hService = ::OpenService(hSCM, m_szServiceName,
        SERVICE_STOP | DELETE);

    if (hService == NULL)
    {
        ::CloseServiceHandle(hSCM);
        MessageBox(NULL, _T("Couldn't open service"),
            m_szServiceName, MB_OK);
        return FALSE;
    }
    SERVICE_STATUS status;
    ::ControlService(hService, SERVICE_CONTROL_STOP, &status);

    BOOL bDelete = ::DeleteService(hService);
    ::CloseServiceHandle(hService);
    ::CloseServiceHandle(hSCM);

    if (bDelete)
        return TRUE;

    MessageBox(NULL, _T("Service could not be deleted"),
        m_szServiceName, MB_OK);
    return FALSE;
}
```

(continued)

```
/////////////////////////////////////////////////////////////////////
// Logging functions
void CServiceModule::LogEvent(LPCTSTR pFormat, ...)
{
    TCHAR   chMsg[256];
    HANDLE  hEventSource;
    LPTSTR  lpszStrings[1];
    va_list    pArg;

    va_start(pArg, pFormat);
    _vstprintf(chMsg, pFormat, pArg);
    va_end(pArg);

    lpszStrings[0] = chMsg;

    if (m_bService)
    {
        /* Get a handle to use with ReportEvent()*/
        hEventSource = RegisterEventSource(NULL, m_szServiceName);
        if (hEventSource != NULL)
        {
            /* Write to event log*/
            ReportEvent(hEventSource, EVENTLOG_INFORMATION_TYPE,
                0, 0, NULL, 1, 0, (LPCTSTR*) &lpszStrings[0], NULL);
            DeregisterEventSource(hEventSource);
        }
    }
    else
    {
        // Since we are not running as a service, just write
            the error to the console.
        _putts(chMsg);
    }
}

/////////////////////////////////////////////////////////////////////
// Service startup and registration
inline void CServiceModule::Start()
{
    SERVICE_TABLE_ENTRY st[] =
    {
        { m_szServiceName, _ServiceMain },
        { NULL, NULL }
    };
    if (m_bService && !::StartServiceCtrlDispatcher(st))
    {
        m_bService = FALSE;
    }
```

```
        if (m_bService == FALSE)
            Run();
}

inline void CServiceModule::ServiceMain(DWORD /* dwArgc */,
    LPTSTR* /* lpszArgv */)
{
    // Register the control request handler.
    m_status.dwCurrentState = SERVICE_START_PENDING;
    m_hServiceStatus = RegisterServiceCtrlHandler(m_szServiceName,
        _Handler);
    if (m_hServiceStatus == NULL)
    {
        LogEvent(_T("Handler not installed"));
        return;
    }
    SetServiceStatus(SERVICE_START_PENDING);

    m_status.dwWin32ExitCode = S_OK;
    m_status.dwCheckPoint = 0;
    m_status.dwWaitHint = 0;

    // When the Run function returns, the service has stopped
    Run();

    SetServiceStatus(SERVICE_STOPPED);
    LogEvent(_T("Service stopped"));
}

inline void CServiceModule::Handler(DWORD dwOpcode)
{
    switch (dwOpcode)
    {
    case SERVICE_CONTROL_STOP:
        SetServiceStatus(SERVICE_STOP_PENDING);
        PostThreadMessage(dwThreadID, WM_QUIT, 0, 0);
        break;
    case SERVICE_CONTROL_PAUSE:
        break;
    case SERVICE_CONTROL_CONTINUE:
        break;
    case SERVICE_CONTROL_INTERROGATE:
        break;
    case SERVICE_CONTROL_SHUTDOWN:
        break;
    default:
```

(continued)

75

```
            LogEvent(_T("Bad service request"));
        }
    }

    void WINAPI CServiceModule::_ServiceMain(DWORD dwArgc,
        LPTSTR* lpszArgv)
    {
        _Module.ServiceMain(dwArgc, lpszArgv);
    }
    void WINAPI CServiceModule::_Handler(DWORD dwOpcode)
    {
        _Module.Handler(dwOpcode);
    }


    void CServiceModule::SetServiceStatus(DWORD dwState)
    {
        m_status.dwCurrentState = dwState;
        ::SetServiceStatus(m_hServiceStatus, &m_status);
    }


    void CServiceModule::Run()
    {
        HRESULT hr;

        _Module.dwThreadID = GetCurrentThreadId();

        HRESULT hRes = CoInitialize(NULL);
    //  If you are running on Windows NT 4.0 or later, you can use the
    //  following call instead to make the EXE free threaded.
    //  This means that calls come in on a random RPC thread.
    //  HRESULT hRes = CoInitializeEx(NULL, COINIT_MULTITHREADED);

        _ASSERTE(SUCCEEDED(hRes));

        // This provides a NULL DACL that will allow access to everyone.
        CSecurityDescriptor sd;
        sd.InitializeFromThreadToken();
        hr = CoInitializeSecurity(sd, -1, NULL, NULL,
            RPC_C_AUTHN_LEVEL_PKT, RPC_C_IMP_LEVEL_IMPERSONATE, NULL,
                EOAC_NONE, NULL);
        _ASSERTE(SUCCEEDED(hr));

        hr = _Module.RegisterClassObjects(CLSCTX_LOCAL_SERVER |
            CLSCTX_REMOTE_SERVER, REGCLS_MULTIPLEUSE);
        _ASSERTE(SUCCEEDED(hr));

        g_hExitEvent = CreateEvent(NULL, TRUE, FALSE, NULL);
        DWORD hListenThreadID;
```

```
        HANDLE hListenThread;
        hListenThread = (HANDLE) _beginthreadex(NULL, 0,
            &ListenThreadProc, (CServiceModule*) this,
            0, (UINT*) &hListenThreadID);


        LogEvent(_T("Service started"));
        SetServiceStatus(SERVICE_RUNNING);

        MSG msg;
        while (GetMessage(&msg, 0, 0, 0))
            DispatchMessage(&msg);

        SetEvent(g_hExitEvent);
        WaitForSingleObject(hListenThread, 15000);
        CloseHandle ((HANDLE) hListenThread);

        _Module.RevokeClassObjects();

        CoUninitialize();
}


/////////////////////////////////////////////////////////////////////////
extern "C" int WINAPI _tWinMain(HINSTANCE hInstance,
    HINSTANCE /*hPrevInstance*/, LPTSTR lpCmdLine, int /*nShowCmd*/)
{
    lpCmdLine = GetCommandLine(); //this line necessary
                                  //for _ATL_MIN_CRT
    _Module.Init(ObjectMap, hInstance, IDS_SERVICENAME);
    _Module.m_bService = TRUE;

    TCHAR szTokens[] = _T("-/");

    LPCTSTR lpszToken = FindOneOf(lpCmdLine, szTokens);
    while (lpszToken != NULL)
    {
        if (lstrcmpi(lpszToken, _T("UnregServer"))==0)
            return _Module.UnregisterServer();

        // Register as Local Server
        if (lstrcmpi(lpszToken, _T("RegServer"))==0)
            return _Module.RegisterServer(TRUE, FALSE);

        // Register as Service
        if (lstrcmpi(lpszToken, _T("Service"))==0)
            return _Module.RegisterServer(TRUE, TRUE);
```

(continued)

```
        lpszToken = FindOneOf(lpszToken, szTokens);
    }

    // Are we Service or Local Server?
    CRegKey keyAppID;
    LONG lRes = keyAppID.Open(HKEY_CLASSES_ROOT, _T("AppID"));
    if (lRes != ERROR_SUCCESS)
        return lRes;

    CRegKey key;
    lRes = key.Open(keyAppID,
        _T("{981BF264-D3D8-11D1-9162-0080C7205DC0}"));
    if (lRes != ERROR_SUCCESS)
        return lRes;

    TCHAR szValue[_MAX_PATH];
    DWORD dwLen = _MAX_PATH;
    lRes = key.QueryValue(szValue, _T("LocalService"), &dwLen);

    _Module.m_bService = FALSE;
    if (lRes == ERROR_SUCCESS)
        _Module.m_bService = TRUE;

    _Module.Start();

    // When we get here, the service has been stopped
    return _Module.m_status.dwWin32ExitCode;
}

unsigned __stdcall CServiceModule::ListenThreadProc(void* p)
{

    CServiceModule* pThis = (CServiceModule*) p;
    _ASSERT(pThis);

    // WinSock needs initialization
    WSADATA WSAData;
    WSAStartup(MAKEWORD(1,1), &WSAData);

    // Assign address fields, and set up to listen on port 80
    SOCKADDR_IN local_sin;
    local_sin.sin_family = AF_INET;
    local_sin.sin_addr.s_addr = INADDR_ANY;
    local_sin.sin_port = htons(80);

    // Create socket
    SOCKET socListen;
```

```
socListen = socket (AF_INET, SOCK_STREAM, 0);
if(socListen == INVALID_SOCKET)
{
    ATLTRACE("socket() failed: %d is the error\r\n",
        WSAGetLastError());
    goto cleanup;
}

//   Bind address to socket
if (bind( socListen, (struct sockaddr FAR *) &local_sin,
    sizeof(local_sin)) == SOCKET_ERROR)
{
    ATLTRACE("bind(sock) failed: %d is the error\r\n",
        WSAGetLastError());
    goto cleanup;
}

if (listen( socListen, MAX_PENDING_CONNECTS ) == SOCKET_ERROR )
{
    ATLTRACE("listen(sock) failed: %d is the error\r\n",
        WSAGetLastError());
    goto cleanup;
}

ATLTRACE("Accepting connections...\r\n");

while(1)
{

    while(1)
    {
        int iu, is;
        struct timeval timeout;
        fd_set setR;
        FD_ZERO(&setR);
        FD_SET(socListen, &setR);

        timeout.tv_sec = 5;
        timeout.tv_usec = 0;

        is = select(iu, &setR, NULL, NULL, &timeout);
        if(is == SOCKET_ERROR)
        {
            ATLTRACE("select failed: %d is the error\r\n",
                WSAGetLastError());
            goto cleanup;
        }
```

(continued)

```
                    else if (is != 0 )break;

                    // Check for termination
                    if(WaitForSingleObject(g_hExitEvent, 0) != WAIT_TIMEOUT)
                    {
                        ATLTRACE("Termination Requested\r\n");
                        goto cleanup;
                    }

                }

                SOCKADDR_IN acc_sin;
                int acc_sin_len;
                acc_sin_len = sizeof(acc_sin);

                SOCKET* pSocket = new SOCKET;

                *pSocket = accept( socListen, (struct sockaddr FAR *) &acc_sin,
                    (int FAR *) &acc_sin_len );

                if (*pSocket == INVALID_SOCKET)
                {
                    ATLTRACE("accept(sock) failed: %d is the error\n",
                        WSAGetLastError());
                    goto cleanup;
                }

                DWORD hJumpThreadID;
                HANDLE hJumpThread;
                hJumpThread = (HANDLE) _beginthreadex(NULL, 0, &JumpThreadProc,
                    pSocket, 0, (UINT*) &hJumpThreadID);
                if (hJumpThread != 0) CloseHandle ((HANDLE) hJumpThread);
        }

cleanup:

    closesocket(socListen);
    WSACleanup();

    _endthreadex(S_OK);

    return 0;
}

unsigned __stdcall CServiceModule::JumpThreadProc(void* p)
{
```

```
SOCKET* pSocket = (SOCKET*) p;

char szRead[MESSAGE_BUFF_SIZE];
memset( (void*) szRead, '\0', MESSAGE_BUFF_SIZE);
char szRequest[MAX_BUFF_SIZE];
memset((void*) szRequest, '\0', MAX_BUFF_SIZE);
char szResponse[MAX_BUFF_SIZE];
memset((void*) szResponse, '\0', MAX_BUFF_SIZE);

const char * szHeader1 = "HTTP/1.1 302 Object Moved\r\nLocation: ";
const char * szHeader2 =
    "\r\nServer: InternetJump/1.0\r\nContent-Type:/
text/html\r\nContent-Length: ";
const char * szBody1 =
    "<head><title>Document Moved</title>/
</head>\r\n<body><h1>Object Moved</h1>This/
document may be found <a HREF=\"";
const char * szBody2 = "\">here</a>";

while (1)
{

    // Receive request
    int ncount_read = 0;
    ncount_read = recv(*pSocket, (char*) szRead,
        MESSAGE_BUFF_SIZE, 0);
    if (ncount_read == SOCKET_ERROR)
    {
        ATLTRACE("recv(sock) failed: %d is the error\n",
            WSAGetLastError());
        break;
    }
    else if (ncount_read > 0)
    {
        szRead[ncount_read] = '\0';
        strcat(szRequest, szRead);
        // Check to see whether we have received all of the request
          if( strstr( szRequest, "\r\n\r\n" ) != NULL )
        {
            // Has the get method been used?
            int isize = strlen( szRequest );
            for( int i = 0; i < isize; i++ )
            {
                if(islower(szRequest[i])) szRequest[i] =
                    _toupper( szRequest[i]);
            }
```

(continued)

```
char *pdest1 = strstr( szRequest, "GET" );

// Extract target of a GET request and
// send back response
if( pdest1 != NULL )
{
    char szGet[MAX_URL_SIZE];
    memset( (void*) szGet, '\0', MESSAGE_BUFF_SIZE);
    pdest1 = pdest1+4;
    char *pdest2 = NULL;
    pdest2 = strstr( pdest1, "HTTP" );
    if( pdest2 != NULL )
    {
        strncat( szGet, pdest1+1, pdest2 - pdest1 - 2 );
        // Map GET to forwarding URL, and create
        // response string
        char szURL[MAX_URL_SIZE];
        memset( (void*) szURL, '\0', MAX_URL_SIZE);

        if (!strcmp(szGet, "MEET"))
            strncat(szURL,
            "http://www.InternetJump.com/Meeting",
            MAX_URL_SIZE);
        if (!strcmp(szGet, "CGI"))
            strncat(szURL,
            "http://hoohoo.ncsa.uiuc.edu/cgi/",
            MAX_URL_SIZE);
        if (!strcmp(szGet, "ARISTOTLE"))
            strncat(szURL,
            "http://paul.spu.edu/~hawk/aristotle.html",
            MAX_URL_SIZE);
        // Put in a default if no map found.
        if (!strcmp(szURL, ""))
            strncat(szURL,
            "http://www.internetjump.com/",
            MAX_URL_SIZE);

        // Create response string
        strcat(szResponse, szHeader1);
        strcat(szResponse, szURL);
        strcat(szResponse, szHeader2);
        size_t istrl = strlen(szBody1) +
            strlen(szURL ) + strlen(szBody2 );
        char strsize[20];
        _itoa( istrl, strsize, 10 );
        strcat(szResponse, strsize);
```

```
                    strcat(szResponse, "\r\n\r\n");
                    strcat(szResponse, szBody1);
                    strcat(szResponse, szURL);
                    strcat(szResponse, szBody2);
                    size_t ist1 =
                        strlen( (const char *) szResponse );
                }
                else break;
            }
            else break;

            // Send back response
            int nbytesleft, npoint, nsize, ncount_sent;
            nsize = strlen( (const char *) szResponse );
            npoint = 0;
            nbytesleft = nsize;
            ncount_sent = 0;
            while(nbytesleft > 0)
            {
                ncount_sent = send(*pSocket, szResponse+npoint,
                    MESSAGE_BUFF_SIZE, 0);
                if ( ncount_sent == SOCKET_ERROR)
                {
                    ATLTRACE(
                        "send(sock) failed: %d is the error\n",
                        WSAGetLastError());
                    break;
                }
                npoint += ncount_sent;
                nbytesleft -= ncount_sent;
            }
            break;


        }
    }
}

closesocket(*pSocket);

delete pSocket;

_endthreadex(S_OK);
return 0;
}
```

Berkeley-Style Socket Routines

The following section contains prototypes of the Berkeley-style socket routines.

socket

SOCKET socket (int *af*, int *type*, int *protocol*);

The socket function creates a socket descriptor of the specified address family *af*, data type *type*, and protocol *protocol*. The address family identifies the format required for interpreting the addresses that are used; for example, AF_INET is the address family for Internet addresses.

Windows sockets 2.0 can support many data types, but traditionally sockets supported only the types SOCK_STREAM and SOCK_DGRAM. The SOCK_STREAM data type provides sequenced, reliable, two-way, connection-based byte streams, and it uses TCP for the Internet address family. The SOCK_DGRAM data type provides connectionless, unreliable datagram communication, and it uses UDP for the Internet address family. The protocol parameter identifies the protocol to be used, and it can be set to zero if the *af* parameter is AF_INET. The socket function returns a descriptor for the new socket, or the value INVALID_SOCKET if an error occurred. The *WSAGetLastError* function can be used to get the specific error code.

setsockopt

int setsockopt (SOCKET *s*, int *level*, int *optname*, const char FAR * *optval*, int *optlen*);

This function allows the user to set the value *optval* of options *optname* associated with a socket *s*. The *optlen* parameter is the size of the *optval* buffer, and the *level* parameter specifies the level at which the option is defined, such as SOL_SOCKET and IPPROTO_TCP. This is a powerful function for fine-tuning the operation of the socket. If the level is set to IPPROTO_TCP, the TCP_NODELAY option determines whether the Nagle algorithm is used to reduce the number of small packets sent by a host by buffering data that is to be sent until a full-sized packet is ready. Using this algorithm usually enhances performance; however, applications that send many small messages, in which time delays between the messages are maintained, might benefit by disabling this algorithm. If the level is set to SOL_SOCKET, the following options can be set:

Value	Type	Description
SO_BROADCAST	BOOL	Allows the socket to be configured for the transmission of broadcast messages.
SO_DEBUG	BOOL	Disables or enables debugging.
SO_DONTLINGER	BOOL	Determines whether the socket will block on close waiting for unsent data to be sent.
SO_DONTROUTE	BOOL	Disables or enables routing.
SO_GROUP_PRIORITY	int	Sets the relative priority for sockets that are part of a socket group.
SO_KEEPALIVE	BOOL	Used to request that a TCP/IP provider enable the use of "keep-alive" packets on TCP connections.
SO_LINGER	struct LINGER	Determines whether the socket will linger on close if unsent data is present.
SO_OOBINLINE	BOOL	Determines whether socket will receive out-of-band data in the normal data stream.
SO_RCVBUF	int	Specifies the buffer size for receives.
SO_REUSEADDR	BOOL	Allows the socket to be bound to an address that is already in use.
SO_SNDBUF	int	Specifies the buffer size for receives.
PVD_CONFIG	Provider Dependent	Used to store configuration information for the service provider associated with the socket.

bind

int bind (SOCKET *s*, const struct sockaddr FAR* *name*, int *namelen*);

This function associates a specific address and port number with a socket. The socket function creates a socket within a name space (*address family*), but it does not assign a name to it. This function takes the created socket as the parameter *s* and assigns an address and port number *name* to it. The parameter *namelen* specifies the length of the name. If no error occurs, this function returns zero.

listen
int listen (SOCKET *s*, int *backlog*);

This function puts the socket in a listening mode to receive incoming connections. The socket *s* has already been bound and is unconnected. The *backlog* parameter specifies the maximum length of the queue of pending connections.

accept
SOCKET accept (SOCKET *s*, struct sockaddr FAR* *addr*, int FAR* *addrlen*);

The *accept* function takes the first connection in the queue of pending connections on the socket *s* and creates a new socket for it. If no error occurs, the function returns a new socket that maintains the new accepted connection; otherwise, a value of INVALID_SOCKET is returned. When the socket is marked as blocking, the accept function blocks the caller until a connection request is present. When the socket is marked as nonblocking, the accept function returns an error if no pending connections are present on the queue. The *addr* parameter and its length *addrlen* are optional parameters that can be used to give the address of the connecting entity.

connect
int connect (SOCKET *s*, const struct sockaddr FAR* *name*, int *namelen*);

The *connect* function is used to create a connection to a remote host. On the server side, we have seen that the *listen* and *accept* functions are used to establish new connection requests from clients. The clients call the *connect* function to make that request. The *connect* function takes as parameters the socket *s* for the unconnected socket, a pointer to a *sockaddr* structure *name*, and the length of this structure. The *sockaddr* structure contains the address and port number of the destination host. For connection-oriented sockets of type SOCK_STREAM, the *connect* function establishes a connection and the socket is ready to send and receive data. If the socket is a connectionless SOCK_DGRAM type, the *connect* function merely establishes a default destination address that is used on subsequent calls to send or receive data.

send

int send (SOCKET *s*, **const char FAR** * *buf*, **int** *len*, **int** *flags***);**

This function sends data to a remote host on the connected socket *s*. The second parameter, *buf*, points to the data that is to be sent; and the third parameter, *len*, is the length of the buffer. If this function returns without any error, it does not mean that the data has been delivered but rather that the data has been queued for transmission. Unless the socket has been placed in a nonblocking mode, the *send* function will block if no buffer space is available to hold the data to be transmitted.

On nonblocking stream-oriented sockets, the *send* function accepts as much of the buffer space as is available. This function returns with the number of bytes written for transmission, or with SOCKET_ERROR if an error occurs. If the *send* function has been passed a datagram socket, the maximum datagram size of the current network must not be exceeded. The *flags* parameter is used to modify the behavior of the send function beyond the options specified for the associated socket. The flag MSG_DONTROUTE means that the data should not be routed, and the MSG_OOB flag is used to inform stream sockets that data should be sent as out-of-band data. (Out-of-band data is an independent transmission channel associated with a pair of connected stream sockets.)

sendto

int sendto (SOCKET *s*, **const char FAR** * *buf*, **int** *len*, **int** *flags*, **const struct sockaddr FAR** * *to*, **int** *tolen***);**

This function is similar to the *send* function (described earlier), but it specifies a destination. The *to* parameter is the address of the target socket; it can be any valid address in the socket's address family. The *tolen* parameter is the size of the address in the *to* parameter. The *sendto* function is typically used on a connectionless socket to send a datagram to a specific peer socket. On a connection-oriented stream socket, the *to* and *tolen* parameters are ignored, making *sendto* identical to the *send* function.

recv

int recv (SOCKET *s*, **char FAR*** *buf*, **int** *len*, **int** *flags***);**

This function is used to read incoming data on a socket. The first parameter is a descriptor that identifies the connected socket. The second and third parameters are the buffer for the incoming data and its length, respectively. The last parameter is a flag that sets how a call is made. If the socket is of the type SOCK_STREAM, this function retrieves as much data as is currently available up to the size of the buffer supplied. For sockets of type SOCK_DGRAM, the *recv* function retrieves data from the first queued datagram. For unreliable protocols such as UDP, any data from the datagram that doesn't fit into the buffer supplied is discarded, and *recv* generates the error WSAEMSGSIZE. If you use a reliable protocol, the service provider retains the data until it is successfully read by calling *recv* again with a large enough buffer. For blocking sockets, the *recv* call waits for data to arrive if no incoming data is currently available. When a nonblocking socket is used and there is no data to read, *recv* returns a value of SOCKET_ERROR. If the MSG_PEEK flag is used, the data is copied into the buffer but is not removed from the input queue. The MSG_OOB flag is used for processing out-of-band data. The *recv* function returns with the number of bytes read, or with SOCKET_ERROR if an error occurred.

recvfrom

int recvfrom (SOCKET *s*, char FAR* *buf*, int *len*, int *flags*, struct sockaddr FAR* *from*, int FAR* *fromlen*);

The *recvfrom* function is similar to the *recv* function, but it also returns the address from which the data was sent. With sockets that are not connection oriented, the optional parameter *from* points to a buffer that holds the source address upon return. When a call is made, the length of the buffer is specified in the *fromlen* parameter. When the function returns, *fromlen* is set to the size of the data received. For connection-oriented sockets, such as those of type SOCK_STREAM, the *from* and *fromlen* parameters are ignored. The *recvfrom* function returns the number of bytes received if no error occurs. If an error occurs, the value of SOCKET_ERROR is returned and a specific error code can be retrieved by calling *WSAGetLastError*. If the connection has been gracefully closed, the return value is zero.

select

int select (int *nfds*, fd_set FAR * *readfds*, fd_set FAR * *writefds*, fd_set FAR * *exceptfds*, const struct timeval FAR * *timeout*);

The *select* function is used to request information on the read, write, or error status of one or more sockets. The first parameter, *nfds*, is ignored by Windows sockets but has been kept in this function to maintain compatibility with the original Berkeley Sockets API.

The next three parameters—*readfds, writefds,* and *exceptfds*—use the fd_set structure, which can be defined as follows for the Windows platform:

```
typedef struct fd_set {
        u_int  fd_count;
        SOCKET   fd_array[FD_SETSIZE];
} fd_set
```

This structure contains an array of sockets and an unsigned *int* to hold the number of sockets set. Because the underlying representation of the fd_set structure can vary for different implementations, a set of macros compatible with those used in the Berkeley API is provided for manipulating it. The *readfds* parameter uses the fd_set structure to contain the sockets that are to be checked for readability.

The *writefds* parameter uses the fd_set structure to contain the sockets that are to be checked for writability. The *exceptfds* parameter identifies the sockets that are to be checked for errors or for the presence of out-of-band data. The *timeout* parameter specifies the maximum time that the *select* function will wait before returning. If this value is *null,* the *select* function will block indefinitely until at least one descriptor meets the specified criteria. If an error occurs, the *select* function returns SOCKET_ERROR. If the *timeout* parameter times out, the *select* function returns zero. Otherwise, it returns the number of sockets that meet the specified criteria.

Readability and Writability for Sockets

Readability means that queued data is available for reading. So, for example, a call to *recv* or *recvfrom* will not block. If a socket is currently in the listen state, readability means that an incoming connection request has been received and thus a call to accept will not block. If the socket is of type SOCK_STREAM, readability can also mean that a request to close the socket has been received.

Writability for a blocking socket means that a call to *send* or *sendto* will succeed, but it can still block if the *len* parameter exceeds the amount of available outgoing buffer space. If the *connect* function is called on a nonblocking socket, a socket is writable after the connection is successfully established.

closesocket

int closesocket (SOCKET *s*);

This function closes an existing socket and frees the resources associated with it. The way *closesocket* works is affected by the socket options SO_LINGER and SO_DONTLINGER, as follows:

Option	Interval	Type of Close	Wait for Close?
SO_DONTLINGER	Don't care	Graceful	No
SO_LINGER	Zero	Hard	No
SO_LINGER	Nonzero	Graceful	Yes

The closing of a socket is called *hard* if the socket is reset immediately; any unsent data is lost. The closing of a socket is called *graceful* if the *closesocket* function blocks on a blocking socket until the remaining data has been sent or until the timeout expires. The *closesocket* function blocks only if SO_LINGER is set with a nonzero timeout on a blocking socket.

shutdown

int shutdown (SOCKET *s*, int *how*);

This function disables sends or receives on a socket. If the *how* parameter is set to SD_RECEIVE, subsequent calls to receive data are disabled. For TCP, if data is still queued or if data arrives subsequently, the socket is reset. If the *how* parameter is set to SD_SEND, subsequent calls to send data are disabled. For TCP, this causes FIN to be sent. Both the sending and receiving of data are disabled if the *how* parameter is set to SD_BOTH. Note that this function does not close the socket or free its resources. If an error occurs, the shutdown returns SOCKET_ERROR; otherwise, it returns *0*.

getpeername

**int getpeername (SOCKET *s*, struct sockaddr FAR* *name*,
int FAR* *namelen*);**

This function retrieves the name of the peer connected to the socket *s* and puts it in the address structure *name*. The *namelen* parameter contains the size in bytes of the name returned.

getsockname

**int getsockname (SOCKET *s*, struct sockaddr FAR* *name*,
int FAR* *namelen*);**

This function gets the current name for the bound or connected socket *s*. It is like the *getpeername* function, but it returns the local address and port bound to the socket and not the remote address and port number. A Windows sockets application cannot assume that the address will be specified until the socket is connected. This function is often used to get the address and port number of a socket that has been connected before being bound.

getsockopt

int getsockopt (SOCKET *s*, int *level*, int *optname*, char FAR* *optval*, int FAR* *optlen*);

This function retrieves the options set with the *setsockopt* function. The *getsockopt* function returns the default value for any option not set with *setsockopt*.

ioctlsocket

int ioctlsocket (SOCKET *s*, long *cmd*, u_long FAR* *argp*);

This function controls the I/O mode of a socket independent of the protocol and communications subsystem. The *cmd* parameter contains the command to perform on the socket *s*, and the *argp* parameter is a parameter for *cmd*. The FIONBIO command disables nonblocking on the socket when *argp* is zero; otherwise, nonblocking is enabled. The FIONREAD command determines the amount of data that can be read on the socket. For sockets of type SOCK_STREAM, the *argp* parameter is set on return to the amount of data read by a single call to *recv*. For sockets of type SOCK_DGRAM, the parameter is set to the size of the first queued datagram. The SIOCATMARK command is used to determine if all out-of-band data has been read. The *argp* is set to TRUE when no out-of-band data is waiting to be read; otherwise, it is set to FALSE. This command applies only to stream-oriented sockets that have been configured with the SO_OOBINLINE option.

inet_addr

unsigned long inet_addr (const char FAR * *cp*);

This function converts a dotted-decimal IP address to an unsigned long value representing the IP address. The IP address is passed in the *cp* parameter and, if it does not contain a legitimate Internet address such as 256.255.255.255, *inet_addr* returns the value INADDR_NONE.

inet_ntoa

char FAR * inet_ntoa (struct in_addr *in*);

This function takes an IP address specified by the *in* parameter and formats it as a dotted-decimal character string. The IP address is passed in as an in_addr structure. The string returned by this function resides in memory allocated by Windows sockets and is guaranteed to be valid only until the next Windows Socket function call.

htonl

u_long htonl (u_long *hostlong*) ;

This function takes a 32-bit number in host byte order and returns a 32-bit number in the network byte order.

NOTE   Different systems use different byte ordering mechanisms. The *x*86 family of processors uses the little-endian byte order, in which the least significant byte of a multibyte integer is stored before the more significant bytes. Other types of processors use the big-endian byte order, in which the most significant byte of a multibyte integer is stored in memory before the less significant bytes. Big-endian byte order is also known as network byte order and is used in TCP/IP networks.

htons

u_short htons (u_short *hostshort*);

This function takes a 16-bit number in host byte order and returns a 16-bit number in network byte order.

ntohl

u_long ntohl (u_long *netlong*);

This function takes a 32-bit number in network byte order and returns a 32-bit number in host byte order. No operation is performed if the *netlong* parameter is already in host byte order.

ntohs

u_short ntohs (u_short *netshort*);

This function takes a 16-bit number in TCP/IP network byte order and returns a 16-bit number in host byte order. If the *netshort* parameter is already in host byte order, no operation is performed.

An Example of HTTP

Now that we've examined TCP/IP and HTTP, lets look at an example of it in operation. I used Network Monitor to capture the network packets that are transferred between two computers. In our example, Microsoft Internet Explorer (which is on one computer) requests the following simple HTML file from another computer running IIS 3.0:

```
<HTML>
<HEAD>
<TITLE>Inside Active Server</TITLE>
</HEAD>
<BODY>
<CENTER>
<FONT SIZE=3>This is a test page</FONT>
</CENTER>
</BODY>
</HTML>
```

The following trace file demonstrates HTTP by using the TCP and IP protocols to transfer the file default.htm. You can see the establishment of the TCP connection and the HTTP *GET* request followed by the HTTP response.

```
*******************************************************************
Frame    Time    Src MAC Addr    Dst MAC Addr    Protocol
8        0.714   ACTIVESR        DC_TECRA_01     TCP
Description
....S., len:    4, seq: 534438438-534438441, ack:         0, win:
Src Other Addr  Dst Other Addr  Type Other Addr
192.168.205.99  DC_TECRA_01     IP

+ FRAME: Base frame properties
+ ETHERNET: ETYPE = 0x0800 : Protocol = IP:  DOD Internet Protocol
  IP: ID = 0x422C; Proto = TCP; Len: 44
     IP: Version = 4 (0x4)
     IP: Header Length = 20 (0x14)
     IP: Service Type = 0 (0x0)
        IP: Precedence = Routine
        IP: ...0.... = Normal Delay
        IP: ....0... = Normal Throughput
        IP: .....0.. = Normal Reliability
     IP: Total Length = 44 (0x2C)
     IP: Identification = 16940 (0x422C)
     IP: Flags Summary = 2 (0x2)
        IP: .......0 = Last fragment in datagram
        IP: ......1. = Cannot fragment datagram
```

(continued)

93

```
        IP: Fragment Offset = 0 (0x0) bytes
        IP: Time to Live = 128 (0x80)
        IP: Protocol = TCP - Transmission Control
        IP: Checksum = 0x9C9E
        IP: Source Address = 192.168.205.99
        IP: Destination Address = 192.168.205.76
        IP: Data: Number of data bytes remaining = 24 (0x0018)
        TCP: ....S., len:    4, seq: 534438438-534438441,
ack:        0, win: 8192, src: 2013  dst:   80
        TCP: Source Port = 0x07DD
        TCP: Destination Port = Hypertext Transfer Protocol
        TCP: Sequence Number = 534438438 (0x1FDAE226)
        TCP: Acknowledgment Number = 0 (0x0)
        TCP: Data Offset = 24 (0x18)
        TCP: Reserved = 0 (0x0000)
        TCP: Flags = 0x02 : ....S.
            TCP: ..0..... = No urgent data
            TCP: ...0.... = Acknowledgment field not significant
            TCP: ....0... = No Push function
            TCP: .....0.. = No Reset
            TCP: ......1. = Synchronize sequence numbers
            TCP: .......0 = No Fin
        TCP: Window = 8192 (0x2000)
        TCP: Checksum = 0x51F7
        TCP: Urgent Pointer = 0 (0x0)
        TCP: Options
                TCP: Option Kind (Maximum Segment Size) = 2 (0x2)
                TCP: Option Length = 4 (0x4)
                TCP: Option Value = 1460 (0x5B4)
        TCP: Frame Padding

00000:  00 80 C7 A6 19 BB 00 A0 24 E5 38 E7 08 00 45 00
    ........$.8...E.
00010:  00 2C 42 2C 40 00 80 06 9C 9E C0 A8 CD 63 C0 A8
    .,B,@........c..
00020:  CD 4C 07 DD 00 50 1F DA E2 26 00 00 00 00 60 02
    .L...P...&....`.
00030:  20 00 51 F7 00 00 02 04 05 B4 05 B4
    .Q.........


*******************************************************************
Frame   Time    Src MAC Addr    Dst MAC Addr    Protocol
9       0.723   DC_TECRA_01     ACTIVESR        TCP
Description
.A..S., len:    4, seq:   9054549-9054552, ack: 534438439, win: 8
Src Other Addr  Dst Other Addr  Type Other Addr
DC_TECRA_01     192.168.205.99  IP
```

```
+ FRAME: Base frame properties
+ ETHERNET: ETYPE = 0x0800 : Protocol = IP:  DOD Internet Protocol
  IP: ID = 0x9006; Proto = TCP; Len: 44
      IP: Version = 4 (0x4)
      IP: Header Length = 20 (0x14)
      IP: Service Type = 0 (0x0)
          IP: Precedence = Routine
          IP: ...0.... = Normal Delay
          IP: ....0... = Normal Throughput
          IP: .....0.. = Normal Reliability
      IP: Total Length = 44 (0x2C)
      IP: Identification = 36870 (0x9006)
      IP: Flags Summary = 2 (0x2)
          IP: .......0 = Last fragment in datagram
          IP: ......1. = Cannot fragment datagram
      IP: Fragment Offset = 0 (0x0) bytes
      IP: Time to Live = 128 (0x80)
      IP: Protocol = TCP - Transmission Control
      IP: Checksum = 0x4EC4
      IP: Source Address = 192.168.205.76
      IP: Destination Address = 192.168.205.99
      IP: Data: Number of data bytes remaining = 24 (0x0018)
      TCP: .A..S., len:    4, seq:   9054549-9054552,
ack: 534438439, win: 8760, src:    80  dst: 2013
          TCP: Source Port = Hypertext Transfer Protocol
          TCP: Destination Port = 0x07DD
          TCP: Sequence Number = 9054549 (0x8A2955)
          TCP: Acknowledgment Number = 534438439 (0x1FDAE227)
          TCP: Data Offset = 24 (0x18)
          TCP: Reserved = 0 (0x0000)
          TCP: Flags = 0x12 : .A..S.
              TCP: ..0..... = No urgent data
              TCP: ...1.... = Acknowledgment field significant
              TCP: ....0... = No Push function
              TCP: .....0.. = No Reset
              TCP: ......1. = Synchronize sequence numbers
              TCP: .......0 = No Fin
          TCP: Window = 8760 (0x2238)
          TCP: Checksum = 0x25CF
          TCP: Urgent Pointer = 0 (0x0)
          TCP: Options
                  TCP: Option Kind (Maximum Segment Size) = 2 (0x2)
                  TCP: Option Length = 4 (0x4)
                  TCP: Option Value = 1460 (0x5B4)
```

(continued)

```
00000:  00 A0 24 E5 38 E7 00 80 C7 A6 19 BB 08 00 45 00
    ..$.8.........E.
00010:  00 2C 90 06 40 00 80 06 4E C4 C0 A8 CD 4C C0 A8
    .,..@...N....L..
00020:  CD 63 00 50 07 DD 00 8A 29 55 1F DA E2 27 60 12
    .c.P....)U...'`.
00030:  22 38 25 CF 00 00 02 04 05 B4
    "8%.......


*********************************************************************
Frame   Time    Src MAC Addr    Dst MAC Addr    Protocol
10      0.724   ACTIVESR        DC_TECRA_01     TCP
Description
.A...., len:    0, seq: 534438439-534438439, ack:    9054550, win:
Src Other Addr  Dst Other Addr  Type Other Addr
192.168.205.99  DC_TECRA_01     IP


+ FRAME: Base frame properties
+ ETHERNET: ETYPE = 0x0800 : Protocol = IP:  DOD Internet Protocol
  IP: ID = 0x432C; Proto = TCP; Len: 40
      IP: Version = 4 (0x4)
      IP: Header Length = 20 (0x14)
      IP: Service Type = 0 (0x0)
          IP: Precedence = Routine
          IP: ...0.... = Normal Delay
          IP: ....0... = Normal Throughput
          IP: .....0.. = Normal Reliability
      IP: Total Length = 40 (0x28)
      IP: Identification = 17196 (0x432C)
      IP: Flags Summary = 2 (0x2)
          IP: .......0 = Last fragment in datagram
          IP: ......1. = Cannot fragment datagram
      IP: Fragment Offset = 0 (0x0) bytes
      IP: Time to Live = 128 (0x80)
      IP: Protocol = TCP - Transmission Control
      IP: Checksum = 0x9BA2
      IP: Source Address = 192.168.205.99
      IP: Destination Address = 192.168.205.76
      IP: Data: Number of data bytes remaining = 20 (0x0014)
      TCP: .A...., len:    0, seq: 534438439-534438439,
  ack:   9054550, win: 8760, src: 2013  dst:   80
      TCP: Source Port = 0x07DD
      TCP: Destination Port = Hypertext Transfer Protocol
      TCP: Sequence Number = 534438439 (0x1FDAE227)
      TCP: Acknowledgment Number = 9054550 (0x8A2956)
      TCP: Data Offset = 20 (0x14)
      TCP: Reserved = 0 (0x0000)
```

```
      TCP: Flags = 0x10 : .A....
          TCP: ..0..... = No urgent data
          TCP: ...1.... = Acknowledgment field significant
          TCP: ....0... = No Push function
          TCP: .....0.. = No Reset
          TCP: ......0. = No Synchronize
          TCP: .......0 = No Fin
      TCP: Window = 8760 (0x2238)
      TCP: Checksum = 0x3D8C
      TCP: Urgent Pointer = 0 (0x0)
      TCP: Frame Padding

00000:  00 80 C7 A6 19 BB 00 A0 24 E5 38 E7 08 00 45 00
    .......$.8...E.
00010:  00 28 43 2C 40 00 80 06 9B A2 C0 A8 CD 63 C0 A8
    .(C,@........c..
00020:  CD 4C 07 DD 00 50 1F DA E2 27 00 8A 29 56 50 10
    .L...P...'..)VP.
00030:  22 38 3D 8C 00 00 00 00 00 00 00 00
    "8=........


****************************************************************
Frame   Time    Src MAC Addr    Dst MAC Addr    Protocol
11      0.725   ACTIVESR        DC_TECRA_01     HTTP
Description
GET Request (from client using port 2013)
Src Other Addr  Dst Other Addr  Type Other Addr
192.168.205.99  DC_TECRA_01     IP

+ FRAME: Base frame properties
+ ETHERNET: ETYPE = 0x0800 : Protocol = IP:  DOD Internet Protocol
  IP: ID = 0x442C; Proto = TCP; Len: 411
      IP: Version = 4 (0x4)
      IP: Header Length = 20 (0x14)
      IP: Service Type = 0 (0x0)
          IP: Precedence = Routine
          IP: ...0.... = Normal Delay
          IP: ....0... = Normal Throughput
          IP: .....0.. = Normal Reliability
      IP: Total Length = 411 (0x19B)
      IP: Identification = 17452 (0x442C)
      IP: Flags Summary = 2 (0x2)
          IP: .......0 = Last fragment in datagram
          IP: ......1. = Cannot fragment datagram
      IP: Fragment Offset = 0 (0x0) bytes
      IP: Time to Live = 128 (0x80)
```

(continued)

```
      IP: Protocol = TCP - Transmission Control
      IP: Checksum = 0x992F
      IP: Source Address = 192.168.205.99
      IP: Destination Address = 192.168.205.76
      IP: Data: Number of data bytes remaining = 391 (0x0187)
      TCP: .AP..., len:  371, seq: 534438439-534438809,
ack:   9054550, win: 8760, src: 2013  dst:    80
      TCP: Source Port = 0x07DD
      TCP: Destination Port = Hypertext Transfer Protocol
      TCP: Sequence Number = 534438439 (0x1FDAE227)
      TCP: Acknowledgment Number = 9054550 (0x8A2956)
      TCP: Data Offset = 20 (0x14)
      TCP: Reserved = 0 (0x0000)
      TCP: Flags = 0x18 : .AP...
          TCP: ..0..... = No urgent data
          TCP: ...1.... = Acknowledgment field significant
          TCP: ....1... = Push function
          TCP: .....0.. = No Reset
          TCP: ......0. = No Synchronize
          TCP: .......0 = No Fin
      TCP: Window = 8760 (0x2238)
      TCP: Checksum = 0x876C
      TCP: Urgent Pointer = 0 (0x0)
      TCP: Data: Number of data bytes remaining = 371 (0x0173)
HTTP: GET Request (from client using port 2013)
      HTTP: Request Method = GET
      HTTP: Uniform Resource Identifier = /default.htm
      HTTP: Protocol Version = HTTP/1.0
      HTTP: Accept = image/gif, image/x-xbitmap, image/jpeg,
          image/pjpeg, application/mswo
      HTTP: Accept-Language = en
      HTTP: Undocumented Header = UA-pixels: 1024x768
          HTTP: Undocumented Header Fieldname = UA-pixels
          HTTP: Undocumented Header Value = 1024x768
      HTTP: Undocumented Header = UA-color: color8
          HTTP: Undocumented Header Fieldname = UA-color
          HTTP: Undocumented Header Value = color8
      HTTP: Undocumented Header = UA-OS: Windows NT
          HTTP: Undocumented Header Fieldname = UA-OS
          HTTP: Undocumented Header Value = Windows NT
      HTTP: Undocumented Header = UA-CPU: x86
          HTTP: Undocumented Header Fieldname = UA-CPU
          HTTP: Undocumented Header Value = x86
      HTTP: If-Modified-Since =
          Thu, 28 Aug 1997 17:37:44 GMT; length=172
      HTTP: User-Agent = Mozilla/2.0 (compatible; MSIE 3.02; Win32)
      HTTP: Host = 192.168.205.76
      HTTP: Connection = Keep-Alive
```

```
00000:   00 80 C7 A6 19 BB 00 A0 24 E5 38 E7 08 00 45 00
         ........$.8...E.
00010:   01 9B 44 2C 40 00 80 06 99 2F C0 A8 CD 63 C0 A8
         ..D,@..../...c..
00020:   CD 4C 07 DD 00 50 1F DA E2 27 00 8A 29 56 50 18
         .L...P...'..)VP.
00030:   22 38 87 6C 00 00 47 45 54 20 2F 64 65 66 61 75
         "8.l..GET /defau
00040:   6C 74 2E 68 74 6D 20 48 54 54 50 2F 31 2E 30 0D
         lt.htm HTTP/1.0.
00050:   0A 41 63 63 65 70 74 3A 20 69 6D 61 67 65 2F 67
         .Accept: image/g
00060:   69 66 2C 20 69 6D 61 67 65 2F 78 2D 78 62 69 74
         if, image/x-xbit
00070:   6D 61 70 2C 20 69 6D 61 67 65 2F 6A 70 65 67 2C
         map, image/jpeg,
00080:   20 69 6D 61 67 65 2F 70 6A 70 65 67 2C 20 61 70
         image/pjpeg, ap
00090:   70 6C 69 63 61 74 69 6F 6E 2F 6D 73 77 6F 72 64
         plication/msword
000A0:   2C 20 2A 2F 2A 0D 0A 41 63 63 65 70 74 2D 4C 61
         , */*..Accept-La
000B0:   6E 67 75 61 67 65 3A 20 65 6E 0D 0A 55 41 2D 70
         nguage: en..UA-p
000C0:   69 78 65 6C 73 3A 20 31 30 32 34 78 37 36 38 0D
         ixels: 1024x768.
000D0:   0A 55 41 2D 63 6F 6C 6F 72 3A 20 63 6F 6C 6F 72
         .UA-color: color
000E0:   38 0D 0A 55 41 2D 4F 53 3A 20 57 69 6E 64 6F 77
         8..UA-OS: Window
000F0:   73 20 4E 54 0D 0A 55 41 2D 43 50 55 3A 20 78 38
         s NT..UA-CPU: x8
00100:   36 0D 0A 49 66 2D 4D 6F 64 69 66 69 65 64 2D 53
         6..If-Modified-S
00110:   69 6E 63 65 3A 20 54 68 75 2C 20 32 38 20 41 75
         ince: Thu, 28 Au
00120:   67 20 31 39 39 37 20 31 37 3A 33 37 3A 34 34 20
         g 1997 17:37:44
00130:   47 4D 54 3B 20 6C 65 6E 67 74 68 3D 31 37 32 0D
         GMT; length=172.
00140:   0A 55 73 65 72 2D 41 67 65 6E 74 3A 20 4D 6F 7A
         .User-Agent: Moz
00150:   69 6C 6C 61 2F 32 2E 30 20 28 63 6F 6D 70 61 74
         illa/2.0 (compat
```

(continued)

```
*******************************************************************
Frame   Time    Src MAC Addr   Dst MAC Addr   Protocol
13      0.726   ACTIVESR       DC_TECRA_01    TCP
Description
.A...., len:    0, seq: 534438810-534438810, ack:    9054550, win:
Src Other Addr  Dst Other Addr  Type Other Addr
192.168.205.99  DC_TECRA_01     IP


+ FRAME: Base frame properties
+ ETHERNET: ETYPE = 0x0800 : Protocol = IP:  DOD Internet Protocol
  IP: ID = 0x452C; Proto = TCP; Len: 40
     IP: Version = 4 (0x4)
     IP: Header Length = 20 (0x14)
     IP: Service Type = 0 (0x0)
         IP: Precedence = Routine
         IP: ...0.... = Normal Delay
         IP: ....0... = Normal Throughput
         IP: .....0.. = Normal Reliability
     IP: Total Length = 40 (0x28)
     IP: Identification = 17708 (0x452C)
     IP: Flags Summary = 2 (0x2)
         IP: .......0 = Last fragment in datagram
         IP: ......1. = Cannot fragment datagram
     IP: Fragment Offset = 0 (0x0) bytes
     IP: Time to Live = 128 (0x80)
     IP: Protocol = TCP - Transmission Control
     IP: Checksum = 0x99A2
     IP: Source Address = 192.168.205.99
     IP: Destination Address = 192.168.205.76
     IP: Data: Number of data bytes remaining = 20 (0x0014)
     TCP: .A...., len:    0, seq: 534438810-534438810,
   ack:   9054550, win:32768, src: 2013  dst:    80
     TCP: Source Port = 0x07DD
     TCP: Destination Port = Hypertext Transfer Protocol
     TCP: Sequence Number = 534438810 (0x1FDAE39A)
     TCP: Acknowledgment Number = 9054550 (0x8A2956)
     TCP: Data Offset = 20 (0x14)
     TCP: Reserved = 0 (0x0000)
     TCP: Flags = 0x10 : .A....
         TCP: ..0..... = No urgent data
         TCP: ...1.... = Acknowledgment field significant
         TCP: ....0... = No Push function
         TCP: .....0.. = No Reset
         TCP: ......0. = No Synchronize
         TCP: .......0 = No Fin
     TCP: Window = 32768 (0x8000)
     TCP: Checksum = 0xDE50
     TCP: Urgent Pointer = 0 (0x0)
     TCP: Frame Padding
```

```
00000:  00 80 C7 A6 19 BB 00 A0 24 E5 38 E7 08 00 45 00
    ........$.8...E.
00010:  00 28 45 2C 40 00 80 06 99 A2 C0 A8 CD 63 C0 A8
    .(E,@........c..
00020:  CD 4C 07 DD 00 50 1F DA E3 9A 00 8A 29 56 50 10
    .L...P......)VP.
00030:  80 00 DE 50 00 00 00 00 00 00 00 00 00
    ...P........


*********************************************************************
Frame    Time     Src MAC Addr    Dst MAC Addr    Protocol
14       0.784    DC_TECRA_01     ACTIVESR        HTTP
Description
Response (to client using port 2013)
Src Other Addr   Dst Other Addr   Type Other Addr
DC_TECRA_01      192.168.205.99   IP

+ FRAME: Base frame properties
+ ETHERNET: ETYPE = 0x0800 : Protocol = IP:  DOD Internet Protocol
  IP: ID = 0x9106; Proto = TCP; Len: 261
      IP: Version = 4 (0x4)
      IP: Header Length = 20 (0x14)
      IP: Service Type = 0 (0x0)
          IP: Precedence = Routine
          IP: ...0.... = Normal Delay
          IP: ....0... = Normal Throughput
          IP: .....0.. = Normal Reliability
      IP: Total Length = 261 (0x105)
      IP: Identification = 37126 (0x9106)
      IP: Flags Summary = 2 (0x2)
          IP: .......0 = Last fragment in datagram
          IP: ......1. = Cannot fragment datagram
      IP: Fragment Offset = 0 (0x0) bytes
      IP: Time to Live = 128 (0x80)
      IP: Protocol = TCP - Transmission Control
      IP: Checksum = 0x4CEB
      IP: Source Address = 192.168.205.76
      IP: Destination Address = 192.168.205.99
      IP: Data: Number of data bytes remaining = 241 (0x00F1)
      TCP: .AP..., len:  221, seq:   9054550-9054770,
  ack: 534438810, win: 8389, src:   80  dst: 2013
      TCP: Source Port = Hypertext Transfer Protocol
      TCP: Destination Port = 0x07DD
      TCP: Sequence Number = 9054550 (0x8A2956)
      TCP: Acknowledgment Number = 534438810 (0x1FDAE39A)
      TCP: Data Offset = 20 (0x14)
      TCP: Reserved = 0 (0x0000)
```

(continued)

```
      TCP: Flags = 0x18 : .AP...
          TCP: ..0..... = No urgent data
          TCP: ...1.... = Acknowledgment field significant
          TCP: ....1... = Push function
          TCP: .....0.. = No Reset
          TCP: ......0. = No Synchronize
          TCP: .......0 = No Fin
      TCP: Window = 8389 (0x20C5)
      TCP: Checksum = 0x6FFA
      TCP: Urgent Pointer = 0 (0x0)
      TCP: Data: Number of data bytes remaining = 221 (0x00DD)
   HTTP: Response (to client using port 2013)
      HTTP: Protocol Version = HTTP/1.0
      HTTP: Status Code = OK
      HTTP: Reason = OK
      HTTP: Server = Microsoft-IIS/3.0
      HTTP: Connection = keep-alive
      HTTP: Date = Thu, 28 Aug 1997 17:56:51 GMT
      HTTP: Content-Type = text/html
      HTTP: Undocumented Header = Accept-Ranges: bytes
          HTTP: Undocumented Header Fieldname = Accept-Ranges
          HTTP: Undocumented Header Value = bytes
      HTTP: Last-Modified = Thu, 28 Aug 1997 17:56:10 GMT
      HTTP: Content-Length = 150

00000:  00 A0 24 E5 38 E7 00 80 C7 A6 19 BB 08 00 45 00
    ..$.8.........E.
00010:  01 05 91 06 40 00 80 06 4C EB C0 A8 CD 4C C0 A8
    ....@...L....L..
00020:  CD 63 00 50 07 DD 00 8A 29 56 1F DA E3 9A 50 18
    .c.P....)V....P.
00030:  20 C5 6F FA 00 00 48 54 54 50 2F 31 2E 30 20 32
    .o...HTTP/1.0 2
00040:  30 30 20 4F 4B 0D 0A 53 65 72 76 65 72 3A 20 4D   00
    OK..Server: M
00050:  69 63 72 6F 73 6F 66 74 2D 49 49 53 2F 33 2E 30
    icrosoft-IIS/3.0
00060:  0D 0A 43 6F 6E 6E 65 63 74 69 6F 6E 3A 20 6B 65
    ..Connection: ke
00070:  65 70 2D 61 6C 69 76 65 0D 0A 44 61 74 65 3A 20
    ep-alive..Date:
00080:  54 68 75 2C 20 32 38 20 41 75 67 20 31 39 39 37
    Thu, 28 Aug 1997
00090:  20 31 37 3A 35 36 3A 35 31 20 47 4D 54 0D 0A 43
    17:56:51 GMT..C
000A0:  6F 6E 74 65 6E 74 2D 54 79 70 65 3A 20 74 65 78
    ontent-Type: tex
```

```
000B0:  74 2F 68 74 6D 6C 0D 0A 41 63 63 65 70 74 2D 52
    t/html..Accept-R
000C0:  61 6E 67 65 73 3A 20 62 79 74 65 73 0D 0A 4C 61
    anges: bytes..La
000D0:  73 74 2D 4D 6F 64 69 66 69 65 64 3A 20 54 68 75
    st-Modified: Thu
000E0:  2C 20 32 38 20 41 75 67 20 31 39 39 37 20 31 37
    , 28 Aug 1997 17
000F0:  3A 35 36 3A 31 30 20 47 4D 54 0D 0A 43 6F 6E 74
    :56:10 GMT..Cont
00100:  65 6E 74 2D 4C 65 6E 67 74 68 3A 20 31 35 30 0D
    ent-Length: 150.
00110:  0A 0D 0A                                          ...
```

```
******************************************************************
Frame    Time     Src MAC Addr    Dst MAC Addr    Protocol
17       0.888    ACTIVESR        DC_TECRA_01     TCP
Description
.A....., len:     0, seq: 534438810-534438810, ack:    9054771, win:
Src Other Addr   Dst Other Addr   Type Other Addr
192.168.205.99   DC_TECRA_01      IP


+ FRAME: Base frame properties
+ ETHERNET: ETYPE = 0x0800 : Protocol = IP:  DOD Internet Protocol
  IP: ID = 0x472C; Proto = TCP; Len: 40
     IP: Version = 4 (0x4)
     IP: Header Length = 20 (0x14)
     IP: Service Type = 0 (0x0)
        IP: Precedence = Routine
        IP: ...0.... = Normal Delay
        IP: ....0... = Normal Throughput
        IP: .....0.. = Normal Reliability
     IP: Total Length = 40 (0x28)
     IP: Identification = 18220 (0x472C)
     IP: Flags Summary = 2 (0x2)
        IP: .......0 = Last fragment in datagram
        IP: ......1. = Cannot fragment datagram
     IP: Fragment Offset = 0 (0x0) bytes
     IP: Time to Live = 128 (0x80)
     IP: Protocol = TCP - Transmission Control
     IP: Checksum = 0x97A2
     IP: Source Address = 192.168.205.99
     IP: Destination Address = 192.168.205.76
     IP: Data: Number of data bytes remaining = 20 (0x0014)
     TCP: .A....., len:     0, seq: 534438810-534438810,
  ack:    9054771, win:32547, src: 2013  dst:    80
     TCP: Source Port = 0x07DD
```

(continued)

```
        TCP: Destination Port = Hypertext Transfer Protocol
        TCP: Sequence Number = 534438810 (0x1FDAE39A)
        TCP: Acknowledgment Number = 9054771 (0x8A2A33)
        TCP: Data Offset = 20 (0x14)
        TCP: Reserved = 0 (0x0000)
        TCP: Flags = 0x10 : .A....
            TCP: ..0..... = No urgent data
            TCP: ...1.... = Acknowledgment field significant
            TCP: ....0... = No Push function
            TCP: .....0.. = No Reset
            TCP: ......0. = No Synchronize
            TCP: .......0 = No Fin
        TCP: Window = 32547 (0x7F23)
        TCP: Checksum = 0xDE50
        TCP: Urgent Pointer = 0 (0x0)
        TCP: Frame Padding

00000:  00 80 C7 A6 19 BB 00 A0 24 E5 38 E7 08 00 45 00
    .......$.8...E.
00010:  00 28 47 2C 40 00 80 06 97 A2 C0 A8 CD 63 C0 A8
    .(G,@........c..
00020:  CD 4C 07 DD 00 50 1F DA E3 9A 00 8A 2A 33 50 10
    .L...P......*3P.
00030:  7F 23 DE 50 00 00 00 00 00 00 00 00
    .#.P........


************************************************************************
Frame   Time    Src MAC Addr    Dst MAC Addr    Protocol
18      0.894   DC_TECRA_01     ACTIVESR        HTTP
Description
Response (to client using port 2013)
Src Other Addr  Dst Other Addr  Type Other Addr
DC_TECRA_01     192.168.205.99  IP

+ FRAME: Base frame properties
+ ETHERNET: ETYPE = 0x0800 : Protocol = IP:  DOD Internet Protocol
  IP: ID = 0x9206; Proto = TCP; Len: 190
      IP: Version = 4 (0x4)
      IP: Header Length = 20 (0x14)
      IP: Service Type = 0 (0x0)
          IP: Precedence = Routine
          IP: ...0.... = Normal Delay
          IP: ....0... = Normal Throughput
          IP: .....0.. = Normal Reliability
      IP: Total Length = 190 (0xBE)
      IP: Identification = 37382 (0x9206)
      IP: Flags Summary = 2 (0x2)
```

```
            IP: .......0 = Last fragment in datagram
            IP: ......1. = Cannot fragment datagram
        IP: Fragment Offset = 0 (0x0) bytes
        IP: Time to Live = 128 (0x80)
        IP: Protocol = TCP - Transmission Control
        IP: Checksum = 0x4C32
        IP: Source Address = 192.168.205.76
        IP: Destination Address = 192.168.205.99
        IP: Data: Number of data bytes remaining = 170 (0x00AA)
        TCP: .AP..., len:  150, seq:  9054771-9054920,
    ack: 534438810, win: 8389, src:   80  dst: 2013
        TCP: Source Port = Hypertext Transfer Protocol
        TCP: Destination Port = 0x07DD
        TCP: Sequence Number = 9054771 (0x8A2A33)
        TCP: Acknowledgment Number = 534438810 (0x1FDAE39A)
        TCP: Data Offset = 20 (0x14)
        TCP: Reserved = 0 (0x0000)
        TCP: Flags = 0x18 : .AP...
            TCP: ..0..... = No urgent data
            TCP: ...1.... = Acknowledgment field significant
            TCP: ....1... = Push function
            TCP: .....0.. = No Reset
            TCP: ......0. = No Synchronize
            TCP: .......0 = No Fin
        TCP: Window = 8389 (0x20C5)
        TCP: Checksum = 0x346F
        TCP: Urgent Pointer = 0 (0x0)
        TCP: Data: Number of data bytes remaining = 150 (0x0096)
    HTTP: Response (to client using port 2013)
        HTTP: Data: Number of data bytes remaining = 150 (0x0096)

00000:  00 A0 24 E5 38 E7 00 80 C7 A6 19 BB 08 00 45 00
        ..$.8.........E.
00010:  00 BE 92 06 40 00 80 06 4C 32 C0 A8 CD 4C C0 A8
        ....@...L2...L..
00020:  CD 63 00 50 07 DD 00 8A 2A 33 1F DA E3 9A 50 18
        .c.P....*3....P.
00030:  20 C5 34 6F 00 00 3C 48 54 4D 4C 3E 0D 0A 3C 48
        .4o..<HTML>..<H
00040:  45 41 44 3E 0D 0A 3C 54 49 54 4C 45 3E 49 6E 73
        EAD>..<TITLE>Ins
00050:  69 64 65 20 41 63 74 69 76 65 20 53 65 72 76 65
        ide Active Serve
00060:  72 3C 2F 54 49 54 4C 45 3E 0D 0A 3C 2F 48 45 41
        r</TITLE>..</HEA
```

(continued)

```
00070:  44 3E 0D 0A 3C 42 4F 44 59 3E 0D 0A 3C 43 45 4E
    D>..<BODY>..<CEN
00080:  54 45 52 3E 0D 0A 3C 46 4F 4E 54 20 53 49 5A 45
    TER>..<FONT SIZE
00090:  3D 33 3E 54 68 69 73 20 69 73 20 61 20 74 65 73
    =3>This is a tes
000A0:  74 20 70 61 67 65 3C 2F 46 4F 4E 54 3E 0D 0A 3C
    t page</FONT>..<
000B0:  2F 43 45 4E 54 45 52 3E 0D 0A 3C 2F 42 4F 44 59
    /CENTER>..</BODY
000C0:  3E 0D 0A 3C 2F 48 54 4D 4C 3E 0D 0A
    >..</HTML>..


******************************************************************
Frame   Time    Src MAC Addr   Dst MAC Addr    Protocol
19      1.089   ACTIVESR       DC_TECRA_01     TCP
Description
.A...., len:    0, seq: 534438810-534438810, ack:    9054921, win:
Src Other Addr  Dst Other Addr  Type Other Addr
192.168.205.99  DC_TECRA_01      IP


+ FRAME: Base frame properties
+ ETHERNET: ETYPE = 0x0800 : Protocol = IP:  DOD Internet Protocol
  IP: ID = 0x492C; Proto = TCP; Len: 40
      IP: Version = 4 (0x4)
      IP: Header Length = 20 (0x14)
      IP: Service Type = 0 (0x0)
          IP: Precedence = Routine
          IP: ...0.... = Normal Delay
          IP: ....0... = Normal Throughput
          IP: .....0.. = Normal Reliability
      IP: Total Length = 40 (0x28)
      IP: Identification = 18732 (0x492C)
      IP: Flags Summary = 2 (0x2)
          IP: .......0 = Last fragment in datagram
          IP: ......1. = Cannot fragment datagram
      IP: Fragment Offset = 0 (0x0) bytes
      IP: Time to Live = 128 (0x80)
      IP: Protocol = TCP - Transmission Control
      IP: Checksum = 0x95A2
      IP: Source Address = 192.168.205.99
      IP: Destination Address = 192.168.205.76
      IP: Data: Number of data bytes remaining = 20 (0x0014)
      TCP: .A...., len:    0, seq: 534438810-534438810,
  ack:   9054921, win:32397, src: 2013  dst:   80
      TCP: Source Port = 0x07DD
      TCP: Destination Port = Hypertext Transfer Protocol
```

```
        TCP: Sequence Number = 534438810 (0x1FDAE39A)
        TCP: Acknowledgment Number = 9054921 (0x8A2AC9)
        TCP: Data Offset = 20 (0x14)
        TCP: Reserved = 0 (0x0000)
        TCP: Flags = 0x10 : .A....
            TCP: ..0..... = No urgent data
            TCP: ...1.... = Acknowledgment field significant
            TCP: ....0... = No Push function
            TCP: .....0.. = No Reset
            TCP: ......0. = No Synchronize
            TCP: .......0 = No Fin
        TCP: Window = 32397 (0x7E8D)
        TCP: Checksum = 0xDE50
        TCP: Urgent Pointer = 0 (0x0)
        TCP: Frame Padding

00000:  00 80 C7 A6 19 BB 00 A0 24 E5 38 E7 08 00 45 00
    ........$.8...E.
00010:  00 28 49 2C 40 00 80 06 95 A2 C0 A8 CD 63 C0 A8
    .(I,@........c..
00020:  CD 4C 07 DD 00 50 1F DA E3 9A 00 8A 2A C9 50 10
    .L...P......*.P.
00030:  7E 8D DE 50 00 00 00 00 00 00 00 00
    ~..P........
```

107

IIS Development with CGI and ISAPI

In Chapter Three, we examined how a web server works and introduced powerful programming protocols for developing Internet applications: TCP/IP and Microsoft Windows sockets. Although you can develop many powerful Internet systems using only TCP/IP and Windows sockets, it is more efficient to use the existing communications infrastructure in web servers. Web servers such as Microsoft Internet Information Server (IIS) offer the following advantages:

- They support a ubiquitous user interface standard.
- They can operate through most Internet firewalls that prevent the use of custom TCP/IP applications.
- They avoid many complex programming issues, such as synchronized access to shared resources and thread pools.

In this chapter, we'll examine how you can build Internet systems around IIS by using the Common Gateway Interface (CGI) and the Internet Server Application Programming Interface (ISAPI).

CGI

In Chapter Three, you saw that web servers use the HTTP protocol to retrieve a Uniform Resource Identifier (URI), which is a formatted string identifying a resource by name, location, or any other characteristic. While these resources are usually text files and images, a Request-URI can also identify a program that generates data. Typically, such a program provides a gateway to resources such as databases.

CGI, which has been in use since 1993, defines a specification for how gateway programs are coded and how they integrate with web servers. A gateway program is any executable that can be invoked by the web server. Although CGI programs are typically written in C, they can also be written in Perl, Fortran, TCL, Unix Shell, and AppleScript.

NOTE You can find information about CGI at the following two web sites: *www.ast.cam.ac.uk/~drtr/draft-robinson-www-interface-01.txt* and *hoohoo.ncsa.uiuc.edu/cgi.*

How CGI Works

CGI involves interaction among three primary components:

- The client that issues the request
- The web server that receives the request
- The gateway program that is executed

A client can issue a request to run the CGI executable program in two ways:

- By using a URL
- By filling out and submitting an HTML form within a web page

When a client issues a request by using a URL—for example, *http://www.yourcompany.com/cgi-bin/myprog.exe?arg1+arg2+arg3*—the executable program myprog.exe runs on the web server at *www.yourcompany.com* with the arguments *arg1*, *arg2*, and *arg3*.

A client can also issue a request by submitting a completed HTML form, such as the one shown in Figure 4-1, which invites a user to request that an electronic newsletter be sent to her e-mail address.

Notice in the figure that the browser address box displays a URL. When the user clicks the button named Send Me Your Newsletter, the following URL is displayed and then sent to the web server: *http://192.168.205.79/ CGI1.exe?Name=John+Doe&Email=jdoe@msn. com.* The beginning of the URL consists of the form action URL *http://192.168.205.79/CGI1.exe,* which is specified in the form's HTML code:

```
<html>
<body>
<BR>
<BR>
```

```
<H2>Fill out this form to have our newsletter e-mailed to you.</H2>
<FORM ACTION=http://192.168.205.79/CGI1.exe METHOD=GET>
    Name:
    <input type=text size=30 name=Name value = "" ><BR>
    Email Address:
    <input type=text size=23 name=Email value = "" ><BR><BR>
    <input type=submit size=20 value="Send me your newsletter">

</FORM>
</body>
</html>
```

The form action URL identifies the location and the name of the CGI executable that will be invoked by the web server. It is appended with a question mark (?) and followed by the form variable names along with the values entered by the user. The equal sign (=) separates the form variable from its value, and the ampersand (&) separates each variable/value pair. Blank spaces are replaced with the plus sign (+) in the generated URL.

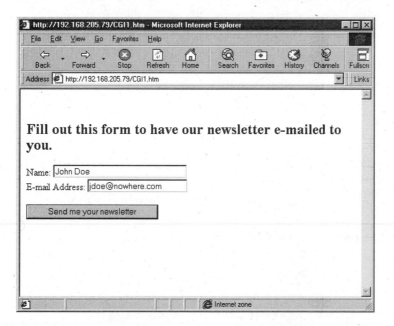

Figure 4-1.
A sample HTML form. When the user clicks the Send Me Your Newsletter button, the URL appears in the Address box.

111

Percent-Encoding

Some characters in a URL require percent-encoding to avoid being modified as they pass through gateways. Percent-encoding simply replaces the character with its hexadecimal value and places a percent sign (%) in front of it. For example, the colon (:) is replaced with " %3A".

When the web server receives this URL, it invokes the CGI executable cgi1.exe, which provides the required service. The web server knows nothing about the services provided by the CGI program; it merely acts as a bridge between the browser and the gateway program. The web server makes information available to the CGI program through environment variables. Because the HTML form in our example uses the *GET* method, the CGI program finds the values of the form variables in the QUERY_STRING environment variable. If our HTML form were to use the *POST* method instead, our CGI program would have to be coded to get the length of the data from the CONTENT_ LENGTH environment variable and then read the data in from the standard input stream, *stdin*. If you have to send a large amount of data from an HTML form to a server, use the *POST* method. Web servers have limits on the amount of data that can be sent using QUERY_STRING.

Because our sample CGI application deals with only a small amount of data, we coded it to use the *GET* method. The code for the following application consists of only 77 lines:

CGI Implementation File

```
#include <stdio.h>
#include <stdlib.h>
#include <string.h>
#include <rpc.h>

#define MAX_SIZE 100
#define MAX_BUFFER 250
char *getenv(const char * env);

bool GetValue(const char * str, char strValue[MAX_SIZE],
    char * strName);

bool GetValue(const char * str, char strValue[MAX_SIZE],
    char * strName )
{
```

```
        char *str1 = strstr(str, strName);
        if (str1 == NULL)
        {
            strcpy(strValue, " ");
            strValue[1] = '\0';
            return false;
        }
        while (strchr((const char *)str1, '+' ))
            strchr((const char *)str1, '+' )[0] = ' ';
        int n1 = strcspn(str1, "=") + 1;
        int n2 = strcspn(str1, "&") + 1;
        if (n2 - n1 - 1 > MAX_SIZE - 1)
        {
            strncpy(strValue, str1 + n1, MAX_SIZE - 1);
            strValue[MAX_SIZE - 1] = '\0';
        }
        else
        {
            strncpy(strValue, str1 + n1, n2 - n1 - 1);
            strValue[n2 - n1 - 1] = '\0';
        }
        return true;
}

void main(int argc, char *argv[])
{

    //Get the environment variable QUERY_STRING.
    const char *strq = getenv("QUERY_STRING");
    if (strq == NULL)
        strq = "Name=John+Doe&Email=jdoe@nowhere.com";

    FILE *stream;
    char strName[MAX_SIZE];
    char strEmail[MAX_SIZE];
    bool b;

    b = GetValue(strq, strName, "Name");
    b = GetValue(strq, strEmail, "Email");

    HANDLE hMutex;
    hMutex = CreateMutex(NULL, false, "CGI1Mutex");
    if (hMutex)
    {
        WaitForSingleObject(hMutex, INFINITE);
        char buffer[MAX_BUFFER];
```

(continued)

113

```
        sprintf(buffer,
            "INSERT INTO EMAIL_TABLE VALUES ('%s', '%s')\n",
            strName, strEmail);
        stream = fopen("cgit.txt", "a");
        fprintf(stream, buffer);
        fclose(stream);
        ReleaseMutex(hMutex);
        CloseHandle(hMutex);
    }

    // You need to print a content type and a blank line.
    printf("Content-Type: text/html\r\n\r\n");
    printf("<html><body>");
    printf("<H3>Thanks %s,<BR><H3>", strName);
    printf("Your request has been successfully processed. ");
    printf("Our newsletter will be sent to your email ");
    printf("address %s shortly.", strEmail);
    printf("</body></html>");
}
```

Notice that this application looks similar to a Windows console application. CGI programs use the same input and output functions as console programs, but the *printf* function writes to an HTML page rather than to the screen. A CGI application sends the HTTP Content Type header to the browser, telling it what type of data is being sent so that the browser can handle the data correctly. You can also include other information in the header, but you must send back a Content-Type header even if you do not send back data. After you print all your headers and separate them by linefeeds or carriage returns (or both), you insert a blank line and print your HTML code. Our HTML code in the program simply informs the user that the request has been successfully processed and confirms this by restating the user's e-mail address, as shown in Figure 4-2.

Our sample does not perform any error checking, and we could improve it by sending back a different HTML response when a failure occurs. The *GetValue* method is a helper function that parses out the QUERY_STRING to get the value for a form variable. This extracts the name and e-mail address of the person requesting the newsletter. The CGI program then generates a SQL statement that inserts this user information into a database. Because this request does not have to be processed in real time, the database does not have to be updated immediately. Instead, we write this statement to a file that can be used later to update the database.

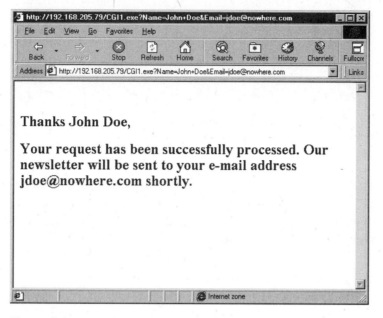

Figure 4-2.
A confirmation generated by CGI code.

We do, however, have to protect this file from being accessed simultaneously by two or more instances of the CGI application. We do this by using a *mutex* object, which is a synchronization object that coordinates mutually exclusive access to a shared resource. A *mutex* object is set to signaled when it is not owned by any thread, and it is set to nonsignaled when it is owned. We can thus prevent two threads from writing to the same file at the same time because only one thread can own a *mutex* object at any given time. Each thread waits for ownership of a *mutex* object before executing the code that accesses the shared resource. After writing to the shared file, the thread releases the *mutex* object to allow another thread to write to the file.

Environment Variables

One of the main tasks of the CGI and ISAPI specification is to pass environment variables to your program. An environment variable is a piece of information about the client request that the server maintains in memory. Every process in Microsoft Windows NT has an environment associated with it; this environment contains information about the state of the program that is currently running in the process and about the operating system. You can see this information by compiling the following program and executing it from the command prompt, as shown on the following page.

```
#include <stdio.h>
#include <stdlib.h>
#include <string.h>

FILE *stream;
char *getenv(const char * env);
void main(int argc, char *argv[])
{
    stream = fopen("environ.txt", "a" );
    for (int i = 0; _environ[i]; i++)
        fprintf(stream, "%s\n", _environ[i]);
    fclose(stream );
    system("type environ.txt" );
}
```

This program generates the file environ.txt, which lists environment variables and their values in a manner similar to the following:

```
CLASSPATH=.;C:\Cafe\JAVA\LIB
COMPUTERNAME=INJ_01
ComSpec=C:\WINNT\system32\cmd.exe
HOMEDRIVE=C:
HOMEPATH=\
INCLUDE=c:\program files\devstudio\vc\include;c:\program
 files\devstudio\vc\atl\include;c:\program
 files\devstudio\vc\mfc\include;C:\MTX\Include
JAVA_HOME=C:\Cafe\JAVA
LIB=c:\program files\devstudio\vc\lib;c:\program
 files\devstudio\vc\mfc\lib;C:\MTX\Lib
LOGONSERVER=\\INJ_01
MSDevDir=C:\Program Files\DevStudio\SharedIDE
NTRESKIT=C:\NTRESKIT
NUMBER_OF_PROCESSORS=1
OS=Windows_NT
Os2LibPath=C:\WINNT\system32\os2\dll;
Path=C:\Program Files\DevStudio\SharedIDE\BIN\;C:\WINNT\system32;
 C:\WINNT;;C:\MSSQL\BINN;C:\MTX;C:\NTRESKIT;c:\program
 files\devstudio\sharedide\bin\ide;c:\program
 files\devstudio\sharedide\bin;c:\program
 files\devstudio\vc\bin;C:\Cafe\BIN;C:\Cafe\JAVA\BIN;
PROCESSOR_ARCHITECTURE=x86
PROCESSOR_IDENTIFIER=x86 Family 5 Model 2 Stepping 12, GenuineIntel
PROCESSOR_LEVEL=5
PROCESSOR_REVISION=020c
SystemDrive=C:
SystemRoot=C:\WINNT
TEMP=C:\TEMP
TMP=C:\TEMP
```

```
USERDOMAIN=INJ
USERNAME=sorensenr
USERPROFILE=C:\WINNT\Profiles\sorensenr
windir=C:\WINNT
_MSDEV_BLD_ENV_=1
```

If we run this program as a CGI application but instead use the URL *http://192.168.205.79/CGI1.exe?Name=John+Doe&Email=jdoe@msn.com*, we get a much larger set of environment variables:

```
COMPUTERNAME=INJ_01
ComSpec=C:\WINNT\system32\cmd.exe
CONTENT_LENGTH=0
GATEWAY_INTERFACE=CGI/1.1
HTTP_ACCEPT=image/gif, image/x-xbitmap, image/jpeg, image/pjpeg,
 application/msword, */*
HTTP_ACCEPT_LANGUAGE=en
HTTP_CONNECTION=Keep-Alive
HTTP_HOST=192.168.205.79
HTTP_REFERER=http://192.168.205.79/cgi1.htm
HTTP_USER_AGENT=Mozilla/2.0 (compatible; MSIE 3.02; Win32)
HTTP_UA_PIXELS=1024x768
HTTP_UA_COLOR=color8
HTTP_UA_OS=Windows NT
HTTP_UA_CPU=x86
HTTPS=off
INCLUDE=C:\MTX\Include
INSTANCE_ID=1
LIB=C:\MTX\Lib
LOCAL_ADDR=192.168.205.79
NTRESKIT=C:\NTRESKIT
NUMBER_OF_PROCESSORS=1
Os2LibPath=C:\WINNT\system32\os2\dll;
OS=Windows_NT
Path=C:\WINNT\system32;C:\WINNT;;C:\MSSQL\BINN;C:\MTX;C:\NTRESKIT
PATH_TRANSLATED=C:\InetPub\wwwroot
PROCESSOR_ARCHITECTURE=x86
PROCESSOR_IDENTIFIER=x86 Family 5 Model 2 Stepping 12, GenuineIntel
PROCESSOR_LEVEL=5
PROCESSOR_REVISION=020c
QUERY_STRING=Name=John+Doe&Email=jdoe@msn.com
REMOTE_ADDR=192.168.205.49
REMOTE_HOST=192.168.205.49
REQUEST_METHOD=GET
SCRIPT_NAME=/CGI1.exe
SERVER_NAME=192.168.205.79
SERVER_PORT=80
```

(continued)

```
SERVER_PORT_SECURE=0
SERVER_PROTOCOL=HTTP/1.0
SERVER_SOFTWARE=Microsoft-IIS/4.0 Beta 3
SystemDrive=C:
SystemRoot=C:\WINNT
USERPROFILE=C:\WINNT\Profiles\Administrator
windir=C:\WINNT
```

Most of these environment variables are useful, but only some of them are relevant to CGI. You can use the larger set of environment variables in your program if you want, but your CGI application might not be portable to other platforms if you do so. The following list describes the environment variables that the CGI specification requires web servers to handle:

AUTH_TYPE is NULL unless the URL requires authentication for access. If authentication is required, this variable contains the method used to validate a user.

CONTENT_LENGTH contains the size of data sent. It informs a CGI program of the amount of data that can be read through *stdin* when the *POST* method is used.

CONTENT_TYPE contains the MIME type of the attached entity—for example, *application/x-www-form-urlencoded*. It has no default value and is used when the *POST* or *PUT* method is called.

GATEWAY_INTERFACE is the CGI version used—for example, CGI 1.1.

HTTP_* represents a group of variables that contain the header lines received from the client. They are prefixed with "*HTTP*" and are placed in the environment space of the server. Individual servers might interpret the header lines differently, and a server might remove some headers (such as those dealing with authentication).

PATH_INFO is additional path information from the client that identifies the resource to be returned by the CGI script.

PATH_TRANSLATED is the server's translated version of the PATH_INFO sent by the client. It maps the virtual path from the client to a physical location on the server's hard drive. Some servers might not support this variable for security reasons and thus return NULL.

QUERY_STRING is the information that follows the question mark (?) in the URL sent from the client.

REMOTE_ADDR is the IP address of the host that is generating the address. The host is not always the client.

REMOTE_HOST is the fully qualified name of the host that is making the request; the host is not necessarily the client. If the server does not have this information, the value is not set.

REMOTE_IDENT is used by servers that support RFC 931 identification to pass the remote user name.

REMOTE_USER is the remote user name when basic authentication is performed. If AUTH_TYPE is NULL, this value is NULL.

REQUEST_METHOD identifies the method used in the request, such as *GET*, *HEAD*, or *POST*. A CGI script can use this variable to retrieve data either from the QUERY_STRING variable, as in the case of the *GET* method, or from *stdin* (standard input) when the *POST* method is used.

SCRIPT_NAME contains a virtual path to the script being executed—for example, cgi-bin/CGI1.exe.

SERVER_NAME identifies the server running the CGI script. The server name can be either a fully qualified name or an IP address.

SERVER_PORT specifies the port number on which the web server was accessed. Web servers usually listen for requests on port 80.

SERVER_PROTOCOL is the name and version of the protocol that the request came in with—for example, HTTP 1.1.

SERVER_SOFTWARE is the name and version of the server software being used—for example, Microsoft IIS 4.0.

ISAPI Applications

Perhaps the greatest weakness of CGI is that it scales poorly. A separate instance of a CGI application is brought into memory every time a client requests it. So if you have hundreds of clients hitting your site, you have hundreds of instances of your CGI program loaded into memory.

ISAPI is a high-performance alternative to CGI. An ISAPI application is a run-time dynamic link library (DLL) that can be loaded once for all clients accessing it. ISAPI applications are usually loaded into the same memory address space as the web server. (However, with IIS 4.0, you can load ISAPI applications into a separate memory address space.) In any event, your ISAPI application must be thread-safe, since multiple requests from different clients can be received simultaneously. ISAPI applications usually run until the web server is restarted, which means that they can run for a long time. You must ensure that ISAPI applications free up resources whenever possible.

How ISAPI Works

An ISAPI program can be invoked in the same way as a CGI program. The following HTML code calls the ISAPI1.DLL application, which is a port of the CGI newsletter request application that we looked at earlier.

```
<html>
<body>
<BR>
<BR>
<H2>Fill out this form to have our newsletter e-mailed to you.</H2>
<FORM ACTION=http://localhost/isapi1.dll? METHOD=GET>
<INPUT TYPE=HIDDEN NAME="MfcISAPICommand" VALUE="Newsletter">
    Name:
    <input type=text size=30 name=Name value = "" ><BR>
    Email Address:
    <input type=text size=23 name=Email value = "" ><BR><BR>
    <input type=submit size=20 value="Send me your newsletter">

</FORM>
</body>
</html>
```

ISAPI applications can support many commands, so the HTML form must specify which one will be used for the request. The following HTML sample form illustrates why this is important:

```
<FORM ACTION="http://www.YourServer.com/scripts/
YourISAPI.dll?YourFunction" METHOD=GET>
Enter your full name: <INPUT NAME="name" VALUE="YourName">
<INPUT TYPE=SUBMIT VALUE="Submit">
</FORM>
```

If you submit this form using Microsoft Internet Explorer 2.0, the following command line is sent to the server:

```
http://www.YourServer.com/scripts/YourISAPI.dll?YourFunction?
name=YourName
```

If you submit this form using Netscape Navigator 2.02, a different command line is sent to the server:

```
http://www.YourServer.com/scripts/YourISAPI.dll?name=YourName
```

Other browsers or versions of them might produce additional variations.

A creative way to get around web browser inconsistencies in the mapping of ISAPI commands is to use the hidden parameter *MfcISAPICommand*, which is used in the code fragment on page 120. The *MfcISAPICommand* parameter assumes that the ISAPI application was created with the MFC ISAPI classes.

N O T E   Using the MFC ISAPI AppWizard is the easiest way to produce ISAPI applications. It also provides an easy way to remove MFC dependencies.

If your HTML form's first available parameter is *MfcISAPICommand*, the parameter's value is the command handler used by the MFC *CHttpServer* object to process the request, no matter which browser you are using.

The following code is the previous CGI1.EXE newsletter application rewritten to use the MFC ISAPI classes:

ISAPI1 Header File

```
#if !defined(AFX_ISAPI1_H__C6BF521A_57F0_11D1_9CEC_E4E161000000
__INCLUDED_)
#define AFX_ISAPI1_H__C6BF521A_57F0_11D1_9CEC_E4E161000000__INCLUDED_

// ISAPI1.H - Header file for your Internet Server
//      ISAPI1 Extension

#define MAX_SIZE 100
#define MAX_BUFFER 250

#include "resource.h"

class CISAPI1Extension : public CHttpServer
{
public:
    CISAPI1Extension();
    ~CISAPI1Extension();

// Overrides
    // ClassWizard generated virtual function overrides
    // NOTE - The ClassWizard will add and remove member
    // functions here.
    //      DO NOT EDIT what you see in these blocks of generated code!
    //{{AFX_VIRTUAL(CISAPI1Extension)
public:
    virtual BOOL GetExtensionVersion(HSE_VERSION_INFO* pVer);
    //}}AFX_VIRTUAL

    // TODO: Add handlers for your commands here.
    HANDLE m_hMutex;
```

(continued)

```
    void Default(CHttpServerContext* pCtxt);
    void Newsletter(CHttpServerContext* pCtxt,
        LPTSTR pszName,  LPTSTR pszEmail);
    bool GetValue( const char * str, char strValue[MAX_SIZE],
        char * strName);

    DECLARE_PARSE_MAP()

    //{{AFX_MSG(CISAPI1Extension)
    //}}AFX_MSG
};

//{{AFX_INSERT_LOCATION}}
// Microsoft Developer Studio will insert additional
// declarations immediately before the previous line.

#endif // !defined(AFX_ISAPI1_H__
// C6BF521A_57F0_11D1_9CEC_E4E161000000__INCLUDED)
```

ISAPI1 Implementation File

```
// ISAPI1.CPP - Implementation file for your Internet Server
//      ISAPI1 Extension

#include "stdafx.h"
#include "ISAPI1.h"


///////////////////////////////////////////////////////////////////////
// The one and only CWinApp object
// NOTE: You may remove this object if you alter your project to no
// longer use MFC in a DLL.

CWinApp theApp;

///////////////////////////////////////////////////////////////////////
// command-parsing map

BEGIN_PARSE_MAP(CISAPI1Extension, CHttpServer)
    // TODO: insert your ON_PARSE_COMMAND() and
    // ON_PARSE_COMMAND_PARAMS() here to hook up your commands.
    // For example:
    DEFAULT_PARSE_COMMAND(Default, CISAPI1Extension)
    ON_PARSE_COMMAND(Default, CISAPI1Extension, ITS_EMPTY)
    ON_PARSE_COMMAND(Newsletter, CISAPI1Extension,
        ITS_PSTR ITS_PSTR)
END_PARSE_MAP(CISAPI1Extension)
```

```
///////////////////////////////////////////////////////////////////////
// The one and only CISAPI1Extension object

CISAPI1Extension theExtension;

///////////////////////////////////////////////////////////////////////
// CISAPI1Extension implementation

CISAPI1Extension::CISAPI1Extension()
{
    m_hMutex = CreateMutex(NULL, false, "ISAPI1Mutex");
}


CISAPI1Extension::~CISAPI1Extension()
{
    CloseHandle(m_hMutex);
}

BOOL CISAPI1Extension::GetExtensionVersion(HSE_VERSION_INFO* pVer)
{
    // Call default implementation for initialization.
    CHttpServer::GetExtensionVersion(pVer);

    // Load description string.
    TCHAR sz[HSE_MAX_EXT_DLL_NAME_LEN+1];
    ISAPIVERIFY(::LoadString(AfxGetResourceHandle(),
        IDS_SERVER, sz, HSE_MAX_EXT_DLL_NAME_LEN));
    _tcscpy(pVer->lpszExtensionDesc, sz);
    return TRUE;
}


///////////////////////////////////////////////////////////////////////
// CISAPI1Extension command handlers

void CISAPI1Extension::Default(CHttpServerContext* pCtxt)
{
    StartContent(pCtxt);
    WriteTitle(pCtxt);

    *pCtxt << _T("This default message was produced by the Internet");
    *pCtxt << _T(
        " Server DLL Wizard. Edit your CISAPI1Extension::Default()");
    *pCtxt << _T(" implementation to change it.\r\n");

    EndContent(pCtxt);
}
```

(continued)

123

```
void CISAPI1Extension::Newsletter(CHttpServerContext* pCtxt,
    LPTSTR pszName,  LPTSTR pszEmail)
{

    StartContent(pCtxt);
    WriteTitle(pCtxt);
    FILE* stream;

    char strName[MAX_SIZE];
    char strEmail[MAX_SIZE];

    bool b = GetValue(pszName, strName, "Name");
    b = GetValue(pszEmail, strEmail, "Email");

    if (m_hMutex)
    {

        WaitForSingleObject(m_hMutex, INFINITE);
        char buffer[MAX_BUFFER];
        sprintf(buffer,
            "INSERT INTO EMAIL_TABLE VALUES ('%s', '%s')\n",
            strName, strEmail);
        stream = fopen( "c:\\isapi1.txt", "a");
        fprintf(stream, buffer);
        fclose(stream);
        ReleaseMutex(m_hMutex);
    }

    // You need to print a content type and a blank line.

    *pCtxt << _T("<html><body>");
    *pCtxt << _T("<H3>Thanks ");
    *pCtxt << strName;
    *pCtxt << _T(",<BR><H3>");
    *pCtxt << _T("Your request has been successfully processed. Our");
    *pCtxt << _T(" newsletter will be sent to your email address ");
    *pCtxt << strEmail;
    *pCtxt << _T(" shortly.");
    *pCtxt << _T("</body></html>");

    EndContent(pCtxt);
}

bool CISAPI1Extension::GetValue(const char * str,
    char strValue[MAX_SIZE], char * strName )
{
    char * str1 = strstr(str, strName );
    if (str1 == NULL)
```

```
        {
            strcpy(strValue, " ");
            strValue[1] = '\0';
            return false;
        }
        while(strchr((const char *)str1, '+' ))
            strchr((const char *)str1, '+' )[0] = ' ';
        int n1 = strcspn(str1, "=")+1;
        int n2 = strcspn(str1, "&")+1;
        if (n2-n1-1 > MAX_SIZE-1)
        {
            strncpy( strValue, str1+n1, MAX_SIZE-1);
            strValue[MAX_SIZE-1] = '\0';
        }
        else
        {
            strncpy( strValue, str1+n1, n2-n1-1 );
            strValue[n2-n1-1] = '\0';
        }
        return true;
}


// Do not edit the following lines, which are needed by ClassWizard.
#if 0
BEGIN_MESSAGE_MAP(CISAPI1Extension, CHttpServer)
    //{{AFX_MSG_MAP(CISAPI1Extension)
    //}}AFX_MSG_MAP
END_MESSAGE_MAP()
#endif    // 0


///////////////////////////////////////////////////////////////////////
// If your extension will not use MFC, you'll need this code
// to make sure the extension objects can find the resource
// handle for the module. If you convert your extension to not
// be dependent on MFC, remove the comments
// around the following AfxGetResourceHandle() and DllMain()
// functions as well as the g_hInstance global.

/****

static HINSTANCE g_hInstance;

HINSTANCE AFXISAPI AfxGetResourceHandle()
{
    return g_hInstance;
}
```

(continued)

```
BOOL WINAPI DllMain(HINSTANCE hInst, ULONG ulReason,
    LPVOID lpReserved)
{
    if (ulReason == DLL_PROCESS_ATTACH)
    {
        g_hInstance = hInst;
    }

    return TRUE;
}


****/
```

STDAFX Header File

```
#if !defined(AFX_STDAFX_H__C6BF5220_57F0_11D1_9CEC_E4E161000000__/
INCLUDED_)
#define AFX_STDAFX_H__C6BF5220_57F0_11D1_9CEC_E4E161000000__INCLUDED_

// stdafx.h : include file for standard system include
// files, or project-specific include files that are used
// frequently but changed infrequently.
//

#include <afx.h>
#include <afxwin.h>
#include <afxmt.h>              // For synchronization objects
#include <afxext.h>
#include <afxisapi.h>

//{{AFX_INSERT_LOCATION}}
// Microsoft Developer Studio will insert additional declarations
// immediately before the previous line.

#endif // !defined(AFX_STDAFX_H__
// C6BF5220_57F0_11D1_9CEC_E4E161000000__INCLUDED)
```

The preceding code was generated by the MFC AppWizard. The wizard created a generic ISAPI application in which most of the ISAPI code is wrapped in two classes: *CHttpServer* and *CHttpServerContext*. The *CHttpServer* object is used to initialize the ISAPI application; only one *CHttpServer* object exists in a module. The *CHttpServer* object creates a *CHttpServerContext* object for each ISAPI request processed by the web server. Thus, multiple *CHttpServerContext* objects are created and run in separate threads to process multiple client requests simultaneously.

Our port of the CGI program required that we add a new method named *Newsletter* to the *CISAPI1Extension* class, which is derived from the *CHttpServer* class. In addition to a *CHttpServerContext* pointer, the *Newsletter* method takes two string variables to hold the name and e-mail address that will be passed from the HTML form. We reused our *GetValue* method to easily extract the value of these variables from the strings generated. We had to add our *Newsletter* method to a parse map to allow the MFC code to map the ISAPI Newsletter command to the *Newsletter* method of *CISAPI1Extension* class. The AppWizard creates a default command, which is invoked if either no command or the Default command is specified in the HTML code. Parse maps also require that the arguments of functions be listed. The following flags indicate the possible values:

```
ITS_EMPTY   - No arguments
ITS_I2      - Short
ITS_I4      - Long
ITS_R4      - Float
ITS_R8      - Double
```

Our porting of the CGI application functionality to ISAPI was simple: It involved simply moving most of the code from the *main* function of the CGI program to our new *Newsletter* method. Because our ISAPI application gets reloaded with only the first request, not with each request, we moved the code to create and destroy the *Mutex* object into the constructor and destructor of the *CISAPI1Extension* class.

Although ISAPI programming is more complex than CGI programming because of its synchronization requirements, it is still a relatively short API. Every ISAPI DLL has two entry points that it must export: *GetExtensionVersion* and *HttpExtensionProc*. The HTTP server calls the function *GetExtensionVersion(HSE_VERSION_INFO *pVer)* when it loads an ISAPI application. This function retrieves the version number of the specification that the DLL extension is based on. The function *HttpExtensionProc(EXTENSION_CONTROL_BLOCK *pECB)* is the second entry point for an ISAPI application. It is called with each request and plays a role similar to the *main* function in the CGI program. The function returns one of several HTTP server extension messages, which are described below:

HSE_STATUS_SUCCESS indicates that the ISAPI application has finished processing and the server can disconnect and free up allocated resources.

HSE_STATUS_SUCCESS_AND_KEEP_CONN indicates that the ISAPI application has finished processing and that if the client supports persistent connections, the server should wait for the next HTTP request. The server is not required to keep the session open, and the application should return this message only if it was able to send the correct content-length header to the client.

HSE_STATUS_PENDING indicates that the ISAPI application has queued the request for processing and will notify the server when it has finished.

HSE_STATUS_ERROR means that the ISAPI application has encountered an error while processing the request and that the server can disconnect and free up allocated resources.

The *HttpExtensionProc* function is passed the EXTENSION_CONTROL_BLOCK data structure as shown here:

```
typedef struct _EXTENSION_CONTROL_BLOCK {
    DWORD       cbSize;
    DWORD       dwVersion
    HCONN       ConnID;
    DWORD       dwHttpStatusCode;
    CHAR        lpszLogData[HSE_LOG_BUFFER_LEN];
    LPSTR       lpszMethod;
    LPSTR       lpszQueryString;
    LPSTR       lpszPathInfo;
    LPSTR       lpszPathTranslated;
    DWORD       cbTotalBytes;
    DWORD       cbAvailable;
    LPBYTE      lpbData;
    LPSTR       lpszContentType;

    BOOL ( WINAPI * GetServerVariable )
        ( HCONN        hConn,
          LPSTR        lpszVariableName,
          LPVOID       lpvBuffer,
          LPDWORD      lpdwSize );

    BOOL ( WINAPI * WriteClient )
        ( HCONN       ConnID,
          LPVOID      Buffer,
          LPDWORD     lpdwBytes,
          DWORD       dwReserved );

    BOOL ( WINAPI * ReadClient )
        ( HCONN       ConnID,
          LPVOID      lpvBuffer,
          LPDWORD     lpdwSize );

    BOOL ( WINAPI * ServerSupportFunction )
        ( HCONN       hConn,
          DWORD       dwHSERRequest,
          LPVOID      lpvBuffer,
```

```
        LPDWORD     lpdwSize,
        LPDWORD     lpdwDataType );
```

`} EXTENSION_CONTROL_BLOCK, *LPEXTENSION_CONTROL_BLOCK;`

The member variables of this structure contain the most commonly needed information for a request, but you can get additional information through the structure's server callback functions. The *cbSize* member variable contains the size of the EXTENSION_CONTROL_BLOCK structure. The *dwVersion* member variable contains the version information of HTTP_FILTER_REVISION. *ConnID* is a unique number assigned by the HTTP server and should not be modified. The *dwHttpStatusCode* member variable contains the status of the completed request. It can be one of the following values:

```
HTTP_STATUS_BAD_REQUEST
HTTP_STATUS_AUTH_REQUIRED
HTTP_STATUS_FORBIDDEN
HTTP_STATUS_NOT_FOUND
HTTP_STATUS_SERVER_ERROR
HTTP_STATUS_NOT_IMPLEMENTED
```

The *lpszLogData* member variable is a char array of size HSE_LOG_BUFFER_LEN. It contains the null-terminated log information string for the current request, which is entered in the HTTP server log. The *lpszMethod*, *lpszQueryString*, *lpszPathInfo*, *lpszPathTranslated*, and *lpszContentType* variables are equivalent to the following CGI variables, which we looked at earlier: REQUEST_METHOD, QUERY_STRING, PATH_INFO, PATH_TRANSLATED, CONTENT_TYPE. The *cbTotalBytes* member variable contains the total number of bytes to be received from the client and is equivalent to the CGI variable CONTENT_LENGTH. The *cbAvailable* member variable indicates the available number of bytes in the buffer pointed to by *lpbData*, which has a limit of 48 KB. If *cbTotalBytes* is not the same as *cbAvailable*, the ISAPI application must use the callback function *ReadClient* to read the rest of the data, starting from an offset of *cbAvailable*.

Asynchronous Write Operations

The member function *ReadClient* performs the same purpose as *stdin* in CGI and reads in data from an HTML form that uses the *POST* method. In the same way that *stdin* is equivalent to *ReadClient*, *stdout* is equivalent to *WriteClient*, and *WriteClient* allows the server to optimize writes to improve performance. With ISAPI 2.0, the *WriteClient* function supports asynchronous write operations. It indicates that the write operation has to be performed asynchronously by using the HSE_IO_ASYNC flag in the *dwReserved* parameter variable. This puts the write operation in an asynchronous thread queue and allows the call to return immediately. The ISAPI application can then continue to do more tasks or return with HSE_STATUS_PENDING, freeing up the server thread pool to handle other requests.

To use this asynchronous capability, the ISAPI application should first make a call to *ServerSupportFunction* with the HSE_REQ_IO_COMPLETION flag and submit a callback function and context value for handling completion of asynchronous operations. When the I/O operation is completed, the server calls this callback function, passing the ECB, context value, and numbers of bytes sent along with any error codes that might have been generated. The ISAPI application calls *ServerSupportFunction* with the HSE_DONE_WITH_SESSION flag to notify the server that it has processed the request.

The *ServerSupportFunction* server callback function can be used to provide some general-purpose functions as well as functions that are specific to HTTP server implementation, such as URL redirection, session management, and common headers/responses. The *GetServerVariable* function in the structure EXTENSION_CONTROL_BLOCK copies information relating to an HTTP connection and to the server itself into a buffer. You can get all the CGI variables with this function; it is equivalent to *getenv* in CGI.

> **NOTE** You can also use the Win32 function *TransmitFile* to perform asynchronous write operations. It relies on the Windows sockets implementation in Windows NT 3.51 and later versions to perform fast transmission of file data over a socket connection.

Saving Space and Memory: Linking Non-MFC DLLs

Although we created our ISAPI newsletter application using the MFC ISAPI AppWizard, we do not necessarily want to link the MFC DLLs to our application. If your ISAPI DLL does not use MFC, it is better to create a non-MFC Win32 DLL. We'll look at the reasons shortly. Linking your ISAPI DLL to MFC, either statically or dynamically, takes up significant disk space and memory. If your DLL does use MFC, you must build either a regular DLL that dynamically links to MFC or a regular DLL that statically links to MFC. You should probably use a regular DLL that dynamically links to MFC because the file size of the DLL will be much smaller and the savings in memory from using the shared version of MFC can be significant. If you statically link your ISAPI DLL to MFC, the DLL will load its own private copy of the MFC library code and the file size of your DLL will be larger.

To demonstrate this, I built our ISAPI newsletter application using the three scenarios I just described. Because our application does not use MFC, we can simply create a non-MFC DLL by removing the *CWinApp* object, *theApp*, and by adding the following code:

```
static HINSTANCE g_hInstance;

HINSTANCE AFXISAPI AfxGetResourceHandle()
{
    return g_hInstance;
}

BOOL WINAPI DllMain(HINSTANCE hInst, ULONG ulReason,
    LPVOID lpReserved)
{
    if (ulReason == DLL_PROCESS_ATTACH)
    {
        g_hInstance = hInst;
    }

    return TRUE;
}
```

We must also add the header file stdio.h and remove the header files afx.h, afxwin.h, afxmt.h, and afxext.h.

We built the two MFC versions by flipping the switch that determines whether the MFC DLLs are statically or dynamically linked. We then used *DumpBin* to show the imports of functions used by the three versions of our ISAPI DLL. The results, shown in the output of *DumpBin* below, clearly demonstrate that the memory footprint of our DLL is much smaller when MFC is not used. The results also show that linking MFC DLLs statically is inefficient because it adds a lot of unnecessary code.

```
======================================================================
IMPORTS of our ISAPI DLL (Size 89KB) when MFC is not used.
KERNEL32.dll   size 364KB
9D   GetACP; 18   CloseHandle; 1DD   ReleaseMutex; 26A
WaitForSingleObject; 1AB   MultiByteToWideChar; 96
FreeEnvironmentStringsA; F4   GetLastError; 179
InitializeCriticalSecti; 196   LocalAlloc; 19A   LocalFree; 4C
DeleteCriticalSection; 18F   LeaveCriticalSection; 58
EnterCriticalSection; 2A1   lstrlenA; 1E5   RtlUnwind; AA
GetCommandLineA; 116   GetProcAddress; FE   GetModuleHandleA; 14C
GetVersion; 16E   HeapFree; 168   HeapAlloc; 171   HeapReAlloc; 1C9
RaiseException; 6B   ExitProcess; 246   TerminateProcess; D3
GetCurrentProcess; 172   HeapSize; D6   GetCurrentThreadId; 24B
TlsSetValue; 248   TlsAlloc; 249   TlsFree; 21E   SetLastError; 24A
TlsGetValue; 21B   SetHandleCount; 12A   GetStdHandle; EF
GetFileType; 128   GetStartupInfoA; FC   GetModuleFileNameA; A3
GetCPInfo; 38   CreateMutexA; 109   GetOEMCP; 229   SetStdHandle;
97   FreeEnvironmentStringsW; E1   GetEnvironmentStrings; E3
```

(continued)

131

GetEnvironmentStringsW; 26E   WideCharToMultiByte; 16C
HeapDestroy; 16A   HeapCreate; 25E   VirtualFree; 27B   WriteFile;
25B   VirtualAlloc; 18D   LCMapStringA; 18E   LCMapStringW;
12B   GetStringTypeA; 12E   GetStringTypeW;
236   SetUnhandledExceptionFi; 183   IsBadReadPtr; 186   IsBadWritePtr;
180   IsBadCodePtr; 210   SetEndOfFile; 8E   FlushFileBuffers;
17B   InterlockedDecrement; 17E   InterlockedIncrement;
31   CreateFileA; 219   SetFilePointer; 190   LoadLibraryA;
F6   GetLocaleInfoA; 1D6   ReadFile; F7   GetLocaleInfoW; ;

USER32.dll size 323KB
183   LoadStringA; 264   wsprintfA;

===

IMPORTS of our ISAPI DLL (Size 164KB) when MFC is statically linked.

KERNEL32.dll   size 364KB
1C9   RaiseException; 168   HeapAlloc; 16E   HeapFree; 172   HeapSize;
A3   GetCPInfo; 9D   GetACP; 109   GetOEMCP; 171   HeapReAlloc;
21B   SetHandleCount; 12A   GetStdHandle; EF   GetFileType;
128   GetStartupInfoA; 96   FreeEnvironmentStringsA;
97   FreeEnvironmentStringsW; E1   GetEnvironmentStrings;
E3   GetEnvironmentStringsW; 16C   HeapDestroy; 16A   HeapCreate;
6B   ExitProcess; 246   TerminateProcess; FE   GetModuleHandleA;
18E   LCMapStringW; 183   IsBadReadPtr; 186   IsBadWritePtr;
180   IsBadCodePtr; 229   SetStdHandle; 12B   GetStringTypeA;
12E   GetStringTypeW; F6   GetLocaleInfoA; F7   GetLocaleInfoW;
4C   DeleteCriticalSection; 248   TlsAlloc;
179   InitializeCriticalSection; 19A   LocalFree; 196   LocalAlloc;
AA   GetCommandLineA; 1E5   RtlUnwind; 15D   GlobalGetAtomNameA;
153   GlobalAddAtomA; 14D   GetVersionExA; F0   GetFullPathNameA;
14F   GetVolumeInformationA; 82   FindFirstFileA; 7E   FindClose;
210   SetEndOfFile; 8E   FlushFileBuffers; 219   SetFilePointer;
27B   WriteFile; 1D6   ReadFile; 31   CreateFileA;
D3   GetCurrentProcess; 11D   GetProcessVersion; 190   LoadLibraryA;
116   GetProcAddress; 98   FreeLibrary; F4   GetLastError;
21E   SetLastError; 27F   WritePrivateProfileStringA;
15B   GlobalFlags; 38   CreateMutexA; 1AA   MulDiv; 14C   GetVersion;
1AB   MultiByteToWideChar; 26E   WideCharToMultiByte;
17E   InterlockedIncrement; 2A1   lstrlenA; 29E   lstrcpynA;
FC   GetModuleFileNameA; 29B   lstrcpyA; 292   lstrcatA;
213   SetErrorMode; 24A   TlsGetValue; 19D   LocalReAlloc;
24B   TlsSetValue; 58   EnterCriticalSection; 162   GlobalReAlloc;
18F   LeaveCriticalSection; 249   TlsFree; 15F   GlobalHandle;
166   GlobalUnlock; 15C   GlobalFree;
236   SetUnhandledExceptionFilter; 18D   LCMapStringA;
25E   VirtualFree; 25B   VirtualAlloc; D5   GetCurrentThread;

18   CloseHandle; 1DD   ReleaseMutex; 26A   WaitForSingleObject;
D6   GetCurrentThreadId; 17B   InterlockedDecrement; 298   lstrcmpiA;
295   lstrcmpA; 157   GlobalDeleteAtom; 155   GlobalAlloc;
160   GlobalLock

USER32.dll size 323KB
167   IsWindow; 1E2   SetActiveWindow; 129   GetSysColor;
190   MapWindowPoints; 234   SystemParametersInfoA;
251   UpdateWindow; 176   LoadIconA; 2   AdjustWindowRectEx;
1F5   SetFocus; 22D   ShowWindow; 12C   GetSystemMetrics;
172   LoadCursorA; 12A   GetSysColorBrush; 89   DestroyMenu;
261   WindowFromPoint; 2B   CharUpperA; B4   EndDialog;
CD   FindWindowA; 152   InvalidateRect; 209   SetRectEmpty;
16E   LoadAcceleratorsA; 242   TranslateAcceleratorA;
1CC   ReleaseCapture; 17E   LoadMenuA; 1FB   SetMenu;
1D2   ReuseDDElParam; 24C   UnpackDDElParam; 164   IsIconic;
A   BringWindowToTop; 131   GetTopWindow; 168   IsWindowEnabled;
15D   IsChild; D8   GetCapture; 25E   WinHelpA; DB   GetClassInfoA;
1BE   RegisterClassA; 128   GetSubMenu; 10E   GetMenuItemID;
109   GetMenu; F3   GetDlgItem; 80   DefWindowProcA;
E4   GetClientRect; 206   SetPropA; 108   GetLastActivePopup;
F9   GetForegroundWindow; 82   DeferWindowPos; C9   EqualRect;
12   CallWindowProcA; 1CF   RemovePropA; 118   GetMessageTime;
1CA   RegisterWindowMessageA; 145   GrayStringA; AA   DrawTextA;
B6   EndPaint; 9   BeginPaint; 1CD   ReleaseDC; EE   GetDC;
10D   GetMenuItemCount; 264   wsprintfA; F0   GetDesktopWindow;
13F   GetWindowTextA; 221   SetWindowTextA; 36   ClientToScreen;
137   GetWindow; F2   GetDlgCtrlID; 13D   GetWindowRect;
1BB   PtInRect; 13A   GetWindowLongA; E1   GetClassNameA;
10A   GetMenuCheckMarkDimensions; 170   LoadBitmapA;
112   GetMenuState; 19B   ModifyMenuA; 1FE   SetMenuItemBitmaps;
30   CheckMenuItem; B0   EnableMenuItem; F8   GetFocus;
11D   GetParent; 11B   GetNextDlgTabItem; 195   MessageBoxA;
B2   EnableWindow; 1EC   SetCursor; 22A   ShowOwnedPopups;
24D   UnregisterClassA; 115   GetMessageA; 245   TranslateMessage;
90   DispatchMessageA; D5   GetActiveWindow; 101   GetKeyState;
1DA   SendMessageA; 11   CallNextHookEx; 255   ValidateRect;
16A   IsWindowVisible; 1AF   PeekMessageA; ED   GetCursorPos;
225   SetWindowsHookExA; 248   UnhookWindowsHookEx;
1B1   PostMessageA; 1B3   PostQuitMessage; 183   LoadStringA;
8   BeginDeferWindowPos; 40   CopyRect; B3   EndDeferWindowPos;
1D3   ScreenToClient; 1D6   ScrollWindow; 20A   SetScrollInfo;
22B   ShowScrollBar; 20C   SetScrollRange; 125   GetScrollPos;
1F6   SetForegroundWindow; 121   GetPropA; 8A   DestroyWindow;
20B   SetScrollPos; 55   CreateWindowExA; 21B   SetWindowLongA;
117   GetMessagePos; 236   TabbedTextOutA; 21E   SetWindowPos;

(continued)

GDI32.dll size 162KB

46   DeleteObject; 143   SaveDC; 141   RestoreDC; 14A   SelectObject;
FA   GetStockObject; 150   SetBkColor; 172   SetTextColor;
161   SetMapMode; 175   SetViewportOrgEx; 11F   OffsetViewportOrgEx;
174   SetViewportExtEx; 144   ScaleViewportExtEx;
178   SetWindowExtEx; 145   ScaleWindowExtEx; BE   GetClipBox;
19   CreateBitmap; C7   GetDeviceCaps; 136   PtVisible;
139   RectVisible; 183   TextOutA; 62   ExtTextOutA;
5B   Escape; EA   GetObjectA; 43   DeleteDC

comdlg32.dll size 181KB

WINSPOOL.DRV size 91KB

69   OpenPrinterA; 3D   DocumentPropertiesA; 1A   ClosePrinter

ADVAPI32.dll size 241KB

117   RegCloseKey; 141   RegSetValueExA; 136   RegQueryValueExA;
12E   RegOpenKeyExA; 11B   RegCreateKeyExA

SHELL32.dll size 1,673KB

F   DragQueryFileA; D   DragFinish

COMCTL32.dll size 452KB

17   ImageList_Destroy; Ordinal   17

```
==========================================================================
```
IMPORTS of our ISAPI DLL (Size 17KB) when MFC is dynamically linked.

MFC42.DLL size 919KB

Ordinal 1168; Ordinal   825; Ordinal   815; Ordinal   600;
Ordinal 1182; Ordinal 1577; Ordinal   269; Ordinal   826;
Ordinal 1176; Ordinal 6412; Ordinal   342; Ordinal 1197;
Ordinal 1570; Ordinal 1253; Ordinal 1255; Ordinal   561;
Ordinal 1116; Ordinal 1578; Ordinal 1243; Ordinal 1575;
Ordinal   599

MSVCRT.dll size 274KB

2B6   strcspn; 2B2   strchr; 2C0   strstr; 42   _EH_prolog;
F   ???2@YAPAXI@Z; 55   __dllonexit; 181   _onexit;
E   ??1type_info@@UAE@XZ; 259   free; 28C   malloc;
9A   _adjust_fdiv; 10B   _initterm; 239   atol; 237   atof;
292   memcpy; 2B9   strlen; 15A   _mbsicmp; 153   _mbschr;
12A   _ismbcspace; 1BA   _strdup; 294   memset; 178   _mbstok;
238   atoi; 2AD   sprintf; 2BC   strncpy; 14F   _mbctoupper;
2A2   realloc; 41   _CxxThrowException; 49   __CxxFrameHandler;
252   fopen; 253   fprintf; 247   fclose

```
KERNEL32.dll size 364KB
4C   DeleteCriticalSection; 179   InitializeCriticalSection;
38   CreateMutexA; 18   CloseHandle; 1DD   ReleaseMutex;
2A1  lstrlenA; 58   EnterCriticalSection; 18F   LeaveCriticalSection;
19A  LocalFree; 26A   WaitForSingleObject; F4   GetLastError;
196  LocalAlloc

USER32.dll size 323KB
183  LoadStringA; 264   wsprintfA
```

ISAPI Filters

ISAPI filters are a totally new concept in web server extensions because they don't have a CGI counterpart. ISAPI filters can intercept specific server events before and after the server handles them. A filter is loaded when the web service starts, and it tells the server what sort of event notifications it is interested in. If these events occur, the filter can process the events, pass the events to other filters, or send the events back to the server after the filter has dealt with them. ISAPI filters are typically used for traffic analysis, compression, encryption, logging, or to provide custom authentication techniques to the web server to enhance security.

The API for filters is similar to the APIs for ISAPI applications. You can also create ISAPI filters with the MFC AppWizard. The MFC code wraps most of the filter API in the classes *CHttpFilter* and *CHttpFilterContext*.

Filter DLLs must support two common entry points: *GetFilterVersion* and *HttpFilterProc*. The prototypes for these functions and the structures they use are as follows:

```
BOOL WINAPI GetFilterVersion(
    HTTP_FILTER_VERSION *pVer
);

DWORD WINAPI HttpFilterProc(
    HTTP_FILTER_CONTEXT *pfc,
    DWORD notificationType,
    VOID *pvNotification
);

typedef struct _HTTP_FILTER_VERSION{DWORD dwServerFilterVersion;
    //INDWORD dwFilterVersion;
    //OUTCHAR lpszFilterDesc[SF_MAX_FILTER_DESC_LEN+1];
    //OUTDWORD dwFlags;
    //OUT} HTTP_FILTER_VERSION, *PHTTP_FILTER_VERSION;
typedef struct _HTTP_FILTER_CONTEXT
```

(continued)

```
{
    DWORD       cbSize;
    DWORD       Revision;
    PVOID       ServerContext;
    DWORD       ulReserved;
    BOOL        fIsSecurePort;
    PVOID       pFilterContext;
    BOOL      (WINAPI * GetServerVariable) (
    struct _HTTP_FILTER_CONTEXT *     pfc,
    LPSTR       lpszVariableName,
    LPVOID      lpvBuffer,
    LPDWORD     lpdwSize
    );
BOOL      (WINAPI * AddResponseHeaders) (
    struct _HTTP_FILTER_CONTEXT *     pfc,
    LPSTR     lpszHeaders,
    DWORD     dwReserved
    );
BOOL      (WINAPI * WriteClient) (
    struct _HTTP_FILTER_CONTEXT *     pfc,
    LPVOID      Buffer,
    LPDWORD     lpdwBytes,
    DWORD       dwReserved
    );
VOID *    (WINAPI * AllocMem) (
    struct _HTTP_FILTER_CONTEXT *     pfc,
    DWORD       cbSize,
    DWORD       dwReserved
    );
BOOL      (WINAPI * ServerSupportFunction) (
    struct _HTTP_FILTER_CONTEXT *     pfc,
    enum SF_REQ_TYPE      sfReq,
    PVOID       pData,
    DWORD       ul1,
    DWORD       ul2
    );
} HTTP_FILTER_CONTEXT, *PHTTP_FILTER_CONTEXT;
```

GetFilterVersion is called when the DLL is loaded; it informs the server of the filter version and the events that the filter is interested in. When these events occur, the server calls the filter's *HttpFilterProc* entry point with appropriate notifications. Some filter notifications are expensive in terms of CPU resources and I/O throughput, and they can have a significant effect on the speed and scalability of the web server. Therefore, filters should register only for notifications that the filters must see. Filters can register to receive notifications for the following events:

Event	Meaning
SF_NOTIFY_SECURE_PORT	Notify application only for sessions over a secure port.
SF_NOTIFY_NONSECURE_PORT	Notify application only for sessions over a nonsecure port.
SF_NOTIFY_READ_RAW_DATA	Allow the application to see the raw data. The data returned will contain both headers and data.
SF_NOTIFY_PREPROC_HEADERS	The server has preprocessed the headers.
SF_NOTIFY_AUTHENTICATION	The server is authenticating the client.
SF_NOTIFY_URL_MAP	The server is mapping a logical URL to a physical path.
SF_NOTIFY_SEND_RAW_DATA	The server is sending raw data back to the client.
SF_NOTIFY_LOG	The server is writing information to the server log.
SF_NOTIFY_END_OF_NET_SESSION	The session with the client is ending.
SF_NOTIFY_ACCESS_DENIED	The server is returning a 401 Access Denied error message.

We can best see the value of ISAPI filters by looking at the working example below—a program named ISAPISPY. It registers for every event notification that the server can process and writes the captured information to a text file. This program is useful for understanding how IIS operates and deals with different Internet browsers.

ISAPISPY Header File

```
#if !defined(AFX_ISAPISPY_H__E013C525_55F1_11D1_8A84_00A024E538E7
__INCLUDED_)
#define AFX_ISAPISPY_H__E013C525_55F1_11D1_8A84_00A024E538E7__INCLUDED_

// ISAPISPY.H - Header file for your Internet Server
//    ISAPISpy Filter

#include "resource.h"

class CISAPISpyFilter : public CHttpFilter
```

(continued)

```
        {
        public:
            CISAPISpyFilter();
            ~CISAPISpyFilter();

        // Overrides
            // ClassWizard generated virtual function overrides
            // NOTE - The ClassWizard will add and remove member
            // functions here.
            //    DO NOT EDIT what you see in these blocks of generated code!
            //{{AFX_VIRTUAL(CISAPISpyFilter)
        public:
            virtual BOOL GetFilterVersion(PHTTP_FILTER_VERSION pVer);
            virtual DWORD OnPreprocHeaders(CHttpFilterContext* pCtxt,
                PHTTP_FILTER_PREPROC_HEADERS pHeaderInfo);
            virtual DWORD OnAuthentication(CHttpFilterContext* pCtxt,
                PHTTP_FILTER_AUTHENT pAuthent);
            virtual DWORD OnUrlMap(CHttpFilterContext* pCtxt,
                PHTTP_FILTER_URL_MAP pMapInfo);
            virtual DWORD OnSendRawData(CHttpFilterContext* pCtxt,
                PHTTP_FILTER_RAW_DATA pRawData);
            virtual DWORD OnReadRawData(CHttpFilterContext* pCtxt,
                PHTTP_FILTER_RAW_DATA pRawData);
            virtual DWORD OnLog(CHttpFilterContext* pfc,
                PHTTP_FILTER_LOG pLog);
            virtual DWORD OnEndOfNetSession(CHttpFilterContext* pCtxt);
            //}}AFX_VIRTUAL

            //{{AFX_MSG(CISAPISpyFilter)
            //}}AFX_MSG

        private:
            CRITICAL_SECTION m_csFile;
            char m_pFileName[MAX_PATH];
        };

        //{{AFX_INSERT_LOCATION}}
        // Microsoft Developer Studio will insert additional declarations
        // immediately before the previous line.

        #endif // !defined(AFX_ISAPISPY_H__
        //E013C525_55F1_11D1_8A84_00A024E538E7__/ INCLUDED)
```

ISAPISPY Implementation File

```
// ISAPISPY.CPP - Implementation file for your Internet Server
//    ISAPISpy Filter

#include "stdafx.h"
#include "ISAPISpy.h"


/////////////////////////////////////////////////////////////////////
// The one and only CWinApp object
// NOTE - You may remove this object if you alter your project
// to no longer use MFC in a DLL.


CWinApp theApp;

FILE *stream;
/////////////////////////////////////////////////////////////////////
// The one and only CISAPISpyFilter object

CISAPISpyFilter theFilter;

/////////////////////////////////////////////////////////////////////
// CISAPISpyFilter implementation

CISAPISpyFilter::CISAPISpyFilter()
{
    InitializeCriticalSection(&m_csFile);
    strcpy(m_pFileName, "C:\\ISAPISpyLog.txt");
}


CISAPISpyFilter::~CISAPISpyFilter()
{
}

BOOL CISAPISpyFilter::GetFilterVersion(PHTTP_FILTER_VERSION pVer)
{
    // Call default implementation for initialization.
    CHttpFilter::GetFilterVersion(pVer);

    // Clear the flags set by base class.
    pVer->dwFlags &= ~SF_NOTIFY_ORDER_MASK;

    // Set the flags we are interested in.
    pVer->dwFlags |= SF_NOTIFY_ORDER_MEDIUM
        | SF_NOTIFY_SECURE_PORT | SF_NOTIFY_NONSECURE_PORT
        | SF_NOTIFY_LOG | SF_NOTIFY_AUTHENTICATION
```

(continued)

```
            | SF_NOTIFY_PREPROC_HEADERS | SF_NOTIFY_READ_RAW_DATA
            | SF_NOTIFY_SEND_RAW_DATA | SF_NOTIFY_URL_MAP
            | SF_NOTIFY_END_OF_NET_SESSION;

    // Load description string.
    TCHAR sz[SF_MAX_FILTER_DESC_LEN+1];
    ISAPIVERIFY(::LoadString(AfxGetResourceHandle(),
        IDS_FILTER, sz, SF_MAX_FILTER_DESC_LEN));
    _tcscpy(pVer->lpszFilterDesc, sz);
    return TRUE;
}

DWORD CISAPISpyFilter::OnPreprocHeaders(CHttpFilterContext* pCtxt,
    PHTTP_FILTER_PREPROC_HEADERS pHeaderInfo)
{
    // TODO: React to this notification accordingly and
    // return the appropriate status code.

    EnterCriticalSection(&m_csFile);
    stream = fopen(m_pFileName, "a");
    fprintf(stream, "\n[--OnEndOfNetSession Start--]\n");
    fprintf(stream, "[No data]");
    fprintf(stream, "\n[==OnEndOfNetSession End==]\n");
    fclose(stream);
    LeaveCriticalSection(&m_csFile);


        return SF_STATUS_REQ_NEXT_NOTIFICATION;
}

DWORD CISAPISpyFilter::OnAuthentication(CHttpFilterContext* pCtxt,
    PHTTP_FILTER_AUTHENT pAuthent)
{
    // TODO: React to this notification accordingly and
    // return the appropriate status code.
    EnterCriticalSection(&m_csFile);
    stream = fopen(m_pFileName, "a");
    fprintf(stream, "\n[--OnAuthentication Start--]\n");
    fprintf(stream, "[User ]");
    fprintf(stream, pAuthent->pszUser);
    fprintf(stream, "\n[Password ]");
    fprintf(stream, pAuthent->pszPassword);
    fprintf(stream, "\n[==OnAuthentication End==]\n");
    fclose(stream);
    LeaveCriticalSection(&m_csFile);

    return SF_STATUS_REQ_NEXT_NOTIFICATION;
}
```

```
DWORD CISAPISpyFilter::OnUrlMap(CHttpFilterContext* pCtxt,
    PHTTP_FILTER_URL_MAP pMapInfo)
{
    // TODO: React to this notification accordingly and
    // return the appropriate status code.
    EnterCriticalSection(&m_csFile);
    stream = fopen(m_pFileName, "a");
    fprintf(stream, "\n[--OnUrlMap Start--]\n");
    fprintf(stream, "[URL ]");
    fprintf(stream, pMapInfo->pszURL);
    fprintf(stream, "\n[Physical Path ]");
    fprintf(stream, pMapInfo->pszPhysicalPath);
    fprintf(stream, "\n[==OnUrlMap End==]\n");
    fclose(stream);
    LeaveCriticalSection(&m_csFile);

    return SF_STATUS_REQ_NEXT_NOTIFICATION;
}


DWORD CISAPISpyFilter::OnSendRawData(CHttpFilterContext* pCtxt,
    PHTTP_FILTER_RAW_DATA pRawData)
{
    // TODO: React to this notification accordingly and
    // return the appropriate status code.

    EnterCriticalSection(&m_csFile);
    char pstrdata[10000];
    strncpy(pstrdata, (char* )pRawData->pvInData, 9990);
    if (pRawData->cbInData < 9990 )
        pstrdata[pRawData->cbInData] = '\0';
    else
        pstrdata[9990] = '\0';
    stream = fopen(m_pFileName, "a");
    fprintf(stream, "\n[--OnSendRawData Start--]\n");
    fprintf(stream, "[Raw data ]\n");
    fprintf(stream, pstrdata);
    fprintf(stream, "\n[==OnSendRawData End==]\n");
    fclose(stream);
    LeaveCriticalSection(&m_csFile);

    return SF_STATUS_REQ_NEXT_NOTIFICATION;
}

DWORD CISAPISpyFilter::OnReadRawData(CHttpFilterContext* pCtxt,
    PHTTP_FILTER_RAW_DATA pRawData)
```

(continued)

```
{
    // TODO: React to this notification accordingly and
    // return the appropriate status code.
    EnterCriticalSection(&m_csFile);
    char pstrdata[10000];
    strncpy(pstrdata, (char* )pRawData->pvInData, 9990);
    if (pRawData->cbInData < 9990 )
        pstrdata[pRawData->cbInData] = '\0';
    else
        pstrdata[9990] = '\0';
    stream = fopen(m_pFileName, "a");
    fprintf(stream, "\n[--OnReadRawData Start----]\n");
    fprintf(stream, "[Raw data ]\n");
    fprintf(stream, pstrdata);
    fprintf(stream, "\n[==OnReadRawData End==]\n");
    fclose(stream);
    LeaveCriticalSection(&m_csFile);
    return SF_STATUS_REQ_NEXT_NOTIFICATION;
}

DWORD CISAPISpyFilter::OnLog(CHttpFilterContext *pCtxt,
    PHTTP_FILTER_LOG pLog)
{
    // TODO: React to this notification accordingly and
    // return the appropriate status code.

    EnterCriticalSection(&m_csFile);
    stream = fopen(m_pFileName, "a");
    fprintf(stream, "\n[--OnLog Start--]\n");
    fprintf(stream, "[ClientHostName ]");
    fprintf(stream, pLog->pszClientHostName);
    fprintf(stream, "\n[ClientUserName ]");
    fprintf(stream, pLog->pszClientUserName);
    fprintf(stream, "\n[ServerName ]");
    fprintf(stream, pLog->pszServerName);
    fprintf(stream, "\n[Operation ]");
    fprintf(stream, pLog->pszOperation);
    fprintf(stream, "\n[Target ]");
    fprintf(stream, pLog->pszTarget);
    fprintf(stream, "\n[Parameters ]");
    fprintf(stream, pLog->pszParameters);
    char buffer[200];
    _ltoa(pLog->dwHttpStatus, buffer, 10);
    fprintf(stream, "\n[HttpStatus ]");
    fprintf(stream, buffer);
    _ltoa(pLog->dwWin32Status, buffer, 10);
    fprintf(stream, "\n[Win32Status ]");
```

```
        fprintf(stream, buffer);
        fprintf(stream, "\n[==OnLog End==]\n");
        fclose(stream);
        LeaveCriticalSection(&m_csFile);

        return SF_STATUS_REQ_NEXT_NOTIFICATION;
}


DWORD CISAPISpyFilter::OnEndOfNetSession(CHttpFilterContext* pCtxt)
{
        // TODO: React to this notification accordingly and
        // return the appropriate status code.
        EnterCriticalSection(&m_csFile);
        stream = fopen(m_pFileName, "a");
        fprintf(stream, "\n[--OnEndOfNetSession Start--]\n");
        fprintf(stream, "[No data]");
        fprintf(stream, "\n[==OnEndOfNetSession End==]\n");
        fclose(stream);
        LeaveCriticalSection(&m_csFile);

        return SF_STATUS_REQ_NEXT_NOTIFICATION;
}


// Do not edit the following lines, which are needed by ClassWizard.
#if 0
BEGIN_MESSAGE_MAP(CISAPISpyFilter, CHttpFilter)
        //{{AFX_MSG_MAP(CISAPISpyFilter)
        //}}AFX_MSG_MAP
END_MESSAGE_MAP()
#endif// 0


/////////////////////////////////////////////////////////////////////
// If your extension will not use MFC, you'll need this code to make
// sure the extension objects can find the resource handle for the
// module.  If you convert your extension to not be dependent on MFC,
// remove the comments around the following AfxGetResourceHandle()
// and DllMain() functions as well as the g_hInstance global.

/****

static HINSTANCE g_hInstance;

HINSTANCE AFXISAPI AfxGetResourceHandle()
{
        return g_hInstance;
}
```

(continued)

```
BOOL WINAPI DllMain(HINSTANCE hInst, ULONG ulReason,
    LPVOID lpReserved)
{
    if (ulReason == DLL_PROCESS_ATTACH)
    {
        g_hInstance = hInst;
    }

    return TRUE;
}

****/
```

ISAPISPY monitors the downloading of an HTML file from a web server. The requested HTML file and output are as follows:

Requested HTML File

```
<HTML>
<HEAD>
<BODY BACKGROUND="/samples/images/back_1.gif">
<TITLE>This is an ISAPISPY Test Page</TITLE>
</HEAD>
<CENTER>
This is a Test
</CENTER>
</BODY>
</HTML>
```

ISAPISPY Output

```
[----------------------OnReadRawData Start--------------]
[Raw data ]
GET /ISAPI_SPY.htm HTTP/1.1
Accept: application/vnd.ms-excel, application/msword,
 application/vnd.ms-powerpoint, image/gif, image/x-xbitmap,
 image/jpeg, image/pjpeg, */*
Accept-Language: en-us
Accept-Encoding: gzip, deflate
User-Agent: Mozilla/4.0 (compatible; MSIE 4.0; Windows NT)
Host: NDCServ1
Connection: Keep-Alive

[==OnReadRawData End==]

[--OnEndOfNetSession Start--]
[No data]
[==OnEndOfNetSession End==]
```

```
[--OnUrlMap Start--]
[URL ]/ISAPI_SPY.htm
[Physical Path ]C:\InetPub\wwwroot\ISAPI_SPY.htm
[==OnUrlMap End==]


[--OnAuthentication Start--]
[User ]
[Password ]
[==OnAuthentication End==]


[--OnSendRawData Start--]
[Raw data ]
HTTP/1.0 401 Access Denied
WWW-Authenticate: Basic realm="NDCServ1"
Content-Length: 24
Content-Type: text/html

Error: Access is Denied.
[==OnSendRawData End==]


[--OnLog Start--]
[ClientHostName ]192.168.205.79
[ClientUserName ]
[ServerName ]192.168.205.49
[Operation ]GET
[Target ]/ISAPI_SPY.htm
[Parameters ]
[HttpStatus ]401
[Win32Status ]5
[==OnLog End==]


[--OnEndOfNetSession Start--]
[No data]
[==OnEndOfNetSession End==]


[--OnReadRawData Start--]
[Raw data ]
GET /ISAPI_SPY.htm HTTP/1.1
Accept: application/vnd.ms-excel, application/msword,
 application/vnd.ms-powerpoint, image/gif, image/x-xbitmap,
 image/jpeg, image/pjpeg, */*
Accept-Language: en-us
Accept-Encoding: gzip, deflate
User-Agent: Mozilla/4.0 (compatible; MSIE 4.0; Windows NT)
Host: NDCServ1
```

(continued)

```
Connection: Keep-Alive
Accept-Language: en-us
Accept-Encoding: gzip, deflate
Authorization: Basic cnNvcmVuc2VuOmlzYXBp

[==OnReadRawData End==]

[--OnEndOfNetSession Start--]
[No data]
[==OnEndOfNetSession End==]

[--OnUrlMap Start--]
[URL ]/ISAPI_SPY.htm
[Physical Path ]C:\InetPub\wwwroot\ISAPI_SPY.htm
[==OnUrlMap End==]

[--OnAuthentication Start--]
[User ]rsorensen
[Password ]isapi
[==OnAuthentication End==]

[--OnSendRawData Start--]
[Raw data ]
HTTP/1.0 200 OK
Server: Microsoft-PWS/2.0
Connection: keep-alive
Date: Thu, 06 Nov 1997 18:46:49 GMT
Content-Type: text/html
Accept-Ranges: bytes
Last-Modified: Thu, 06 Nov 1997 18:44:47 GMT
Content-Length: 176

[==OnSendRawData End==]

[--OnSendRawData Start--]
[Raw data ]
<HTML>
<HEAD>
<BODY BACKGROUND="/samples/images/back_1.gif">
<TITLE>This is an ISAPISPY Test Page</TITLE>
</HEAD>
<CENTER>
This is a Test
</CENTER>
</BODY>
</HTML>

[==OnSendRawData End==]
```

```
[--OnLog Start--]
[ClientHostName ]192.168.205.79
[ClientUserName ]rsorensen
[ServerName ]192.168.205.49
[Operation ]GET
[Target ]/ISAPI_SPY.htm
[Parameters ]
[HttpStatus ]200
[Win32Status ]0
[==OnLog End==]

[--OnReadRawData Start--]
[Raw data ]
GET /samples/images/back_1.gif HTTP/1.1
Accept: */*
Referer: http://NDCServ1/ISAPI_SPY.htm
Accept-Language: en-us
Accept-Encoding: gzip, deflate
User-Agent: Mozilla/4.0 (compatible; MSIE 4.0; Windows NT)
Host: NDCServ1
Connection: Keep-Alive
Authorization: Basic cnNvcmVuc2VuOmlzYXBp

[==OnReadRawData End==]

[--OnEndOfNetSession Start--]
[No data]
[==OnEndOfNetSession End==]

[--OnUrlMap Start--]
[URL ]/samples/images/back_1.gif
[Physical Path ]C:\InetPub\wwwroot\samples\images\back_1.gif
[==OnUrlMap End==]

[--OnAuthentication Start--]
[User ]rsorensen
[Password ]isapi
[==OnAuthentication End==]

[--OnSendRawData Start--]
[Raw data ]
HTTP/1.0 200 OK
Server: Microsoft-PWS/2.0
Connection: keep-alive
Date: Thu, 06 Nov 1997 18:46:50 GMT
Content-Type: image/gif
```

(continued)

```
Accept-Ranges: bytes
Last-Modified: Fri, 09 Aug 1996 06:30:00 GMT
Content-Length: 10282

[==OnSendRawData End==]

[--OnSendRawData Start--]
[Raw data ]
GIF87ad
[==OnSendRawData End==]

[--OnSendRawData Start--]
[Raw data ]
Ð Ý
Z`…""AmWð__Š"_zâ·³2pAÿ*,-ƒ:Ý _V *    R¦_$D/?,,
JÉg_ÏðR_+(A"kp,,„¶_¼"ÑD~_„K5a?¢Ï_|`__¦__& ·
_"•"¦ x¦™_
[==OnSendRawData End==]

[--OnLog Start--]
[ClientHostName ]192.168.205.79
[ClientUserName ]rsorensen
[ServerName ]192.168.205.49
[Operation ]GET
[Target ]/samples/images/back_1.gif
[Parameters ]
[HttpStatus ]200
[Win32Status ]0
[==OnLog End==]
```

This concludes our analysis of IIS development with CGI and ISAPI. You have seen how these interfaces simplify Internet application development by allowing the developer to build on the capabilities of web servers. The next chapter will examine Active Server Pages (ASP). ASP abstracts more effectively than CGI and ISAPI the technical details of extending IIS, thus allowing a more complete adoption of a people-oriented programming paradigm.

CHAPTER FIVE

Active Server Pages

The introduction of Active Server Pages (ASP) with Internet Information Server (IIS) 3.0 gave developers a new alternative to common gateway interface (CGI) and Internet Server application programmer interface (ISAPI) for developing web applications. ASP is a server-side scripting environment that allows you to create dynamic content using script commands that can be written within HTML files. This provides a simpler interface than CGI and ISAPI for programming web applications and offers a more natural way of mixing ASP-generated presentation output with your HTML presentation code. You can easily convert an HTML file to an ASP file by changing the .htm extension to the .asp extension. ASP passes all files with the .asp extension through a Microsoft ActiveX scripting engine before sending them on to the client web browser. The scripting engine executes scripts on the server and sends only outputted HTML back to the browser, so the client need not be aware that ActiveX scripting is being used on the server.

One of the great advantages of server-side processing is that you do not need to be concerned with the types of browsers that might be used to view your site. Most, if not all, browsers can interpret the HTML code generated from the ASP script. This contrasts with client-side processing, in which VBScript, JavaScript, JScript (Microsoft's JavaScript implementation), and Dynamic HTML must be executed within the client browser. Some of these scripting languages are not supported by popular browsers or they behave differently in different versions of the browsers.

Simple ASP Scripts

The following is a simple ASP script that writes *Hello World* three times to the client browser, increasing the font size each time.

```
<%@ LANGUAGE = "VBScript" %>
<HTML>
<HEAD><TITLE> Hello World - ASP Sample</TITLE></HEAD>
<BODY BGCOLOR=#FFFFFF>
<% for i = 3 to 6 %>
    <FONT SIZE=<% = i %>>Hello World</FONT><BR>
<% next %>
<BR>
<BR>
</BODY>
</HTML>
```

This example uses VBScript. Except for the script between the < % and % > tags, this is a standard HTML file. A client browser can request this file using a URL such as *http://192.168.205.79/hello.asp*. Notice that the first line of the file specifies the scripting language. If we use JScript instead of VBScript, our example looks like this:

```
<%@ LANGUAGE = "JScript" %>
<HTML>
<HEAD><TITLE> Hello World - ASP Sample</TITLE></HEAD>
<BODY BGCOLOR=#FFFFFF>
<% for (i = 3; i < 7; i++) {%>
    <FONT SIZE=<% = i %>>Hello World</FONT><BR>
<%}%>
<BR>
<BR>
</BODY>
</HTML>
```

To execute the ASP page, the ASP run time must create a program from the mix of HTML and script code by compiling the source page to produce a pure script file. First each contiguous block of HTML is placed in an array that ASP creates for the page. The compilation process then replaces each HTML block with a call to the ASP internal function *WriteBlock(offsetOfTheBlock)*. Script blocks are left intact. As a result, the ASP page, which consists of a mixture of HTML and script code, is transformed into a program consisting of calls to

WriteBlock and user-created script code. The following generated HTML output is sent back to the browser after either of the script examples above has been executed on the server.

```
<HTML>
<HEAD><TITLE> Hello World - ASP Sample</TITLE></HEAD>
<BODY BGCOLOR=#FFFFFF>

    <FONT SIZE=3>Hello World</FONT><BR>

    <FONT SIZE=4>Hello World</FONT><BR>

    <FONT SIZE=5>Hello World</FONT><BR>

    <FONT SIZE=6>Hello World</FONT><BR>

<BR>
<BR>
</BODY>
</HTML>
```

Script Languages

You can configure ASP with a default script language that will be applied if no other language is specified in the script. In IIS 4.0, you can do this on the App Options tab of Internet Service Manager (ISM). In IIS 3.0, you can set it in the registry using the *DefaultScriptLanguage* value at the following location:

```
HKEY_LOCAL_MACHINE\SYSTEM\CurrentControlSet\Services\
W3SVC\ASP\Parameters
```

ASP achieves language independence through the ActiveX scripting standard, which allows any compliant scripting host to use compliant scripting engines from multiple vendors. The vendors can independently determine the language, syntax, and execution model of the script without needing cooperation from the programmers who develop the scripting host. The scripting engine and the scripting host are COM objects that must support the ActiveX scripting interfaces. The scripting engine is required to implement the *IActiveScript* interface and might implement the *IActiveScriptParse* interface. The scripting host is the application or program that plugs in the particular ActiveX scripting engine; it is required to implement the *IActiveScriptSite* interface. The script itself is usually a block of text, but it can be pcode, machine-specific executable byte code, or any binary blob that the scripting engine can execute.

ActiveX scripting even allows ASP to mix scripting languages within files, as shown here:

```
<HTML>
<HEAD><TITLE> Hello World - ASP Sample</TITLE></HEAD>
<BODY BGCOLOR=#FFFFFF>
<% i = 2%>

<%i = NextSizeJ(i)%>
<FONT SIZE= <%=i%>>Hello World</FONT><BR>
<%i = NextSizeVB(i)%>
<FONT SIZE= <%=i%>>Hello World</FONT><BR>
<%i = NextSizeJ(i)%>
<FONT SIZE= <%=i%>>Hello World</FONT><BR>
<%i = NextSizeVB(i)%>
<FONT SIZE= <%=i%>>Hello World</FONT><BR>

<SCRIPT LANGUAGE=JScript RUNAT=Server>
function NextSizeJ(l)
{
    l = l + 1;
    return l;
}
</SCRIPT>

<SCRIPT LANGUAGE=VBScript RUNAT=Server>
    Function NextSizeVB(k)
        NextSizeVB = k + 1
    End Function
</SCRIPT>

<BR>
<BR>
</BODY>
</HTML>
```

While this ASP file produces the same output as the other *Hello World* examples above, it uses a mix of VBScript and JScript. The following tag specifies that the script enclosed within the tag should be processed with the VBScript engine and that this should be done on the server:

```
<SCRIPT LANGUAGE=VBScript RUNAT=Server>
```

The scripting host within ASP uses code similar to the following to retrieve a pointer to the *IActiveScript* interface of the VBScript scripting engine.

```
HRESULT hr;
IActiveScript* pAS = NULL;
CLSID clsid;
OLECHAR wstrProgID[] = OLESTR("VBScript");
hr = CLSIDFromProgID(wstrProgID, &clsid);
if (SUCCEEDED(hr))
{
    hr = CoCreateInstance(clsid, 0, CLSCTX_ALL,
        IID_IActiveScript, (void**)&pAS);
}
```

You can see that the value of the SCRIPT LANGUAGE tag ("VBScript") is passed in as the ProgID of the scripting engine object to be created. ASP also passes in the ProgID "JScript" to create an instance of the JScript scripting engine.

ActiveX Scripting Methods

The *IActiveScript* interface is the pivotal interface for ActiveX scripting, and every scripting engine must implement it.

IActiveScript

```
interface IActiveScript : public IUnknown
    {
    public:
        virtual HRESULT STDMETHODCALLTYPE SetScriptSite(
            /* [in] */ IActiveScriptSite __RPC_FAR *pass) = 0;

        virtual HRESULT STDMETHODCALLTYPE GetScriptSite(
            /* [in] */ REFIID riid,
            /* [iid_is][out] */ void __RPC_FAR *__RPC_FAR
                *ppvObject) = 0;

        virtual HRESULT STDMETHODCALLTYPE SetScriptState(
            /* [in] */ SCRIPTSTATE ss) = 0;

        virtual HRESULT STDMETHODCALLTYPE GetScriptState(
            /* [out] */ SCRIPTSTATE __RPC_FAR *pssState) = 0;
```

(continued)

153

```
virtual HRESULT STDMETHODCALLTYPE Close( void) = 0;
virtual HRESULT STDMETHODCALLTYPE AddNamedItem(
    /* [in] */ LPCOLESTR pstrName,
    /* [in] */ DWORD dwFlags) = 0;

virtual HRESULT STDMETHODCALLTYPE AddTypeLib(
    /* [in] */ REFGUID rguidTypeLib,
    /* [in] */ DWORD dwMajor,
    /* [in] */ DWORD dwMinor,
    /* [in] */ DWORD dwFlags) = 0;

virtual HRESULT STDMETHODCALLTYPE GetScriptDispatch(
    /* [in] */ LPCOLESTR pstrItemName,
    /* [out] */ IDispatch __RPC_FAR *__RPC_FAR *ppdisp) = 0;

virtual HRESULT STDMETHODCALLTYPE GetCurrentScriptThreadID(
    /* [out] */ SCRIPTTHREADID __RPC_FAR *pstidThread) = 0;

virtual HRESULT STDMETHODCALLTYPE GetScriptThreadID(
    /* [in] */ DWORD dwWin32ThreadId,
    /* [out] */ SCRIPTTHREADID __RPC_FAR *pstidThread) = 0;

virtual HRESULT STDMETHODCALLTYPE GetScriptThreadState(
    /* [in] */ SCRIPTTHREADID stidThread,
    /* [out] */ SCRIPTTHREADSTATE __RPC_FAR *pstsState) = 0;

virtual HRESULT STDMETHODCALLTYPE InterruptScriptThread(
    /* [in] */ SCRIPTTHREADID stidThread,
    /* [in] */ const EXCEPINFO __RPC_FAR *pexcepinfo,
    /* [in] */ DWORD dwFlags) = 0;

virtual HRESULT STDMETHODCALLTYPE Clone(
    /* [out] */ IActiveScript __RPC_FAR *__RPC_FAR
        *ppscript) = 0;
};
```

This interface contains most of the important methods that are required of a scripting engine. The *SetScriptSite* method must be called first on the *IActiveScript* interface. It is used to pass a pointer to the *IActiveScriptSite* interface (which is implemented by the host) to the scripting engine. This allows the scripting engine to make calls back to the scripting host to notify it of events. We will examine the *IActiveScriptSite* interface when we look at the requirements of a scripting host in greater detail. A scripting engine transitions through various states during its operation. The *SetScriptState* method uses the following enumeration to specify the different states:

```
typedef enum tagSCRIPTSTATE
{
    SCRIPTSTATE_UNINITIALIZED = 0,
    SCRIPTSTATE_INITIALIZED = 5,
    SCRIPTSTATE_STARTED = 1,
    SCRIPTSTATE_CONNECTED = 2,
    SCRIPTSTATE_DISCONNECTED = 3,
    SCRIPTSTATE_CLOSED = 4
} SCRIPTSTATE;
```

When the scripting engine is first created, it is not initialized. Before it can be initialized, it must have a pointer to the host's *IActiveScriptSite* interface and one of the following methods must have been called: *IPersist*::Load*, *IPersist*::InitNew*, or *IActiveScriptParse::InitNew*. In the initialized state, the scripting engine still cannot run because it is not connected to host objects and sinking events. In this initialized state, it queues code that the host passes to it through the *ParseScriptText* method of the *IActiveScriptParse* interface. This code is executed as soon as the scripting engine transitions to the started state. The scripting engine can execute code in the started state, but it is not yet connected to the events of the objects added by the scripting host through the *AddNamed-Item* method of the *IActiveScript* interface. To be fully operational, the scripting engine must transition to the connected state, in which the script is both loaded and connected for sinking events from host objects.

Eventually, the scripting engine transitions to the closed state in which it is inoperative. (Most methods return errors.) In the meantime, it might be put into a disconnected state, which means that the script is loaded and has a run-time state but is temporarily disconnected from sinking events from host objects. A scripting engine can also be put in the closed state using the *Close* method, which causes the scripting engine to abandon any currently loaded script, release any interface pointers that it has to other objects, and enter a closed state.

The *IActiveScript* interface method *AddTypeLib* adds a type library to the namespace for the script. In this way, a set of predefined items such as class definitions, typedefs, and named constants can be added to the run-time environment that is available to the script. The SCRIPTTYPELIB_ISCONTROL flag is set in this method call to indicate that the type library describes an ActiveX control used by the scripting host. The *IActiveScript* interface also allows the scripting host to expose automation objects to the scripting engine using the *AddNamedItem* method. This method adds the name of a root-level item to the scripting engine's name space. A root-level item is an object with properties and methods, an event source, or both. The *AddNameItem* method allows the association of the following flags with the root-item item:

```
SCRIPTITEM_ISPERSISTENT
- item should be saved if the scripting engine is saved
SCRIPTITEM_ISSOURCE
- item sources events that the script can sink
SCRIPTITEM_ISVISIBLE
- item's name is available in the name space of the script,
 allowing access to the properties, methods, and events of the item.
SCRIPTITEM_GLOBALMEMBERS
- item is a collection of global properties and methods associated
 with the script. It is left to the scripting engine to deal with
 name conflicts.
SCRIPTITEM_NOCODE
- item is a name being added to the script's name space and should
 not be treated as an item for which code should be associated.
SCRIPTITEM_CODEONLY
- item represents a code-only object. The host has no IUnknown to
 be associated with this code-only object.
```

The *GetScriptDispatch* method of the *IActiveScript* interface allows the scripting host to retrieve the *IDispatch* interface for all the methods and properties associated with the running script. These methods and properties might have been added dynamically to the script through the use of the *IActiveScript-Parse* interface.

IActiveScriptParse

```
interface IActiveScriptParse : public IUnknown
    {
    public:
        virtual HRESULT STDMETHODCALLTYPE InitNew( void) = 0;

        virtual HRESULT STDMETHODCALLTYPE AddScriptlet(
            /* [in] */ LPCOLESTR pstrDefaultName,
            /* [in] */ LPCOLESTR pstrCode,
```

```
    /* [in] */ LPCOLESTR pstrItemName,
    /* [in] */ LPCOLESTR pstrSubItemName,
    /* [in] */ LPCOLESTR pstrEventName,
    /* [in] */ LPCOLESTR pstrDelimiter,
    /* [in] */ DWORD dwSourceContextCookie,
    /* [in] */ ULONG ulStartingLineNumber,
    /* [in] */ DWORD dwFlags,
    /* [out] */ BSTR __RPC_FAR *pbstrName,
    /* [out] */ EXCEPINFO __RPC_FAR *pexcepinfo) = 0;

virtual HRESULT STDMETHODCALLTYPE ParseScriptText(
    /* [in] */ LPCOLESTR pstrCode,
    /* [in] */ LPCOLESTR pstrItemName,
    /* [in] */ IUnknown __RPC_FAR *punkContext,
    /* [in] */ LPCOLESTR pstrDelimiter,
    /* [in] */ DWORD dwSourceContextCookie,
    /* [in] */ ULONG ulStartingLineNumber,
    /* [in] */ DWORD dwFlags,
    /* [out] */ VARIANT __RPC_FAR *pvarResult,
    /* [out] */ EXCEPINFO __RPC_FAR *pexcepinfo) = 0;
};
```

A scripting engine does not need to support the *IActiveScriptParse* interface to be compliant with the ActiveX scripting standard because it might support one of the *IPersist** interfaces instead (*IPersistStorage, IPersistStreamInit,* or *IPersistPropertyBag*). However, the two main scripting engines used with ASP do support the *IActiveScriptParse* interface. The code below verifies that VBScript and JScript both support the interface. You can check to see whether any other scripting engine supports this interface by modifying this code.

```
HRESULT hr;
IActiveScript* pASJ = NULL;
CLSID clsid;
OLECHAR wstrProgIDJ[] = OLESTR("JScript");
hr = CLSIDFromProgID(wstrProgIDJ, &clsid);
if (SUCCEEDED(hr))
{
    hr = CoCreateInstance(clsid, 0, CLSCTX_ALL,
        IID_IActiveScript, (void**)&pASJ);
}
```

(continued)

157

```
IActiveScriptParse* pASParseJ = NULL;
hr = pASJ->QueryInterface(IID_IActiveScriptParse,
    (void**)&pASParseJ);
ASSERT(!FAILED(hr));

IActiveScript* pASVB = NULL;
OLECHAR wstrProgIDVB[] = OLESTR("VBScript");
hr = CLSIDFromProgID(wstrProgIDVB, &clsid);
if (SUCCEEDED(hr))
{
    hr = CoCreateInstance(clsid, 0, CLSCTX_ALL,
        IID_IActiveScript, (void**)&pASVB);
}
IActiveScriptParse* pASParseVB = NULL;
hr = pASVB->QueryInterface(IID_IActiveScriptParse,
    (void**)&pASParseVB);
ASSERT(!FAILED(hr));
```

The *IActiveScriptParse* interface allows text code scriptlets to be added to the script and expression text that will be evaluated at run time. This is accomplished using the *AddScriptlet* and *ParseScriptText* methods. The *AddScriptlet* method enables the host to dynamically add code scriptlets to the script. This allows code embedded in HTML documents to be attached to intrinsic events. The *ParseScriptText* method is used to parse a given code scriptlet, add declarations to the name space, and evaluate code as needed. The scriptlet can be an expression, a list of statements, or anything that can be interpreted by the scripting engine. The *dwFlags* parameter of the *ParseScriptText* method can specify with the value SCRIPTTEXT_ISEXPRESSION that the scriptlet is an expression. Since expressions are executed immediately, it is illegal to use this flag when the scripting engine is only in the initialized state. The *pvarResult* parameter contains the address of a buffer that receives the results of the scriptlet processing. If the *dwFlags* flag is not set with the value SCRIPTTEXT_ISEXPRESSION, the caller will not expect any result and the *pvarResult* parameter will be NULL. The following definition of a new function in VBScript is an example of this kind of scriptlet.

```
Function NextSizeVB(k)
    NextSizeVB = k + 1
End Function
```

This scriptlet only defines a new function that can be called at a later time. It therefore does not return any result. The code in this kind of scriptlet must be a valid, complete portion of code. If we leave out *End Function*, the parser must generate a parse error because a function declaration was started but not completed.

IActiveScriptSite

```
interface IActiveScriptSite : public IUnknown
    {
    public:
        virtual HRESULT STDMETHODCALLTYPE GetLCID(
            /* [out] */ LCID __RPC_FAR *plcid) = 0;

        virtual HRESULT STDMETHODCALLTYPE GetItemInfo(
            /* [in] */ LPCOLESTR pstrName,
            /* [in] */ DWORD dwReturnMask,
            /* [out] */ IUnknown __RPC_FAR *__RPC_FAR *ppiunkItem,
            /* [out] */ ITypeInfo __RPC_FAR *__RPC_FAR *ppti) = 0;

        virtual HRESULT STDMETHODCALLTYPE GetDocVersionString(
            /* [out] */ BSTR __RPC_FAR *pbstrVersion) = 0;

        virtual HRESULT STDMETHODCALLTYPE OnScriptTerminate(
            /* [in] */ const VARIANT __RPC_FAR *pvarResult,
            /* [in] */ const EXCEPINFO __RPC_FAR *pexcepinfo) = 0;

        virtual HRESULT STDMETHODCALLTYPE OnStateChange(
            /* [in] */ SCRIPTSTATE ssScriptState) = 0;

        virtual HRESULT STDMETHODCALLTYPE OnScriptError(
            /* [in] */ IActiveScriptError __RPC_FAR
                *pscripterror) = 0;

        virtual HRESULT STDMETHODCALLTYPE OnEnterScript( void)
            = 0;

        virtual HRESULT STDMETHODCALLTYPE OnLeaveScript( void)
            = 0;
    };
```

ASP is a scripting host and therefore must support the *IActiveScriptSite* interface. A pointer to this interface is passed to the scripting engine with the *IActiveScript* interface method *SetScriptSite*. The scripting engine uses this pointer to call the *IActiveScriptSite* interface methods *OnScriptTerminate, OnStateChange, OnScriptError, OnEnterScript,* and *OnLeaveScript* to inform ASP as these events occur. The scripting engine uses the *GetItemInfo* method to obtain information about any items added with the *IActiveScript* interface method *AddNamedItem.* This information is the address of a pointer to the item's *IUnknown* or *ITypeInfo* interface.

The simplicity of VBScript and JScript and their ability to integrate these ActiveX Scripting languages with HTML tags are compelling reasons for using ASP. However, perhaps the most compelling reason is the rich services provided by ASP's intrinsic objects and Active Server Components. We will now examine these services, which are included in IIS 4.0.

Built-In Objects

ASP has the following six built-in objects:

- *Request*
- *Response*
- *Server*
- *ObjectContext*
- *Application*
- *Session*

Intrinsic objects are automatically accessible within every ASP script name space and do not require instantiation. They provide most of the common services that a web application developer needs, and they provide simpler interfaces than those exposed in CGI and ISAPI. The *Request* and *Response* objects provide services for managing information sent to and from the web server. The *Server* object is used to manage the environment in which scripts are run. The *Application* and *Session* objects are used to manage user state, and the *ObjectContext* object allows you to commit or abort a transaction initiated by an ASP script.

Request Object

The *Request* object retrieves the information that the client browser passed to the server during an HTTP request and stores this information in the following collections:

- *QueryString*
- *Form*
- *Cookies*
- *ClientCertificate*
- *ServerVariables*

The syntax for accessing this information is as follows:

```
Request[.collection|property|method](variable)
```

You can also retrieve variables directly without the collection name by calling *Request(variable)*. But the same name might exist in more than one collection. ASP searches collections for the name in this order: *QueryString, Form, Cookies, ClientCertificate,* and *ServerVariables*. It uses the first one that it finds. You should use the *ServerVariables* collection names when retrieving environment variables. This piece of code retrieves all the HTTP Server variables:

```
<HTML>
<HEAD><TITLE>ASP Request Object Sample </TITLE></HEAD>
<BODY BGCOLOR=#FFFFFF>
<H3>HTTP Server Variables retrieved with the Request Object</H3>

<% For Each key in Request.ServerVariables %>
    <li><strong><% = key %> </li></strong>  - 
    <em><% = Request.ServerVariables(key) %></em><BR>
<% Next %>

</BODY>
</HTML>
```

The code presents the following output to the user:

```
HTTP Server Variables retrieved with the Request Object

ALL_HTTP - HTTP_ACCEPT:*/* HTTP_ACCEPT_LANGUAGE:en-us HTTP_CONNECTION:
Keep-Alive HTTP_HOST:localhost HTTP_USER_AGENT:Mozilla/4.0
 (compatible; MSIE 4.01; Windows NT) HTTP_COOKIE:
ScriptLanguagePreference=VBScript; ComponentPreference=VB5;
ASPSESSIONIDQGGQQQBP=HDBJFLKCMEIBGFHGDNLJBJJA
HTTP_ACCEPT_ENCODING:gzip, deflate
ALL_RAW - Accept: */* Accept-Language: en-us Connection: Keep-Alive
Host: localhost User-Agent: Mozilla/4.0 (compatible; MSIE 4.01;
 Windows NT) Cookie: ScriptLanguagePreference=VBScript;
ComponentPreference=VB5; ASPSESSIONIDQGGQQQBP=
HDBJFLKCMEIBGFHGDNLJBJJA Accept-Encoding: gzip, deflate
APPL_MD_PATH - /LM/W3SVC/1/Root/demo
APPL_PHYSICAL_PATH - D:\Inetpub\Samples\
AUTH_PASSWORD -
AUTH_TYPE -
AUTH_USER -
CERT_COOKIE -
CERT_FLAGS -
CERT_ISSUER -
CERT_KEYSIZE -
CERT_SECRETKEYSIZE -
CERT_SERIALNUMBER -
CERT_SERVER_ISSUER -
CERT_SERVER_SUBJECT -
CERT_SUBJECT -
CONTENT_LENGTH - 0
CONTENT_TYPE -
GATEWAY_INTERFACE - CGI/1.1
HTTPS - off
HTTPS_KEYSIZE -
HTTPS_SECRETKEYSIZE -
HTTPS_SERVER_ISSUER -
HTTPS_SERVER_SUBJECT -
INSTANCE_ID - 1
INSTANCE_META_PATH - /LM/W3SVC/1
LOCAL_ADDR - 127.0.0.1
LOGON_USER -
PATH_INFO - /demo/srvrequest.asp
PATH_TRANSLATED - D:\Inetpub\Samples\srvrequest.asp
QUERY_STRING -
REMOTE_ADDR - 127.0.0.1
```

```
REMOTE_HOST - 127.0.0.1
REMOTE_USER -
REQUEST_METHOD - GET
SCRIPT_NAME - /demo/srvrequest.asp
SERVER_NAME - localhost
SERVER_PORT - 80
SERVER_PORT_SECURE - 0
SERVER_PROTOCOL - HTTP/1.1
SERVER_SOFTWARE - Microsoft-IIS/4.0
URL - /demo/srvrequest.asp
HTTP_ACCEPT - */*
HTTP_ACCEPT_LANGUAGE - en-us
HTTP_CONNECTION - Keep-Alive
HTTP_HOST - localhost
HTTP_USER_AGENT - Mozilla/4.0 (compatible; MSIE 4.01; Windows NT)
HTTP_COOKIE - ScriptLanguagePreference=VBScript;
ComponentPreference=VB5; ASPSESSIONIDQGGQQQBP=HDBJFLKCMEIBGFHGDNLJBJJA
HTTP_ACCEPT_ENCODING - gzip, deflate
```

While you can access information from the client in this way, other collections within the *Request* object provide a simpler interface for parsing out this information. The user normally sends information to the server using either an HTML form or by appending information to the end of a URL. You use the *Form* and *QueryString* collections to extract this information. The following HTML file presents a *Form* collection to a user and asks for the user's name and password:

```
<HTML>
<HEAD><TITLE>ASP Request Object Sample</TITLE></HEAD>
<BODY BGCOLOR=#FFFFFF>
<H3>Request Form Sample</H3>
<HR>

<FORM METHOD=POST ACTION="form1.asp">
    <BR>Your Name:
    <BR><INPUT TYPE=TEXT SIZE=50 MAXLENGTH=50 NAME="name"><BR>
    <BR>Your Password:
    <BR><INPUT TYPE=TEXT SIZE=50 MAXLENGTH=50 NAME="password"><BR>
    <BR><INPUT TYPE=SUBMIT VALUE="Submit Form">
        <INPUT TYPE=RESET VALUE="Reset Form">
</FORM>
<BR>
<BR>
</BODY>
</HTML>
```

This HTML file uses the *POST Form* method and specifies the ASP file form1.asp for the *Form* action value. The file uses the *Request Form* collection to retrieve the value of the name and password and returns a response to the user indicating whether the password was correct, as shown below:

```
<HTML>
<HEAD><TITLE>ASP Request Object Sample</TITLE></HEAD>
<BODY BGCOLOR=#FFFFFF>
<H3>Request Form Sample</H3>
<HR>
<%
    Dim str
    If Request.Form("password") <> "pass" Then
        str = "the password you entered is incorrect!"
    Else
        str = "the password you entered is correct!"
    End If
%>
<%=Request.Form("name")%><BR>
<%=str%>
</BODY>
</HTML>
```

Similarly, you use the *ClientCertificate* collection to retrieve the values of fields stored in the client certificate. The *Cookies* collection stores the values of cookies sent in the HTTP request. The *Request* object has a *TotalBytes* property, which specifies the total number of bytes that the client is sending in the body of the request. It also has a *BinaryRead* method, which enables you to do low-level reads of data sent from the client using the *POST* method. The *BinaryRead* method stores the content of a request in a safe array, as in the following example:

```
<%
Dim data
Dim Numbytes
Numbytes = Request.TotalBytes
data = Request.BinaryRead(Numbytes)
%>
```

Response Object

You use the *Response* object to send information back to the client. It has only one collection to set the values of cookies, but it has nine properties and eight methods. It is concerned with inserting information into HTML pages, sending cookies, redirecting browsers, setting the page properties, and determining whether information is buffered before it is sent back to the client browser. The following example sends a cookie to a client browser and uses the *Response* object's *Write* method to inform the user that this has happened.

```
<%
Response.Cookies("Type") = "Test Cookie"
Response.Cookies("Type").Expires = "Dec 31, 1998"
%>
<HTML>
<HEAD><TITLE>ASP Response Object Sample</TITLE></HEAD>
<BODY BGCOLOR=#FFFFFF>
<H3>Response Cookie Sample</H3>
<HR>
<% Response.Write("You have been sent a test cookie")
   Response.Write(" that will expire on Dec 31, 1998") %>
</BODY>
</HTML>
```

If you want to write out binary data instead of character data, you can use the *BinaryWrite* method to avoid having ASP do any character conversion on the data before it is sent back.

The properties of the *Response* object are as follows:

- *Buffer*
- *CacheControl*
- *Charset*
- *ContentType*
- *Expires*
- *ExpiresAbsolute*
- *IsClientConnected*
- *Pics*
- *Status*

The methods of the *Response* object are as follows:

- *AddHeader*
- *AppendToLog*
- *BinaryWrite*
- *Clear*
- *End*
- *Flush*
- *Redirect*
- *Write*

You use the *Buffer* property in conjunction with the *Clear, Flush,* and *End* methods to gain greater control over how a client receives information from your script. If this property is set to True and you do not call the *Clear, Flush,* and *End* methods, the entire script is processed before any content is sent back to the client browser. However, if you call the *Flush* method, all content that has been buffered up to that point is immediately sent back to the client browser. This can be useful for scripts that do not have quick execution times.

For example, if your script needs to process a large volume of data, you can use the *Flush* method to send back the first screen of processed data immediately so that the user can view the information while your script continues processing the rest of the data. If the processing takes a long time, you can use the *IsClientConnected* property to determine whether the client has disconnected from the server since the last *Response.Write.* In this way, you can be sure that the client is still connected before you continue to process the rest of the script.

The *Clear* method erases HTML that has been buffered up to that point, except for response headers. This method is particularly useful for handling error conditions. For example, if you detect an error that compromises the integrity of the data that you have generated, you can use the *Clear* method to prevent it from being sent back to the user. You can call the *End* method to send back the current buffered data and stop processing the remaining contents of the file.

You use the *ContentType, PICS,* and *Status* properties to set the value of these headers, and you use the *AddHeader* method to add a new HTML header with a specified value. The HTTP protocol requires that all headers be sent before content, so you must call the *AddHeader* method in your script before any HTML code is sent to the client. You can enable buffering to avoid this restriction and to be able to call the *AddHeader* method anywhere before a call to the *Flush* method. Note that the *AddHeader* method does not replace an existing header of the same name.

The *Redirect* method causes the browser to attempt to connect to a different URL by sending the header *HTTP/1.0 302 Object Moved* and by adding a Location header with the value of the URL passed in this method. The *Charset* property appends the name of the character set to the content-type header in the response object. For example, the script *< % Response.Charset("ISO-LATIN-7") % >* produces the following content-type header:

```
content-type:text/html; charset=ISO-LATIN-7
```

You use the *AppendToLog* method to add a string to the end of the web server log entry for this request. The maximum length of this string is 80 characters, and it should not contain any comma characters because fields in the IIS log are comma-delimited. The *Expires* property is the length of time before a page cached on a browser expires. Alternatively, you can use the *ExpiresAbsolute* property value to specify the exact date and time that a page will expire. If you want proxy servers to cache the output generated by ASP, you must set the *CacheControl* property to public.

Server Object

The *Server* object provides access to the server's four methods and one property, which act as general utilities for web application development. The object's only property, *ScriptTimeout*, specifies the amount of time that a script can run before it times out. The timeout will not take effect while a server component is processing, and it cannot be set to a value less than the default timeout value specified in the metabase. The *HTMLEncode* method provides an easy way to apply HTML coding to strings. Since HTML uses text tags to specify how content is displayed in the browser, you cannot use this same text as part of your content. The HTML specification provides a way to encode these characters so that they are displayed correctly in a browser.

```
<HTML>
<HEAD>
<TITLE>Simple HTML File </TITLE>
</HEAD>
<BODY BGCOLOR=#FFFFFF>
This is a simple HTML File
</BODY>
</HTML>
```

For example, to display as text the contents of the simple HTML file above, you use the *HTMLEncode* method as follows:

```
<% = Server.HTMLEncode("<HTML><HEAD><TITLE>Simple HTML File </TITLE></
HEAD><BODY BGCOLOR=#FFFFFF>This is a simple HTML File </BODY></
HTML>") %>
```

It produces this HTML encoded text:

```
&lt;HTML&gt;&lt;HEAD&gt;&lt;TITLE&gt;Simple HTML File
&lt;/TITLE&gt;&lt;/HEAD&gt;&lt;BODY BGCOLOR=#FFFFFF&gt;
This is a simple HTML File &lt;/BODY&gt;&lt;/HTML&gt;
```

The *URLEncode* method is similar to the *HTMLEncode* method, but it applies URL encoding rules, including escape characters, to a specified string. If you enter *John Doe* and *pass;* in the HTML Form example above after changing its *Form* method to *GET*, you see the following URL in the browser:

```
http://localhost/form1.asp?name=John+Doe&password=pass%3B
```

167

Note how spaces are replaced with the + character and how the semicolon character is replaced with *%3B.* This URL encoding is necessary to conform to HTTP transport requirements. The *MapPath* method maps the specified virtual path (either the absolute path on the current server or the path relative to the current page) into a physical path. If you add the following to the Form example above, you get a physical path such as *D:\Inetpub\Samples\form1.asp:*

```
<%=server.mappath(Request.ServerVariables("PATH_INFO"))%>
```

The *CreateObject* method creates an instance of a server component in which the ProgID of the server component is passed in as a parameter, as follows:

```
Server.CreateObject( progID )
```

This is the most important member of the server component. You should use it instead of the generic *CreateObject* function. We will examine this method in more detail later on when we look at ASP's installable components.

ObjectContext Object

The *ObjectContext* object has two events and two methods that extend ASP with transaction processing capabilities. This object comes with IIS 4.0 as a result of the integration of IIS and Microsoft Transaction Server (MTS). We will examine MTS in detail in the next chapter, so we will touch on it only briefly here. The basic principle in transaction processing is that all the elements of a transaction succeed or fail together. ASP uses the @TRANSACTION directive to specify that an ASP page will run in a transaction. The page will not finish processing until the transaction either succeeds completely or fails. If no element within a transaction fails, the *ObjectContext*'s *SetComplete* method completes the transaction. The transaction aborts if the *SetAbort* method is called by the script or by any components participating in the transaction. If the transaction commits, IIS raises an *OnTransactionCommit* event and processes the script's *OnTransactionCommit* subroutine, if the routine exists. Similarly, IIS raises an *OnTransactionAbort* event if the transaction is aborted and processes any existing *OnTransactionAbort* script subroutine.

Application Object

Web applications sometimes require that information be shared among users connected to a web site. The *Application* object was designed for this purpose. This simple yet powerful object has two collections, two methods, and two events. When we speak of ASP applications, we do not mean executable files such as Microsoft Word or Microsoft Excel, but rather a logical grouping of files that have the .asp extension.

An *Application* object is any file that is executed within a defined set of directories within a web site. When you create this object using ISM, you define a name space for it. You designate its starting-point directory, and every file and directory under that directory in your web site is considered part of the object until another starting-point directory is found. In this way, directory boundaries define the scope of an *Application* object. The object begins when the first user requests one of these files and ends when the web server is shut down. ISM also allows you to isolate an *Application* object so that it runs in a separate memory space from the web server. This ensures that other applications and the web server itself keep running even if the isolated application stops responding or fails.

Information is stored in the *Application* object using two collections, *Contents* and *StaticObjects*. Which collection an object belongs to depends on whether the object was added using a script command or the *<OBJECT>* tag. You add objects and other variables to the *Contents* collections in a script as follows:

```
<%
Set Application("Obj") = Server.CreateObject("MyObject")
Application("Message") = "Hello World"
Application("TotalCount") = 8573
%>
```

It's also easy to retrieve a value or call a method of an object in the *Contents* collection:

```
<%=Application("TotalCount")%>
<%=Application("Obj").Method1()%>
```

You access the methods of objects belonging to the *StaticObjects* collection in the same way, but creating them is different. You create objects in the *StaticObjects* collection using the *<OBJECT>* tag in a file named global.asa, which is in the root directory of the application. Every ASP application can have only one such file. This file also handles the two application events, *Application_OnStart* and *Application_OnEnd*, as shown here:

```
<OBJECT RUNAT=Server SCOPE=Session ID=Obj PROGID="MyObject">
</OBJECT>
<SCRIPT LANGUAGE=VBScript RUNAT=Server>
    SUB Application_OnStart
    END SUB
</SCRIPT>
```

(continued)

```
<SCRIPT LANGUAGE=VBScript RUNAT=Server>
    SUB Application_OnEnd
    END SUB
</SCRIPT>
<SCRIPT LANGUAGE=VBScript RUNAT=Server>
    SUB Session_OnStart
    END SUB
</SCRIPT>
<SCRIPT LANGUAGE=VBScript RUNAT=Server>
    SUB Session_OnEnd
    END SUB
</SCRIPT>
```

When the application starts, the server runs the *Application_OnStart* event script but it does not yet create the objects declared with the *<OBJECT>* tag. To conserve server resources, these objects are created only when the server processes a script that calls that object. Because users might try to change the value of an application variable at the same time, the application object provides the *Lock* and *Unlock* methods to synchronize access to the variables in the *Application* object. These two methods are used as follows:

```
<%
Application.Lock
Application("TotalCount") = Application("TotalCount") + 1
Application.Unlock
%>
```

Session Object

The *Session* object is similar to the *Application* object in that it manages state. However, the *Session* object manages state only for individual users and not for groups of users. A typical use of the *Session* object is for recording all the items that a user selects from a shopping mall site. After selecting items, the user proceeds to a check-out web page, where the items and prices can be displayed. The variables in the *Session* object are preserved even if the user leaves the web site and visits other sites. If the user returns to your site before the session times out, he can continue where he left off.

The *Session* object has two collections, four properties, one method, and two events. The collection objects *Contents* and *StaticObjects* and the events *Session_OnEnd* and *Session_OnStart* serve the same purpose that they do in an *Application* object. The *Abandon* method allows you to destroy all *Session* objects so that you can free up server resources without having to wait for them to time out. If a page contains the script *< % Session. Abandon %>*, the session variables are not destroyed until all the scripts on that page have been processed. This allows you to continue using the session variables for the duration of that page.

The four properties of the *Session* object are *CodePage*, *LCID*, *SessionID*, and *Timeout*. The *Timeout* property allows you to set the timeout value for a user session. It has a default value of 20 minutes, which means that the session automatically terminates if the user does not request a page from the application within that period. The *CodePage* property sets the character set that is used to display dynamic content. For example, the code page 1252 is ANSI, which is used for most Western languages. Similarly, the LCID property specifies the location identifier that is used to display dynamic content.

You saw in Chapter Three that HTTP is a stateless protocol, which means that every request is treated independently without any knowledge of previous requests. So how does ASP manage user state? The first time a user requests an .asp file within a given application, ASP uses a complex algorithm to generate a unique cookie for the user. This cookie is stored on the user's computer, and you can use the *SessionID* property to access its value. By checking this property every time a user visits your site, ASP matches these cookies to specific user sessions. To prevent someone from intercepting the value of your cookie in transit, you can use Secure Sockets Layer (SSL) encryption. The creation and checking of these cookies requires some overhead, and you can disable this for your web server or for a specific page using the *< %@ EnableSessionState=False %>* tag.

Sometimes a user's browser might not support cookies or might have disabled them. In this case, you cannot use ASP session management. You can develop your own mechanism by adding parameters to URLs on your page or by adding hidden values to a form. IIS 4.0 also ships with an ISAPI Cookie Conversion Filter sample that implements a workaround for browsers that don't use cookies.

Case Study: InternetJump Meeting

Our case study in Chapter Three examined the *http://www.InternetJump.com* web site, which provides a free URL forwarding service to convert a long URL such as *http://paul.spu.edu/~hawk/aristotle.html* to something like *Fast.to/ Aristotle.*

InternetJump Meeting is another free service from that site. You can see it at *www.internetjump.com/meeting*. It allows two or more people to communicate over the Web in real time. It also allows people to use HTML code so that they can communicate using formatted text, images, and links. To use this system, each user needs only a simple web browser, a meeting name, and a meeting password. The users arrange to connect at a specified time to *www.internetjump.com/meeting*. (They can also use the short URL *Fast.to/Meet*.) After they each enter the meeting name, password, and their first name, they can communicate by simply typing comments and then clicking the Add Comment Or Refresh button. This adds their comments to the web page so that the other participants can read them. They can use HTML tags to show images, links, or formatted text in their comments. To simply see if others have contributed new comments or responses, they can click the Add Comment Or Refresh button periodically.

Up to seven comments are displayed on each page, and all messages are cleared at the end of each day. The first page is a public meeting place; it does not require a meeting name or password. To hold a private meeting, a user can simply tell the other participants when the meeting will take place and give them the meeting name and password. A user can make up any meeting name and password; each must be a single word. To determine who is participating in a private meeting, a user can see the IP address of clients who have recently visited the meeting page.

This might sound like a fairly sophisticated web application, but ASP makes it easy to implement. All the code is contained in one file named meet.asp, which is shown here.

```
<HTML>
<title>InternetJump Meeting !</title>
<BODY>
<META HTTP-EQUIV="Expires" CONTENT="Wed, 15 June 1994 17:30:00 GMT">
<CENTER>
<body bgcolor="#FAFAD2" link="#008080" vlink="#800000">
<A HREF="http://fast.to/meeting" TARGET="_top"><font color=
"#000000" size="5" face="Brush
Script MT">InternetJump Meeting !</font></A>

<%
nShowIP = Request.Form("ShowIP")
strName = Request.Form("Name")
strComment = Request.Form("Comment")
strMeeting = Request.Form("Meeting")
strPassword = Request.Form("Password")
strDate =MID(Now(), 1,8)
strMeetingID = strMeeting & strPassword & strDate & "Meet"
```

```
strTotalCount = strMeeting & strPassword & strDate & "Count"
strIPID = strMeeting & strPassword & strDate & "IP"
strIP = "<OPTION>" & Request.ServerVariables("REMOTE_ADDR") &
    " - " & CStr(Now() & "<BR>")
Application.Lock()
Application(strIPID) = Application(strIPID) & strIP
Application.Unlock()
If Len(strComment) > 0 Then
    Application.Lock()
    If Application(strTotalCount) = 0 Then
        Application(strMeetingID)= "<BR>" & strName &
            "   -   " & strComment
        Application(strTotalCount) = 7
        Application(strIPID) = strIP
    Else
        Application(strTotalCount) = Application(strTotalCount) - 1
        Application(strMeetingID)= Application(strMeetingID) &
            "<BR>" & strName & "   -   " & strComment
    End If
    Application.Unlock()
End If
%>

<FORM ACTION=http://localhost/iissamples/issamples/meet.asp
METHOD=POST>
<font color="#800040" size="3"><Strong>Meeting</Strong></font>
<input type=text size=15 name=Meeting value =<%=strMeeting%>>
<A HREF="http://www.InternetJump.com" TARGET="_top">
    <IMG SRC="/Jump.gif" BORDER=0></A>
<font color="#800040" size="3"><Strong>Password</Strong></font>
<input type=text size=15 name=Password value =<%=strPassword%>><BR>
<font color="#800040" size="3">
    <Strong>Comments -  Check IP Address of Users</Strong>
</font>
<INPUT TYPE="radio" NAME="ShowIP" VALUE="1" ><BR>
<textarea name="Comment" value = "" rows=2 cols=70></textarea><BR>
<input type=submit size=25 value="Add Comment or Refresh">
<font color="#800040" size="3"><Strong>First Name</Strong></font>
<input type=text size=10 name=Name value=<%=strName%>><BR>
</FORM>

<HR></HR>
<font color="#000000" size="4" face="MS Sans Serif">
```

(continued)

173

```
<%
If nShowIP <> 1 Then
    Application.Lock()
    Response.Write("<Strong>Comments Clear at 0 - :")
    Response.Write(Application(strTotalCount))
    Response.Write("</Strong>")
    Response.Write(Application(strMeetingID))
    Application.Unlock()
Else
    If Len(strMeeting) > 0 Then
        Application.Lock()
        Response.Write("<SELECT MULTIPLE SIZE=3>")
        Response.Write(Application(strIPID))
        Response.Write("</SELECT><BR>")
        Response.Write("<Strong>Comments Clear at 0 - :")
        Response.Write(Application(strTotalCount))
        Response.Write("</Strong>")
        Response.Write(Application(strMeetingID))
        Application.Unlock()
    Else
        Application.Lock()
        Response.Write("<SELECT MULTIPLE SIZE=3>")
        Response.Write("<Option> Showing IP addresses only")
        Response.Write(" works for private meetings that have")
        Response.Write(" been given a name.")
        Response.Write("</SELECT><BR>")
        Response.Write("<Strong>Comments Clear at 0 - :")
        Response.Write(Application(strTotalCount))
        Response.Write("</Strong>")
        Response.Write(Application(strMeetingID))
        Application.Unlock()
    End if
End if
%>
</font>
</CENTER>
</HTML>
</BODY>
```

The system is implemented with only three intrinsic ASP objects: *Request, Response,* and *Application.* In the middle of this file is the following HTML code, which displays a Form.

```
<FORM ACTION=http://localhost/iissamples/issamples/meet.asp
METHOD=POST>
```

```
<font color="#800040" size="3"><Strong>Meeting</Strong></font>
<input type=text size=15 name=Meeting value =<%=strMeeting%>>
<A HREF="http://www.InternetJump.com" TARGET="_top">
    <IMG SRC="/Jump.gif" BORDER=0></A>
<font color="#800040" size="3"><Strong>Password</Strong></font>
<input type=text size=15 name=Password value =<%=strPassword%>><BR>
<font color="#800040" size="3">
    <Strong>Comments -  Check IP Address of Users</Strong>
</font>
<INPUT TYPE="radio" NAME="ShowIP" VALUE="1" ><BR>
<textarea name="Comment" value = "" rows=2 cols=70></textarea><BR>
<input type=submit size=25 value="Add Comment or Refresh">
<font color="#800040" size="3"><Strong>First Name</Strong></font>
<input type=text size=10 name=Name value=<%=strName%>><BR>
</FORM>
```

This code has a couple of interesting features. First, the Form is initialized with various VBScript variables, which we will examine in a moment. Second, the Form action URL actually references the same file that it is listed in. This lets you confine the ASP application to just one file and to repopulate the Form each time it appears so that the user has to enter the meeting name, password, and first name only once. We'll use the ASP intrinsic *Request* object's *Form* collection to extract this information from the Form and assign it to the VBScript variables that will initialize the Form the next time:

```
<%
nShowIP = Request.Form("ShowIP")
strName = Request.Form("Name")
strComment = Request.Form("Comment")
strMeeting = Request.Form("Meeting")
strPassword = Request.Form("Password")
strDate =MID(Now(), 1,8)
strMeetingID = strMeeting & strPassword & strDate & "Meet"
strTotalCount = strMeeting & strPassword & strDate & "Count"
strIPID = strMeeting & strPassword & strDate & "IP"
strIP = "<OPTION>" & Request.ServerVariables("REMOTE_ADDR") &
    " - " & CStr(Now() & "<BR>")
%>
```

We'll also generate some additional variable names to uniquely identify and timestamp each meeting. We'll use the VBScript *Now* method to get the current date and time and then use the VBScript *MID* method to extract just the current date. The meeting identifier variable name is a concatenation of the meeting name, meeting password, date, and the word *Meet*. Similarly, we'll create a unique total count variable name to hold the total number of comments submitted for that meeting. We'll also create the variable name *strIPID*, which will contain the IP addresses of all users visiting the meeting. The last line of code above uses the *Request* object's *ServerVariables* collection to extract each IP address from the HTTP header submitted by the user's browser.

When a user enters a comment, the web server must save this information so that it can represent it to the other participants. We must also save the total count and the list of IP addresses extracted. We'll maintain this state using the *Application* intrinsic object, as shown below.

```
<%
Application.Lock()
Application(strIPID) = Application(strIPID) & strIP
Application.Unlock()
If Len(strComment) > 0 Then
    Application.Lock()
    If Application(strTotalCount) = 0 Then
        Application(strMeetingID)= "<BR>" &
            strName & "   -   " & strComment
        Application(strTotalCount) = 7
        Application(strIPID) = strIP
    Else
        Application(strTotalCount) = Application(strTotalCount) - 1
        Application(strMeetingID)= Application(strMeetingID) &
            "<BR>"  & strName & "   -   " & strComment
    End If
    Application.Unlock()
End If
%>
```

The *Application* variable names are taken from the unique identifiers that we created. Access to the *Application* object is protected using the *Lock* and *Unlock* methods to prevent two or more users from changing the variables at the same time. We'll use the VBScript *Len* method to check whether a user is simply refreshing the page or has added a comment. If the user has only refreshed the page, we will not increment the total message count. We will, however, add the IP address to our list of IP addresses for this meeting. If the total number of comments is greater than seven, we'll clear the values of our variables and start over again. This will conserve web server resources and speed uploading of the page. The final piece of code, shown below, uses the *Write* method of the *Response* object to send the calculated output to the participants:

```
<%
If nShowIP <> 1 Then
    Application.Lock()
    Response.Write("<Strong>Comments Clear at 0 - :")
    Response.Write(Application(strTotalCount))
    Response.Write("</Strong>")
    Response.Write(Application(strMeetingID))
    Application.Unlock()
Else
    If Len(strMeeting) > 0 Then
        Application.Lock()
        Response.Write("<SELECT MULTIPLE SIZE=3>")
        Response.Write(Application(strIPID))
        Response.Write("</SELECT><BR>")
        Response.Write("<Strong>Comments Clear at 0 - :")
        Response.Write(Application(strTotalCount))
        Response.Write("</Strong>")
        Response.Write(Application(strMeetingID))
        Application.Unlock()
    Else
        Application.Lock()
        Response.Write("<SELECT MULTIPLE SIZE=3>")
        Response.Write("<Option> Showing IP addresses only")
        Response.Write(" works for private meetings that have")
        Response.Write(" been given a name.")
        Response.Write("</SELECT><BR>")
        Response.Write("<Strong>Comments Clear at 0 - :")
        Response.Write(Application(strTotalCount))
        Response.Write("</Strong>")
        Response.Write(Application(strMeetingID))
        Application.Unlock()
    End if
End if
%>
```

We'll first check whether the user wants to see the IP addresses of recent visitors. If not, we'll simply send back the comments received, along with the number of additional comments remaining to be entered before the comment list will be cleared. If the user wants to see IP addresses, we'll check to see whether this is a public or private meeting. If it is private, we'll display the IP address in a Select box. If it is public, we'll inform the user that the showing of IP addresses is enabled only for private meetings.

The InternetJump Meeting application clearly shows the power of ASP intrinsic objects, and the code on the preceding page demonstrates the simplicity of their use. Figure 5-1 shows this application in operation. You can also visit *www.internetjump.com* to try it out for yourself.

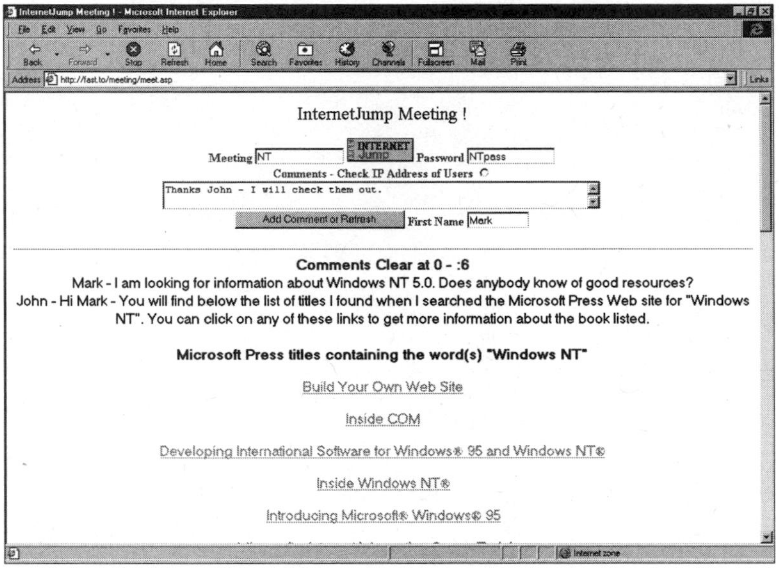

Figure 5-1.
The InternetJump Meeting application uses ASP intrinsic objects.

Installable Components for ASP

The InternetJump Meeting application was created entirely using ASP intrinsic objects and VBScript. However, many of your web applications will have to be coded in C++ due to their performance requirements and complexity. The *Server* ASP intrinsic object allows you to plug C++ components into the ASP environment. In fact, its *CreateObject* method lets you create any COM component to access its properties or invoke its methods. These COM components (also known as ActiveX components) can be written in C++, Java, Microsoft Visual Basic, or any other language that supports a binary interface.

Most COM components that you use will be created and destroyed within the scope of a single page. The ASP thread that processes that page will be the only one that needs to communicate with the component. Your component should therefore support the Apartment COM threading model. It can also support the Both-threading model because it includes the Apartment threading model. You should avoid using free-threaded components because they run in the SYSTEM context rather than in the context of the logged-on user. This prevents the use of Microsoft Windows NT security to control access to objects. Free-threaded components are also not recommended because they must be registered with MTS before they can access the ASP *ObjectContext* object. You should not use components with the Single-threading model because calls to all Single-threaded objects are serialized through the single COM Main thread and adversely affect application performance. Single-threaded components are also problematic in terms of security and the use of intrinsics.

If you are using the same component in many scripts for the same user, it might be a good idea to create the component as a *Session* variable. In this way, the component can maintain state across multiple calls and you will not incur the performance cost of creating and destroying it each time. Sessions are single threaded, which means that only a single system thread within a session can be active at any one point in time. Sessions map to Activities in MTS and use the same notion of logical threads instead of system threads to describe their activity. A logical thread is a conceptual entity whose execution can run on different threads. However, within a logical thread, only one system thread is active at any one point in time. The use of frames is an example of how this can be applied to sessions. In this case, you can have two or more ASP files within the same session being requested simultaneously by the frames in the browser. Each file can be executing on different system threads, but the ASP run time prevents them from executing simultaneously. In this way, a session is confined to a single logical thread even though multiple system threads are involved.

Objects added to the session on one thread should be accessible by other threads with the same session. If you use an Apartment model component in a session, the session must be locked down to a single physical thread because Apartment-thread objects cannot be passed to other threads. A component with the Both-threading model does not have this disadvantage because it can be passed to multiple threads. All components with the Both-threaded model should also aggregate the free-threaded marshaler to avoid any marshaling or thread switches when calls are made between threads.

Objects with the Both-threading model are considered thread-safe by COM. But since *Session* objects are not accessed by multiple threads simultaneously, they do not need to be thread-safe. Your Both-threaded components should still be thread-safe because there is no guarantee that sessions will remain single threaded in future versions of ASP.

Only Both-threaded components should be used in the *Application* ASP intrinsic object because Apartment-threaded components are problematic. If you try to add Apartment-threaded components with the *CreateObject* function, you will get an error, but you can add them using the *<OBJECT>* tag. Using Apartment-threaded components in the *Application* object is not recommended because it leads to slow access and because they run in the System security context rather than in the context of the current user.

The following sections describe the components that ship with IIS 4.0. They are designed to facilitate the generic tasks of web application developers.

Ad Rotator Component

The Ad Rotator component automates the rotation of advertisement images on a web page each time a user opens or reloads the page. A Rotator Schedule file specifies the size of the advertisement space, the image files to use, and the percentage of time that each file should be displayed. You can record how many users click each advertisement in the web server activity logs by setting the URL parameter in the Rotator Schedule file to direct users to a Redirection File.

Content Rotator Component

The Content Rotator component is like the Ad Rotator, except that it automatically rotates any HTML content on a web page rather than just images. You can use this component to rotate through a list of quotations, hyperlinks, images, or anything that can be represented using HTML tags. A Content Schedule File determines which HTML content string is displayed each time a user requests the web page.

Browser Capabilities Component

The Browser Capabilities component is used to determine the capabilities of the client's web browser from the User Agent HTTP header received. It compares the header to entries in the Browscap.ini file. If it finds a match, it assumes the properties of the browser listed. If it doesn't find a match, it uses the default

browser properties listed or sets every property to the string UNKNOWN if
no default browser settings were specified. You can add new browser definitions
to the browscap.ini file if required. The following are the listings for Microsoft
Internet Explorer 4.0 and the default browser capability settings:

```
[Internet Explorer 4.0]
browser=IE
Version=4.0
majorver=4
minorver=0
frames=TRUE
tables=TRUE
cookies=TRUE
backgroundsounds=TRUE
vbscript=TRUE
javascript=TRUE
javaapplets=TRUE
ActiveXControls=TRUE
Win16=False
beta=False
AK=False
SK=False
AOL=False
Crawler=False
CDF=True


[Default Browser Capability Settings]
browser=Default
Version=0.0
majorver=#0
minorver=#0
frames=False
tables=True
cookies=False
backgroundsounds=False
vbscript=False
javascript=False
javaapplets=False
ActiveXControls=False
AK=False
SK=False
AOL=False
```

(continued)

```
beta=False
Win16=False
Crawler=False
CDF=False
AuthenticodeUpdate=
```

The ASP script below uses the Browser Capabilities component to check whether the browser supports frames, tables, cookies, VBScript, and JavaScript:

```
<HTML>
<HEAD><TITLE>Browser Properties</TITLE></HEAD>
<BODY BGCOLOR=#FFFFFF>

<% Set bc = Server.CreateObject("MSWC.BrowserType") %>

<H3>Does your browser support Frames? </H3>
<TABLE BORDER=1>
<TR><TD>Browser Type</TD>        <TD><%= bc.Browser %></TD>
<TR><TD>What Version</TD>        <TD><%= bc.Version %></TD>
<TR><TD>Major Version</TD>       <TD><%= bc.Majorver %></TD>
<TR><TD>Minor Version</TD>       <TD><%= bc.Minorver %></TD>
<TR><TD>Frames</TD>              <TD><%=
    CStr(CBool(bc.Frames)) %></TD>
<TR><TD>Tables</TD>              <TD><%=
    CStr(CBool(bc.Tables)) %></TD>
<TR><TD>Cookies</TD>             <TD><%=
    CStr(CBool(bc.cookies)) %></TD>
<TR><TD>VBScript</TD>            <TD><%=
    CStr(CBool(bc.VBScript)) %></TD>
<TR><TD>JavaScript</TD>          <TD><%=
    CStr(CBool(bc.Javascript)) %></TD>
</TABLE>
<BR>
<BR>
</BODY>
</HTML>
```

Database Access Component

The Database Access component uses ActiveX Data Objects (ADO) to access information in a database or other tabular data structure through an OLEDB data provider. ADO comes with an OLEDB provider to enable it to access ODBC-compliant relational databases. You can create your own OLEDB provider if you need to access a custom data store. You must include the file ADOVBS-.INC or ADOJAVS.INC if your scripting language is VBScript or JScript, respectively, to use the constants specified in the ADO Reference.

Content Linking Component

The Content Linking component helps web developers produce applications such as online newspapers, magazines, and books. It creates a *Nextlink* object that automatically generates tables of contents and navigational links to previous and subsequent web pages. A Content Linking List text file is used to specify the list of web pages to be displayed and the order in which this should occur.

File Access Component

The File Access component is used to manipulate the computer's file sytem. The *FileSystemObject* object's methods allow you to open, copy, delete, or move files. The component also exposes the following file properties: *DateCreated, DateLastAccessed, DateLastModified, Drive, Name, ParentFolder, Path, ShortName, ShortPath, Size, Type,* and *Attributes.*

Collaboration Data Objects for NTS Component

You use the Collaboration Data Objects for NTS component to send and receive mail items. It use the following objects:

Object	Description
AddressEntry	Defines addressing information that is valid for a given messaging system.
Attachment	Represents a file or a message that is an attachment to a message.
Attachments collection	Contains zero or more *Attachment* objects.
Folder	Represents a folder or a container in a message store.
Message	Represents a single message, item, document, or form in a folder.
Messages collection	Contains zero or more *Message* objects.
NewMail	Provides the capability to send a message with few lines of code.
Recipient	Represents a recipient of a message.
Recipients collection	Contains zero or more *Recipient* objects and specifies the recipients of a message.
Session	Contains sessionwide settings and options.

The following simple piece of code demonstrates how to send an e-mail message using the *NewMail* object:

```
Dim objMail As CDONTS.NewMail
Set objMail = CreateObject("CDONTS.NewMail")
objMail.From = "testme@test.com"
objMail.To = "testyou@test.com"
objMail.Subject = "Test Message"
objMail.Body = "This is a test message."
objMail.Send
Set objMail = Nothing
```

Page Counter Component

The Page Counter component counts and displays the number of times a web page has been opened. Its *Hits* method displays the number of times that a specified URL has been opened. The *PageHit* method increments the hit count, and the *Reset* method sets the hit count for a specified page to 0. The hit count value is kept in memory so that it can be accessed quickly, but the object also writes the number of hits to a text file at regular intervals to preserve the hit count value in case of a server shutdown.

Permission Checker Component

The Permission Checker component uses the password authentication protocols provided in IIS to determine whether a user has been granted permission to read a file. Its *HasAccess* method indicates whether the user has permission. You can use this component to avoid displaying hyperlinks to files that a user does not have permission to access.

Four additional components—MyInfo, Status, System, and Tools—provide compatibility for applications that were developed on the Macintosh and deployed on computers running Microsoft Windows.

ASP Performance

ASP is implemented as an ISAPI application and therefore outperforms CGI in terms of speed and scalability. IIS 4.0's integration with MTS also gives you the option of running ISAPI applications, including ASP, in a separate process space from the web server. This slows things down somewhat, but it is still faster than CGI. It has the benefit of protecting the web server from crashing if any ISAPI or Active Server Component becomes unstable. Another advantage of putting your components in an isolated process is that you can unload and update them without having to restart your entire web server.

When an ASP file is called, a preprocessor splits the file into separate pieces for each of the languages used. The scripting engines, which compile and execute the code, are started if they are not already running. If the script is running, it is cloned. If the script is not running, the compiled code might have been cached, in which case it is reused. Each line is parsed separately, so it is more efficient to do such things as Dim all your variables in one line rather than Dim them on separate lines. You should use the latest versions of the scripting engines because they might include performance enhancements. VBScript and JScript, in particular, improved their speed in version 3 over previous versions. Large blocks of HTML text can be block-copied to the client, so it might be wise to avoid mixing HTML code and script code unnecessarily and to strip comments out before you go to production.

If you are not using sessions, you should disable the session capability. The server will create a session by default when a user who does not have a session requests a page. If you are using sessions, you should store generic information about the user there to avoid recalculating it in multiple scripts. For example, you might store the browser type that the client is using in a session variable. If the browser type supports client-side scripts, it is also a good idea to offload scripting to the client. This will use the client's CPU and lighten the load on the server. This might not be a good idea if the script code is large and significantly increases the amount of data that must go over the wire.

Avoid frequent requests for Server Variables. Every time you ask for a Server Variable using the *Request* object, all server variables are retrieved from the server. It is more efficient to capture them all with one call and reuse this information throughout your script. If you ever need to have a reference to an object that might not get called, use the *<OBJECT>* tag instead of *Server.CreateObject.* If you do this, the object will not actually get created if it does not get called. Finally, it is a good idea to use the *IsClientConnected* method of the *Response* object to avoid processing scripts for disconnected clients.

CHAPTER SIX

Microsoft Transaction Server

Our analysis of Internet development on the Microsoft Windows NT platform has so far focused on COM, DCOM, TCP/IP, Windows sockets, HTTP, and ASP. These technologies provide many of the generic requirements of Internet systems, including interprocess communication, synchronization of shared resources, and component invocation. In the future, COM+ will add a service layer to the COM foundation to simplify the handling of transactions, data binding, persistence, events, security, load balancing, queued components, and an in-memory database. Microsoft Transaction Server (MTS) offers some of these services today. (MTS will be plugged into the COM+ infrastructure, and the MTS programming interfaces will probably remain mostly as they are today.) This chapter explains why you need MTS and introduces its main components. It also examines how MTS works and discusses some of the programming issues involved in building MTS applications using the MTS API.

Why Do You Need MTS?

MTS is a component-based transaction processing system in Windows NT that builds powerful services on top of the COM technologies we have discussed so far. COM and its distributed version, DCOM, greatly simplify the building of multitier systems. However, you probably need a number of key features that COM does not provide in order to take care of the following:

▪ **Transaction processing**   Multitier systems can be more difficult to implement than two-tier client-server systems, partly because of increased complexity in handling transactions. When many components are distributed across a number of computers, errors can occur in numerous ways. These errors might be within the business domain or might be due to hardware, software, or network failures. When an error interrupts a transaction, the state of the system can easily be compromised. Systems must rely on transaction processing software to ensure application integrity in these situations. While two-tier client-server systems can leverage the inherent transaction protection capabilities of databases, multitier systems require additional software to ensure the integrity of transactions at the component level.

- *Scalability* Many popular web sites receive more than a million hits per day. Whether these sites use Active Server Pages (ASP), ISAPI, or CGI, the number of hits requires the use of server-side components that consume server resources. References to components might have to be maintained for an extended period of time if ASP session variables are used. To make these systems scale more effectively, you must use software techniques that allow the automatic release of stateless server components from memory when they are not being actively used. This should be transparent to the clients that have references to these components. You can also achieve improved scalability by sharing server resources among many clients using database connection pools and object recycling.

- *Deployment and administration* Because distributed systems consist of many components running on different computers, you need software that easily deploys your components across your enterprise. You might also need to administer these components on a regular basis, so you need software that lets you change their configurations from a central location or remotely.

- *Security* Many systems require different levels of security access for different clients. This can be difficult to implement in a distributed system because it usually requires incorporating security checks at the component level, across process spaces and machine boundaries. You need additional software to simplify implementation of these security checks.

- *Load balancing and fail-over protection* Most Internet systems need to accommodate severe spikes in demand. Using a load balancing mechanism is a common way to handle these fluctuations. Such a mechanism can also protect against server failures. If one web server crashes, the other servers can automatically assume its load to ensure the continuation of service.

Let's look briefly at the components in MTS and then explore how they help in the areas just described above.

MTS Components

MTS consists of the following main components: application components, the Transaction Server Executive, resource managers, resource dispensers, and the MTS Explorer.

Application Components

Application components encapsulate the business logic of your application. For example, if you are engaged in electronic commerce, your application components might take care of tasks such as processing orders, updating inventory, and scheduling delivery. These components are language-independent COM in-process server DLLs that you can easily create using development tools such as Microsoft Visual Basic, Microsoft Visual C++, and Microsoft Visual J++. You should design application components for a single user because MTS takes responsibility for serving them up to multiple users. This greatly simplifies development of these components. MTS does, however, place the following requirements on application components beyond those required by COM:

- The component must have a standard class factory and must support the *IClassFactory* interface. *IClassFactory::CreateInstance* must return a unique instance of an MTS object.

- The component DLL must implement and export the standard *DllGetClassObject* function.

- The component must export only interfaces that use standard marshaling.

- All component interfaces and coclasses must be described by a type library.

- The component must export the *DllRegisterServer* function and perform self-registration of its CLSID, ProgID, interfaces, and type library in this routine.

- For custom interfaces that cannot be marshaled using standard automation support, you must build the proxy-stub DLL with MIDL version 3.00.44 or later (provided with the Microsoft Platform SDK for Windows NT 4.0); use the -Oicf compiler switch; and link the DLL with the mtxih.lib library provided by MTS. The mtxih.lib library must be the first file that you link to your proxy-stub DLL. If the component has both a type library and a proxy-stub DLL, MTS uses the proxy-stub DLL.

■ You cannot use an MTS object as part of an aggregate of other objects, although you can create an MTS object that is implemented as an aggregation of objects. The function *CoCreateInstance* returns CLASS_E_NOAGGREGATION if you try to create an MTS object with another controlling *IUnknown*.

These extra requirements allow MTS to provide additional services on top of the COM foundation. To take advantage of transactions within MTS, your application components must use the MTS API. Because MTS application components are COM components, they have location transparency. This allows you to easily access them within a distributed environment. MTS automatically loads your application component into an MTS process environment, but you can also configure MTS to load it into a client application process instead.

Transaction Server Executive

The Transaction Server Executive provides run-time services for the application components. These services include handling transactions, resources, context management, security, and thread management. The Transaction Server Executive is a DLL that loads into the processes hosting the application components and runs in the background.

Resource Managers

A resource manager is a system service that manages durable data. The Transaction Server Executive works with resource managers to ensure that any changes to state caused by transactions are not lost if the system fails. Transactions can involve multiple resource managers that can reside on different computers. Resource managers cooperate with a transaction manager called the Distributed Transaction Coordinator (DTC) to ensure the integrity of these transactions. The DTC coordinates all the activities of the multiple resource managers operating within every transaction to ensure that if any of these activities fail, the system will return to the state it was in before the transaction was initiated.

Resource Dispensers

Resource dispensers are like resource managers except that they manage nondurable state on behalf of the application components. MTS provides two resource dispensers, the ODBC resource dispenser and the Shared Property

Manager. The ODBC resource dispenser manages pools of database connections that the application components can use. This greatly speeds up database interaction because the application components can use existing open database connections without having to reestablish them each time. The ODBC resource dispenser automatically reclaims and reuses these connections in a way that is transparent to the application components. This means that they do not need any special code to use this service. The Shared Property Manager provides synchronized access to data properties so that different components can share common information maintained in memory. This type of functionality is typically used when you have highly volatile data that does not need to be saved, such as stock market information.

MTS Explorer

The MTS Explorer is the graphical user interface tool that allows you to manage MTS packages and components that are executing in the MTS run-time environment. MTS applications can be distributed among many machines since MTS provides services for component-to-component communication across a network using DCOM. This brings up complex deployment issues, such as treating a large number of small components as a single application with shared security rights and distributing them on the network. The MTS Explorer handles most of these issues using a simple graphical user interface. At deployment time, components are assembled into packages that have security roles. These packages can be mapped to Windows NT groups and user accounts and thus specify who can call which components in the package. The packages can be transferred between machines through point-and-click operations.

How MTS Works

Now that you know why you need MTS and have learned about its main components, let's examine in more detail the services that MTS provides and how they work.

Transaction Processing

Multitier distributed systems do not always need the transaction processing features of MTS. For example, to display free content on your web site, you might use distributed components that do not need any transactional processing capabilities. However, this does not mean that these systems do not need MTS, since MTS provides many features in addition to transaction processing.

You need a transaction processing system when the interaction between clients and servers involves transactions. A transaction is a completed set of operations between parties that changes the state of those parties in some measurable way. For example, the purchase of a plane ticket is a transaction that involves the operations of transferring money and transferring a ticket. The financial state of both the airline company and the traveler changes in a tangible way after these operations occur. We do not use the term *transaction* to describe something like an inquiry about flight times because no significant change of state occurs for the parties.

ACID Properties

If your system is transactional, it must pass the "ACID" test. ACID is an acronym for "atomic, consistent, isolated, and durable."

Atomic   When we speak of a transaction as atomic, we mean that all of its operations must succeed or fail as a unit. If any part of a transaction fails, all of its operations should be rolled back as if they had never occurred. For example, in the case of buying an electronic airplane ticket, at least two operations are involved: the airline company bills the traveler's credit card, and the airline company updates its passenger database. The company's computer system must wrap both of these operations in a single transaction to ensure the integrity of the system. If the company's software succeeds in charging the traveler's credit card but fails to update the passenger database, the credit card operation must be rolled back because the transaction failed.

Consistent   An operation within a system is consistent if it adheres to that system's rules of behavior. When a transaction modifies the state of the system, it must preserve the system's internal integrity. Only correct transformations of state should occur. For example, an accounting system works on the assumption that no two people have the same social security number. An operation is inconsistent if it uses the same social security number for two different people. Such an operation can complete successfully but will compromise the state of the system and lead to unpredictable consequences.

Consistency requires correct transaction design. For example, a company's human resource system might require that every record in the personnel database table have a corresponding record in the payroll database table and in the healthcare database table. If an employee is terminated, three distinct update or delete record operations are required. The consistency property requires that a transaction never consist of only one or two of these operations. All three operations must be included in a transaction profile to preserve the integrity of the system. This consistency cannot be guaranteed by MTS alone because transaction boundaries are determined by software developers and not by MTS.

Isolated   Operations are isolated if they behave as if they occur one after another, even though the server must actually execute these operations concurrently to ensure its scalability. A withdrawal of a bank account balance is a typical example. If transactions are not isolated and two transactions try to clear the $1000 balance in an account, both transactions will query for the amount of money in the account and both will see $1000. They will therefore both withdraw $1000. Because the transactions are not isolated, the first transaction will clear the account and the second one will overdraw it by $1000. If these transactions occur serially, the first transaction will clear the account and the second will find a zero balance. Because transactions must be isolated, however, the transactions must occur *as if* they happen in a serialized fashion. For example, the first transaction can put a lock on the database table that contains the account balance. The second transaction's query will return a zero balance after this lock is released, so it will not overdraw the account.

Durable   We defined a transaction as a set of completed operations between parties that changes the state of the parties in some measurable way. A transaction is durable if it does not lose the state when the system fails. This requires that the state be persisted in some durable form, such as on a hard disk.

MTS and the ACID Properties

How does MTS fulfill the requirements of the ACID properties? The process is quite complex. For example, in the case of buying an airplane ticket, we might have four application components involved called A, B, C, and D.

1. Component A checks to see whether a seat is available on the plane; if so, it reserves a seat.

2. Component B checks to see whether the passenger's credit card number is valid; if so, it bills the fare to the credit card.

3. Component C changes the status of the reserved seat to a purchased seat.

4. Component D issues the ticket to the passenger.

Because the operations of these four components are part of a single transaction, we must coordinate them to ensure that they succeed or fail as a unit. Each component must let MTS know whether it succeeds or fails. Because these components might access resource managers such as Microsoft SQL Server to query and update databases, MTS must also be able to tie the operations of the resource managers into the transaction. To do so, MTS creates an additional context object for each interface within the application components. This context object manages information about each application component, such as its transactional state, its membership in an activity, and its security properties. When the component's interface is released, MTS releases the context object. The component gets access to the context object through the following MTS API function:

```
HRESULT GetObjectContext (IObjectContext** ppInstanceContext);
```

This API function retrieves a pointer to the *IObjectContext* interface, which is defined as follows:

```
interface IObjectContext : public IUnknown
{
public:
    virtual HRESULT STDMETHODCALLTYPE CreateInstance(
        /* [in] */ REFCLSID rclsid,
        /* [in] */ REFIID riid,
        /* [retval][iid_is][out] */ LPVOID __RPC_FAR *ppv) = 0;

    virtual HRESULT STDMETHODCALLTYPE SetComplete( void) = 0;

    virtual HRESULT STDMETHODCALLTYPE SetAbort( void) = 0;

    virtual HRESULT STDMETHODCALLTYPE EnableCommit( void) = 0;

    virtual HRESULT STDMETHODCALLTYPE DisableCommit( void) = 0;

    virtual BOOL STDMETHODCALLTYPE IsInTransaction( void) = 0;

    virtual BOOL STDMETHODCALLTYPE IsSecurityEnabled( void) = 0;

    virtual HRESULT STDMETHODCALLTYPE IsCallerInRole(
        /* [in] */ BSTR __MIDL_0000,
        /* [retval][out] */ BOOL __RPC_FAR *__MIDL_0001) = 0;

};
```

You can see that the *IObjectContext* object supports the transactional methods *SetComplete* and *SetAbort*. If your component is not happy with the outcome of its operation, it will call *SetAbort*. Otherwise, it will call *SetComplete*, indicating that it is ready to commit its operation. If your component is not ready to commit, it can call the *DisableCommit* method. This will cause any attempts to commit this transaction to abort. When your component is in a position to commit again, it will call either *EnableCommit* or *SetComplete* to allow transactions that it is a part of to commit.

This ability to disable committing is important because the component's state might be inconsistent between method calls. For example, a component that assigns team members to tasks might have a method named *Assign*, which might be invoked many times by a client. Let's say that the component also has the constraint that every team member must be assigned at least one task before any of the assigned tasks can be committed. In this case, the component will call *DisableCommit* when *Assign* is first called. It will then call *EnableCommit* after it verifies that every team member has been assigned a least one task. This ensures that the component operations will never be committed when the component's state is inconsistent with its own rules of behavior.

The *IObjectContext* method *IsInTransaction* is important because even if you design your component to require a transaction, a user might not configure it correctly for transactions within MTS. The *IsInTransaction* method lets you verify that your component is actually running in a transaction. If this method returns FALSE, indicating that the component is not running in a transaction, you can alert the user that there is a problem. While the MTS context object has a security property built in, it is not always enabled. For example, it is not enabled if your component is configured to run in the client's process space or if the component and the client are in the same security package boundary. For this reason, the *IObjectContext* interface has a method named *IsSecurity-Enabled* to determine whether security is enabled. You use the *IsCallerInRole* method to determine whether the direct caller of the currently executing method is associated with a specific MTS role. An MTS role designates specific access permissions to a group of components in MTS called a package. We will examine MTS packages and roles in detail later on. The *IsCallerInRole* method is reliable only when security is enabled.

Finally, the *IObjectContext* interface has a method named *CreateInstance*, which allows your component to create other components in such a way that the new component's context is derived from the current component's *ObjectContext* and the declarative properties of the new component. If your component has a transaction, the transaction attribute of the new component determines whether the new component executes within the scope of that transaction.

In the airplane ticket example, we had four components within one transaction. All of these components would be registered in MTS and configured with a Requires A Transaction or Supports Transactions setting. Component A is created by the client and in turn creates components B, C, and D. To automatically group the operations of all these components into a single transaction, component A simply uses the *IObjectContext* method *CreateInstance* instead of the COM *CoCreateInstance* method when creating components B, C, and D. MTS propagates the transaction context to all the other components as they are created. It does this using the DTC. If a single transaction updates multiple databases in a distributed environment, the atomic property requires that the DTC have a way to ensure that all databases commit together. To guarantee this, the DTC uses the Two-Phase Commit protocol, which requires that all databases first write their updates to a log file before they commit. In this way, if any database fails in the process of committing, it can repair itself from the log file when it recovers. The DTC communicates with all the database resource managers to enforce this protocol.

Scalability

How can you build more scalable distributed solutions using MTS? A server becomes overloaded when it does not have enough resources to supply the demand from clients. These resources include component instances, database connections, memory, threads, processes, and network connections. To build a more scalable system, you can adopt one (or both) of these strategies:

- Design the system so that its activity can be distributed over a number of servers.

- Design the system so that the available resources on each server can be shared more effectively among users.

MTS lets you adopt the first strategy because MTS is based on COM. MTS application components are COM components, so they have location transparency (as you learned in Chapter Two). This means that you can configure different MTS application components to execute on different servers. These components can use the DTC to tie their operations into single transactions.

MTS also helps you to adopt the second strategy by extending COM through its interception mechanism. COM+ will modify how this works, but let's examine how it works in COM so that you can understand the principles involved. When you install an application component in MTS, the registry settings for the component are modified. For example, if you have a COM component named Test.obj in the DLL C:\Test.dll, it will have the following registry settings before it is installed in MTS:

HKEY_CLASSES_ROOT\CLSID\ {D3054266-E78D-11D1-919E-0080C7205DC0}

Subkey	Value
InprocServer32	C:\TEST.DLL
ProgID	Test.obj
TypeLib	{D3054266-E78D-11D1-919E-0080C7205DC0}
LocalServer32	

You can see that the component's ProgID is mapped to the in-process server Test.dll. Any calls to the *CoCreateInstance* function will cause Test.dll to be loaded into the process space of the caller. To install this component in MTS, you must first create an MTS package, which we will call Package1. You can do this using the MTS Explorer. You can install Test.dll into this package by simply dropping the file into the package window displayed in the MTS Explorer. This will result in the following new registry settings for Package1 and the component Test.obj:

HKEY_CLASSES_ROOT\CLSID\ {D3054266-E78D-11D1-919E-0080C7205DC0}

Subkey	Value
InprocServer32	
ProgID	Test.obj
TypeLib	{D3054266-E78D-11D1-919E-0080C7205DC0}
LocalServer32	C:\WINNT\System32\mtx.exe /p:{511CDD2B-E792-11D1-919E-0080C7205DC0}

HKEY_CLASSES_ROOT\AppID\
{511CDD2B-E792-11D1-919E-0080C7205DC0}

Subkey	Value
RunAs	Interactive User

HKEY_LOCAL_MACHINE\SOFTWARE\
Microsoft\Transaction Server\Packages\
{511CDD2B-E792-11D1-919E-0080C7205DC0}

Subkey	Value
Activation	Local
Authentication	4
Authorization	0100048034000000500000000000000014
Description	
Latency	180
Name	Package1
NeverShutdown	N
SecurityEnabled	N
System	N
UserId	Interactive User

HKEY_LOCAL_MACHINE\SOFTWARE\
Microsoft\Transaction Server\Packages\
{511CDD2B-E792-11D1-919E-0080C7205DC0}\
Components\{D3054266-E78D-11D1-919E-0080C7205DC0}

Subkey	Value
Authentication	4
SecurityEnabled	Y

HKEY_LOCAL_MACHINE\SOFTWARE\
Microsoft\Transaction Server\Components\
{D3054266-E78D-11D1-919E-0080C7205DC0}

Subkey	Value
Description	
DllServer	C:\Test.dll
Enabled	Y
Inproc	N
Libid	{D3054266-E78D-11D1-919E-0080C7205DC0}
Local	Y
Origin	Install
Package	{511CDD2B-E792-11D1-919E-0080C7205DC0}
ProgID	Test.obj
Remote	N
SupportsInternet	N
System	N
Transaction	Not supported
Typelib	C:\Test.dll

You can see that many new registry entries are created when the component is installed in MTS. The values for InprocServer32 and LocalServer32 are relevant to our discussion here. Notice that the value for InprocServer32, which used to be C:\Test.dll, is now blank. However, the value for LocalServer32, which was blank, is now C:\WINNT\System32\mtx.exe /p:{511CDD2B-E792-11D1-919E-0080C7205DC0}. When *CoCreateInstance* is called for the Test.obj component, the mtx.exe program is loaded and is passed the argument /p:{511CDD2B-E792-11D1-919E-0080C7205DC0}. This argument is the UUID of Package1, which also has registry settings above. The registry key

```
HKEY_LOCAL_MACHINE\SOFTWARE\Microsoft\Transaction Server\
Packages\{511CDD2B-E792-11D1-919E-0080C7205DC0}\Components\
{D3054266-E78D-11D1-919E-0080C7205DC0}
```

lists the Class ID of the Test.obj component as a member of Package1. The DllServer value under the registry key

```
HKEY_LOCAL_MACHINE\SOFTWARE\Microsoft\Transaction Server\
Components\{D3054266-E78D-11D1-919E-0080C7205DC0}
```

points to the location of this component (C:\Test.dll). MTS loads this DLL into the process space created for Package1 and creates the Test.obj component on behalf of the client.

You will recall from Chapter Two that *CoCreateInstance* is a helper function that implements the following:

```
CoGetClassObject(rclsid, dwClsContext, NULL,
    IID_IClassFactory, &pCF);
hresult = pCF->CreateInstance(pUnkOuter, riid, ppvObj);
pCF->Release();
```

When *CoGetClassObject* is called for a component that is installed in MTS, it does not return a reference to the component's class factory; it returns a reference to an MTS-provided class factory. The client calls the *CreateInstance* method of this MTS *IClassFactory* interface pointer, which in turn calls the *CreateInstance* method of the component's real class factory when needed. In the process, MTS also creates a context wrapper and a context object for the interface requested within the component. The context object maintains information about the component, such as its security properties and transactional state, as we discussed earlier. The context wrapper provides a level of indirection between the client and the application component. A pointer to the context wrapper is returned to the client instead of a pointer to the component's interface. If the client calls *QueryInterface* on the context wrapper pointer to retrieve another interface of the component, MTS automatically returns another context wrapper pointer for this new interface.

An application component should never pass out a pointer to its interface directly to the caller. This would compromise the ability of MTS to intercept any calls on the methods of this interface. If your application component wants to pass a self-reference pointer to the interface's context wrapper to receive callbacks from a client or another object, it can use the following MTS API to do so:

```
void* SafeRef (REFIID riid, UNKNOWN* pUnk);
```

The *riid* parameter is a reference to the interface ID of the interface required, and the *pUnk* parameter is a reference to the interface of the component. This function gives a pointer to the context wrapper associated with the interface specified in the *riid* parameter. This pointer is safe to pass to a client or other object. Note that the client or object that obtains a safe reference must release the safe reference after it is finished with it.

How MTS Improves Scalability

MTS can intercept communication between the client and the application component. This ability is the basis for improving the scalability of your system. MTS improves scalability in three key ways, explained in the following sections.

It delays instantiation of components until they are needed.   In object-oriented programming, it is common to create references early on to the components that you will need so that they can be easily accessed later. This programming style conflicts with the pattern generally used in developing transaction processing (TP) monitor systems, in which you try to minimize the number of components in memory on the server at all times. This requires that you delay creating components until they are actually needed. MTS allows you to combine the benefits of both of these programming styles. When a client creates a component installed within MTS, the component is not actually created on the server. Rather, the client gets back a reference to a context wrapper for the component. Only when the client calls a method on the object's interface does MTS actually create the object. This mechanism is called Just-in-Time Activation.

It activates and deactivates application components to release them from memory when they are not being used.   A natural extension of delaying the instantiation of components until they are needed is deactivating them when they are not being used. For example, if a component has completed a transaction, it might not need to maintain any state in memory. You can free up the server resources required to maintain the component in memory, including any expensive resources it might have acquired during its operations, such as database connections. Note that the context object for the component remains in memory across one or more deactivation and reactivation cycles. The client still has a reference to the component even though the component is deactivated, and the component can be automatically reactivated when the client calls any of its methods.

When an application component is created, MTS creates a surrogate process space for it using the program Mtx.exe. Creating this space is time consuming, so MTS keeps the process space in memory in case other calls are made to the component. However, if this process space is idle—if no calls are made to the components it contains—it is better to destroy it to free up server resources. You can use the MTS Explorer to specify the amount of time a server process should run idle before it is destroyed. You can also specify that the process space never be destroyed.

It recycles a pool of application components.   A future version of MTS will further extend the mechanisms described above by maintaining a pool of instantiated components in memory that can be served up to any client. This can be particularly advantageous if instantiation of the component is expensive. For example, if you have a component that represents a car, it might have many properties that must be initialized and that will not change throughout the operation of the program. Example properties are the number of the car's wheels, whether it has ABS brakes, whether it has power steering, and so forth. Other properties might have states that can change during the life of the component, such as the amount of gas in the car or the speed at which the car is traveling. An activated component must reset all the properties that have changed to their default values before the client uses it. A freshly activated component will therefore look identical to a newly created one. It does not have to reset properties that have not changed. Consequently, the activated component can be served up to a client more quickly.

The current version of MTS exposes an API that allows you to automatically take advantage of object recycling when it becomes available. This API is encapsulated in the *IObjectControl* interface, which has methods for component activation, deactivation, and object pooling.

```
interface IObjectControl : public IUnknown
    {
    public:
        virtual HRESULT STDMETHODCALLTYPE Activate(void) = 0;

        virtual void STDMETHODCALLTYPE Deactivate(void) = 0;

        virtual BOOL STDMETHODCALLTYPE CanBePooled(void) = 0;

    };
```

If an application component implements the *IObjectControl* interface, MTS calls its method at the appropriate times. If the component is activated, MTS calls the *Activate* method. The implementation of this method is specific to the functionality of each component. C++ programmers usually initialize their objects in the constructor of the class. They do not do this for MTS components for two reasons. First, an object's context isn't available during the object's construction, so context-specific initialization has to be performed in the *Activate* method, not in the component's constructor. Second, if a component can be recycled, its constructor is not called each time it is served up to a client. The *Activate* method is called each time, so object initialization of variables can be performed. Similarly, you should use the *Deactivate* method instead of the destructor method of the class to "clean up" when an object is no longer used by the client. MTS calls the *Deactivate* method when an object returns from a method that called *SetComplete* or *SetAbort* or when the root of the object's transaction causes the transaction to complete. After the *Deactivate* method is called, the MTS run-time environment calls the *CanBePooled* method. If this method returns TRUE, a future version of MTS will place the deactivated object in an object pool for reuse. If the *CanBePooled* method returns FALSE, the object is released in the usual way and its destructor is called. The component developer must ensure that implementation of the *Activate* and *Deactivate* methods makes any component taken from the pool indistinguishable to the client from a component that is freshly created. A component is always freshly created if no more objects are left in the pool to be recycled.

The current version of MTS does not implement object recycling, but it does support database connection pooling using the ODBC resource dispenser. This is a valuable feature for improving the scalability of a system because it eliminates the expense of establishing a new database connection every time a component is created or activated. The ODBC 3.0 Driver Manager is the ODBC resource dispenser, and the Driver Manager DLL is installed with MTS. Any MTS components that use the standard ODBC interfaces or use objects that can wrap ODBC (such as ADO) automatically use this feature.

Deployment and Administration

Distributed solutions are naturally more complex to deploy and administer than monolithic applications. MTS reduces this complexity considerably with the MTS Explorer. You access the MTS Explorer as a snap-in hosted by the Microsoft Management Console. The MTS Explorer lets you attach to any computer within your enterprise that has MTS installed, thus allowing you to administer the machine remotely. The MTS Explorer offers options for controlling the global settings for the computer and the individual settings for its packages, components, and remote components. It also displays transaction statistics, trace messages from the DTC, and a list of current transactions within MTS applications.

At the computer level, you can modify the transaction timeout for all transactions running within MTS. The timeout value is measured in seconds, with a default value of *60*. If you set the timeout value to 0, transactions will not time out at all. You might want to do this for debugging purposes. You can also regulate the refresh rate for general display, transactions display, and trace messages, as well as the size and location of the DTC log file. In addition, you can specify a remote server name and a replication share name. The replication share name identifies the name of the Microsoft Cluster Server (MSCS) virtual server that is used for fail-over support. The remote server name identifies the computer that you want your client executables to access.

At the package level, you can enable or disable authorization checking and specify whether the package will run under the identity of the interactive user (the user who is currently logged on or a specific user). You can use the MTS Explorer to specify whether the components in a package are loaded into the process space of the client or loaded into a surrogate process space created by MTS on the server. If you opt to load the components into the process space of the client, the client must be on the computer on which the package is installed and there will be no component tracking, role checking, or process isolation.

At the component level, you can enable or disable authorization checking and specify the level of transaction support associated with the application components. You can specify one of the following values:

- **Requires A Transaction** The component must execute within the scope of a transaction. When a new object is created, its object context inherits the transaction from the context of the client. MTS automatically creates a new transaction for the object if the client does not have a transaction.

- **Requires A New Transaction** The component must execute within its own transaction, and a new object should not inherit the transaction from the context of its client. MTS automatically creates a new transaction for the object when a new object is created.

- **Supports Transactions** The component can execute within the scope of its client's transactions, but if a client does not have a transaction, a new context for the object is created without one.

- **Does Not Support Transactions** The component should not run within the scope of transactions. When a new object is created, its object context is always created without a transaction.

The business logic of your application should determine which transaction option you select. For example, you might want to select the Requires A New Transaction option for an auditing component that monitors who accesses sensitive information to avoid having somebody roll back the operation of this component. You can also set the transaction attribute of your component programmatically in the component's .idl file using the values in the Mtxattr.h header file, as in the example below:

```
#include <mtxattr.h>
[
    uuid(915D57FA-ED15-11D1-91AB-0080C7205DC0),
    helpstring("Example Class"),
    TRANSACTION_REQUIRED
]
coclass Example
{
    [default] interface IExample;
};
```

After you configure your application with the appropriate settings, you might want to lock the package before you deploy it. The MTS Explorer lets you disable changes to a package or the deletion of a package. You can export the package by right-clicking on it and selecting the Export option. This creates a file with a .pak extension that is ready to distribute to any other server. You can use the MTS Explorer to import this .pak file to another server. This will set up your application on the other server with all of the components configured correctly.

If the client and server computers have MTS installed, you can push and pull components between them. To push components, you add the appropriate computer to your MTS Explorer and then add your components to the remote computer's Remote Components folder. Similarly, you can pull components to your computer by adding them to your Remote Components folder. You must satisfy the following requirements to push or pull components:

- The DLLs and type library files for the components must be on a shared network directory visible to both the client and the server.
- You must log on using a Windows NT account that is a member of the Administrators role of the System package on the target computer.
- The target computer's System package identity must map to a Windows NT account that is in the Reader role for your System package.
- Security must be enabled for the System package on both computers.

If MTS is not installed on a client computer, you can configure the client by using an MTS-generated client executable. This executable copies the necessary proxy-stub DLLs and type libraries to the client computer and updates the client system registry with information needed by DCOM, including the name of the server computer that was specified in the MTS Explorer on the server computer. The client applications can then access the MTS application on this remote server computer.

Security

Incorporating security into a distributed application can be one of the more difficult features to implement. MTS provides two security mechanisms for doing this: programmatic security and declarative security. These security features apply only to packages with components running under the Server activation setting and not to components activated in the creator's process.

Both forms of security are based on the idea of MTS roles. A role is an abstraction that defines a logical group of users of your application. At development time, you can use these roles to define declarative authorization and programmatic security logic. For example, production manager and sales manager can be two roles with different security rights to the sales and production resources of your application. At deployment time, you can bind these roles to Windows NT users or to groups of users using the MTS Explorer. Any Windows NT users who are not assigned to a role with access privileges to a package will not have permission to access that package.

MTS security authorization occurs between packages rather than between components within a package. A security authorization check occurs when a client calls into a package or when one package calls another. All components within a package run under the identity established for the package. Because security authorization is checked only when a method call crosses a package, you must be careful that all the components in a package can safely call each other without requiring security checks. Even though components in a package mutually trust one another, MTS also lets you restrict access from a client to specific components in the same package. This means that different clients can be given different security access rights to make direct calls on components in a package, even though these components can make calls to one another. When components in a package need to use an external resource such as a database, it might be a good idea to use the package identity for security access. If database access occurs using the identity of the package, all the users mapped to roles for that package can use that database. This can improve the performance of your system because it allows database connections to be recycled among all the users of the package.

You can use the MTS Explorer to specify the following types of security checks for a package:

- *Connect*   Security checking occurs only for the initial connection.
- *Call*   Security checking occurs on every call for the duration of the connection.
- *Packet*   The sender's identity is encrypted to ensure that all the data received is from the sender.
- *Packet Integrity*   The sender's identity and signature are encrypted to ensure that packets haven't been changed during transit.
- *Packet Privacy*   The entire packet, including the data and the sender's identity and signature, are encrypted for maximum security.

MTS programmatic security is based on two functions of the *IObjectContext* interface, *IsCallerInRole* and *IsSecurityEnabled*. Once your component code verifies that security has been enabled using the *IsSecurityEnabled* method, you can use the *IsCallerInRole* method to check whether the current user is a member of the role required for access. Note that the *IsCallerInRole* method applies only to the direct caller of the currently executing method. The following code snippet shows how you can use the programmatic security methods:

```
#include <mtx.h>

IObjectContext* pObjectContext = NULL;
BOOL bIsInRole;
HRESULT hr = NULL;

try
{
    hr = GetObjectContext(&pObjectContext);
    if (FAILED(hr)) throw "error";
    if (pObjectContext->IsSecurityEnabled())
    {
        BSTR bstrRole = SysAllocString(L"Sales");
```

(continued)

```
        hr = pObjectContext->IsCallerInRole(bstrRole,
            & bIsInRole);
        SysFreeString(bstrRole);
        if (FAILED(hr)) throw "error";
        if (!bIsInRole)
        {
            // Do not allow access.
            pObjectContext->SetAbort();
        }
        else
        {
            //  Allow access.
            pObjectContext->SetComplete();
        }
    }
    else
    {
        // Security is disabled.
        pObjectContext->SetAbort();
    }
}
catch(...)
{
    // handle error;
    pObjectContext->SetAbort();
}

if (pObjectContext) pObjectContext->Release();
```

To have an MTS component implement a more fine-grained security check, you can use *ISecurityProperty*:

```
interface ISecurityProperty : public IUnknown
    {
    public:
        virtual HRESULT STDMETHODCALLTYPE GetDirectCreatorSID(
            PSID __RPC_FAR *pSID) = 0;

        virtual HRESULT STDMETHODCALLTYPE GetOriginalCreatorSID(
            PSID __RPC_FAR *pSID) = 0;

        virtual HRESULT STDMETHODCALLTYPE GetDirectCallerSID(
            PSID __RPC_FAR *pSID) = 0;
```

```
virtual HRESULT STDMETHODCALLTYPE GetOriginalCallerSID(
    PSID __RPC_FAR *pSID) = 0;

virtual HRESULT STDMETHODCALLTYPE ReleaseSID(
    PSID pSID) = 0;

};
```

This interface uses the Windows NT security identifier (SID), which is a unique value that identifies a user or group. The *GetDirectCallerSID* method gets the SID of the external process that called the currently executing method. *GetDirectCreatorSID* retrieves the SID of the external process that directly created the current object. The *GetOriginalCallerSID* method retrieves the SID of the base process that initiated the call sequence from which the current method was called. *GetOriginalCreatorSID* retrieves the SID of the base process that initiated the activity in which the current object is executing. Finally, the *ReleaseSID* method releases the SID returned by one of the other *ISecurityProperty* methods.

Load Balancing and Fail-Over Protection

Load balancing is a mechanism that allows you to distribute the demand placed on any application over a number of MTS servers. With static load balancing, you statically configure a client to access different servers. With dynamic load balancing, clients are dynamically directed to the server that is currently the least busy. Fail-over is a mechanism that allows the workload of one server to be transferred automatically to another server in the event of a failure. MTS fail-over is accomplished through the integration of MTS with Microsoft Cluster Server, which we will examine in Chapter Eight.

The current version of MTS supports only static load balancing. You can accomplish static load balancing by specifying different remote server names when you create MTS client setup executables. By distributing these executables evenly among your clients, you statically direct clients to different servers. If the client is a web server on the same server as MTS, you have another option for static load balancing. The Microsoft Domain Name Server (DNS) can map a domain name such as *www.yourserver.com* to different IP addresses in a round-robin fashion. For example, DNS can send the first user to the IP address 182.34.54.200, the second user to 182.34.54.201, and the third to 182.34.54.202. In this fashion, you can achieve load balancing over the three servers.

Case Study: An MTS Shopping Application

A virtual shopping mall is a place where you would need to use MTS. We'll create a simple shopping application to demonstrate the use of the MTS APIs. Our application will consist of three components: a client component to buy items, an orders component to process orders, and a billing component to bill the client. The user will use the client component to buy an item, which will update Orders and Billing tables in a SQL Server database. After the Orders and Billing components have updated the database, the user will see a message box that allows him to confirm or cancel the transaction. If the user cancels the transaction, the operations of the Orders and Billing components will be rolled back. Otherwise, the operations of these components will be committed. The Billing component will use the MTS resource dispenser, Shared Property Manager, to quickly generate receipt numbers.

A client application can be written in Visual Basic as follows:

```
Private Sub BuyItem_Click()
Dim objTxCtx As Object
Dim objOrders As Object
Dim objBilling As Object

    Set objTxCtx = CreateObject("TxCtx.TransactionContext")
    Set objOrders = objTxCtx.CreateInstance("Orders.Orders.1")
    Set objBilling = objTxCtx.CreateInstance("Billing.Billing.1")
    Dim lAccountNo, lItemNo, lQuantity, lReceipt As Long
    lAccountNo = CLng(AccountNo.Text)
    lItemNo = CLng(ItemNo.Text)
    lQuantity = CLng(Quantity.Text)
    lReceipt = 0
    objOrders.Order lAccountNo, lItemNo, lQuantity
    objBilling.Bill lAccountNo, lAmount, lReceipt
    If MsgBox("Your transaction has been processed. " + _
        "Please confirm your acceptance.", vbYesNo) = vbYes Then
        objTxCtx.Commit
        MsgBox "Your receipt number is " + CStr(lReceipt)
    Else
        objTxCtx.Abort
        MsgBox "Your transaction has been canceled."
    End If

End Sub
```

This application uses the *ITransactionContext* object to scope the transaction from the client. We begin the transaction by instantiating an instance of the *TxCtx.TransactionContext* object, and we end the transaction by calling either Commit or Abort on the object. The *TxCtx.TransactionContext* object is an MTS component whose transaction attribute is set to *Requires a new transaction,* which means that a *TransactionContextEx* object is always the root of a transaction.

The Orders and Billing components are implemented in a DLL named AShop.dll. The shell of this DLL and generic code for the Orders and Billing components were generated using the ATL AppWizard. The Interface Definition Language (IDL) code for the completed DLL is as follows:

```
// AShop.idl : IDL source for AShop.dll
//

// This file will be processed by the MIDL tool to
// produce the type library (AShop.tlb) and marshalling code.
#include <mtxattr.h>
import "oaidl.idl";
import "ocidl.idl";

    [
        object,
        uuid(14315CE4-ED42-11D1-91AB-0080C7205DC0),
        dual,
        helpstring("IOrders Interface"),
        pointer_default(unique)
    ]
    interface IOrders : IDispatch
    {
        [id(1), helpstring("method Order")]
            HRESULT Order([in] long lAccountNo,
            [in] long lItemNo, [in] long lQuantity);
    };
    [
        object,
        uuid(14315CE6-ED42-11D1-91AB-0080C7205DC0),
        dual,
        helpstring("IBilling Interface"),
        pointer_default(unique)
    ]
    interface IBilling : IDispatch
```

(continued)

211

```
    {
        [id(1), helpstring("method Bill")]
            HRESULT Bill([in] long lAccountNo,
            [in] long lAmount, [out] long* plReceipt);
    };
[
    uuid(14315CD1-ED42-11D1-91AB-0080C7205DC0),
    version(1.0),
    helpstring("AShop 1.0 Type Library")
]
library ASHOPLib
{
    importlib("stdole32.tlb");
    importlib("stdole2.tlb");

    [
        uuid(14315CE5-ED42-11D1-91AB-0080C7205DC0),
        helpstring("Orders Class"),
        TRANSACTION_REQUIRED
    ]
    coclass Orders
    {
        [default] interface IOrders;
    };
    [
        uuid(14315CE7-ED42-11D1-91AB-0080C7205DC0),
        helpstring("Billing Class"),
        TRANSACTION_REQUIRED
    ]
    coclass Billing
    {
        [default] interface IBilling;
    };
};
```

Notice that we included the mtxattr.h header so that we could use the TRANSACTION_REQUIRED attribute to automatically configure the transaction property when the component is installed in MTS. Also notice that the Orders component exposes just one method, *Order,* and that the Billing component exposes one method, *Bill.* The methods are implemented as follows:

Implementation of COrders

```cpp
// Orders.cpp : Implementation of COrders
#include "stdafx.h"
#include "AShop.h"
#include "Orders.h"
#include <sql.h>
#include <sqlext.h>
#include <mtx.h>
#include <mtxspm.h>
#define RETURN_BUF_SIZE  512
#define SQLSUCCEEDED(rc) (rc == SQL_SUCCESS || \
                          rc == SQL_SUCCESS_WITH_INFO)
//////////////////////////////////////////////////////////////////
// COrders

STDMETHODIMP COrders::Order(long lAccountNo, long lItemNo,
    long lQuantity)
{
    // TODO: Add your implementation code here.

    HRESULT hr = E_FAIL;
    HENV henv = NULL;
    HDBC hdbc = NULL;
    HSTMT hstmt = NULL;
    CComPtr<IObjectContext> pObjectContext;
    try
    {
        hr = GetObjectContext(&pObjectContext);
        RETCODE rc = SQL_SUCCESS;
        SQLTCHAR szSqlStmt[300];

        // Obtain the ODBC environment and connection.
        rc = SQLAllocEnv(&henv);
        if (!SQLSUCCEEDED(rc)) throw "Error";

        rc = SQLAllocConnect(henv, &hdbc);
        if (!SQLSUCCEEDED(rc)) throw "Error";

        rc = SQLConnect(hdbc,
        (unsigned char *)  _TEXT("pubs"), SQL_NTS,
        (unsigned char *) _TEXT("sa"), SQL_NTS,
        (unsigned char *) _TEXT(""), SQL_NTS);
        if (!SQLSUCCEEDED(rc)) throw "Error";
```

(continued)

```
            rc = SQLAllocStmt(hdbc, &hstmt);
            if (!SQLSUCCEEDED(rc)) throw "Error";

            // Update orders.
            wsprintf((TCHAR *)szSqlStmt,
                _TEXT("INSERT INTO Orders VALUES(%ld, %ld, %ld)"),
                    lAccountNo, lItemNo, lQuantity);
            rc = SQLExecDirect(hstmt, szSqlStmt, SQL_NTS);
            if (!SQLSUCCEEDED(rc)) throw "Error";

            pObjectContext->SetComplete();

            hr = S_OK;
        }
        catch(...)
        {
            if (pObjectContext)
                pObjectContext->SetAbort();
        }

        if (hstmt)
            SQLFreeStmt(hstmt, SQL_DROP);

        if (hdbc) {
            SQLDisconnect(hdbc);
            SQLFreeConnect(hdbc);
        }

        if (henv)
            SQLFreeEnv(henv);

        return hr;
    }
```

Implementation of CBilling

```
// Billing.cpp : Implementation of CBilling
#include "stdafx.h"
#include "AShop.h"
#include "Billing.h"
#include <sql.h>
#include <sqlext.h>
#include <mtx.h>
#include <mtxspm.h>
#define RETURN_BUF_SIZE      512
#define SQLSUCCEEDED(rc) (rc == SQL_SUCCESS || \
                            rc == SQL_SUCCESS_WITH_INFO)
```

```
// add mtxguid.lib
//////////////////////////////////////////////////////////////////
// CBilling

STDMETHODIMP CBilling::Bill(long lAccountNo, long lAmount,
    long * plReceipt)
{
    // TODO: Add your implementation code here.
    HRESULT hr = E_FAIL;
    RETCODE rc = SQL_SUCCESS;
    HENV henv = NULL;
    HDBC hdbc = NULL;
    HSTMT hstmt = NULL;
    SQLTCHAR szSqlStmt[300];
    CComPtr<IObjectContext> pObjectContext;
    try
    {

        hr = GetObjectContext(&pObjectContext);

        long lrec = 0;
        *plReceipt = -1;

        // Obtain the ODBC environment and connection.
        rc = SQLAllocEnv(&henv);
        if (!SQLSUCCEEDED(rc)) throw "Error";

        rc = SQLAllocConnect(henv, &hdbc);
        if (!SQLSUCCEEDED(rc)) throw "Error";

        rc = SQLConnect(hdbc,
            (unsigned char *) _TEXT("pubs"), SQL_NTS,
            (unsigned char *) _TEXT("sa"), SQL_NTS,
            (unsigned char *) _TEXT(""), SQL_NTS);
        if (!SQLSUCCEEDED(rc)) throw "Error";
        rc = SQLAllocStmt(hdbc, &hstmt);
        if (!SQLSUCCEEDED(rc)) throw "Error";

        // Update billing.
        wsprintf((TCHAR *)szSqlStmt,
            _TEXT("INSERT INTO Billing VALUES(%ld, %ld)"),
            lAccountNo, lAmount);
        rc = SQLExecDirect(hstmt, szSqlStmt, SQL_NTS);
        if (!SQLSUCCEEDED(rc)) throw "Error";
```

(continued)

```
            lrec = GetNextReceipt();
            if (lrec == -1) throw "Error";
            *plReceipt = lrec;

            pObjectContext->SetComplete();

            hr = S_OK;
        }
    catch(...)
    {
          if (pObjectContext)
                pObjectContext->SetAbort();
    }
    if (hstmt)
        SQLFreeStmt(hstmt, SQL_DROP);

    if (hdbc) {
        SQLDisconnect(hdbc);
        SQLFreeConnect(hdbc);
    }

    if (henv)
        SQLFreeEnv(henv);

    return hr;

}

long CBilling::GetNextReceipt()
{
    HRESULT hr = E_FAIL;
    ISharedPropertyGroupManager* pPropGpMgr = NULL;
    ISharedPropertyGroup* pPropGp = NULL;
    ISharedProperty* pPropNextReceipt = NULL;
    long lreceipt = -1;
    CComPtr<IObjectContext> pObjectContext;
    try
    {
        hr = GetObjectContext(&pObjectContext);
        VARIANT_BOOL fAlreadyExists = VARIANT_FALSE;
        LONG lIsolationMode = LockMethod;
        LONG lReleaseMode = Process;
        LONG lNextValue = 0L;
        BSTR stName, stNextReceipt;
```

```
        VARIANT vNext;

    hr = pObjectContext->CreateInstance
        (CLSID_SharedPropertyGroupManager,
        IID_ISharedPropertyGroupManager,
        (void**)&pPropGpMgr);
    if (hr != S_OK) throw "Error";

    stName = SysAllocString(L"Receipt");
    hr = pPropGpMgr->CreatePropertyGroup(stName,
        &lIsolationMode, &lReleaseMode, &fAlreadyExists,
        &pPropGp);
    SysFreeString(stName);
    if (hr != S_OK) throw "Error";
    stNextReceipt = SysAllocString(L"NextReceipt");
    hr = pPropGp->CreateProperty(stNextReceipt,
        &fAlreadyExists, &pPropNextReceipt);
    SysFreeString(stNextReceipt);
    If (hr != S_OK) throw "Error";

    vNext.vt = VT_I4;
    hr = pPropNextReceipt->get_Value(&vNext);
    if (hr != S_OK) throw "Error";
    lNextValue = vNext.lVal++;
    hr = pPropNextReceipt->put_Value(vNext);
    if (hr != S_OK) throw "Error";

    pObjectContext->SetComplete();
    lreceipt = vNext.lVal;
    lreceipt = lreceipt + 1000;
    }
    catch(...)
    {
        pObjectContext->SetAbort();
    }

    if (pObjectContext) pObjectContext->Release();
    if (pPropGpMgr) pPropGpMgr->Release();
    if (pPropGp) pPropGp->Release();
    if (pPropNextReceipt) pPropNextReceipt->Release();
    return lreceipt;
}
```

The implementations of the *Order* and *Bill* methods are similar. Both use the ODBC API to obtain a connection to a SQL Server database. You can create the appropriate tables in the database with the following script:

```
/****** Object:  Table dbo.Billing ******/
CREATE TABLE dbo.Billing (
    AccountNo int NULL ,
    Amount float NULL
)
GO


/****** Object:  Table dbo.Orders  ******/
CREATE TABLE dbo.Orders (
    AccountNo int NULL ,
    ItemNo int NULL ,
    Quantity int NULL
)
GO
```

Both components should be installed in the same package so that the ODBC connection pooling mechanism will recycle database connection pointers to the database. The *Billing* component includes a method named *GetNextReceipt*, which generates unique receipt numbers. We implemented this method using the MTS Shared Property Manager resource dispenser. This allows different instances of our components to share in-memory data within the same package. We specified a beginning receipt value of 1000 for our sample application, and we incremented it by one each time. For a production system, the beginning value should be higher than any receipt number already given.

Case Study: The MTSAutoStart Service

The current version of MTS does not support asynchronous processing of transactions. This will likely appear in a future version of MTS or in COM+. A busy web site can use this kind of capability to automatically queue requests for transactions at peak moments to avoid a system overload. We can implement this technique today by combining the asynchronous capabilities of Microsoft Message Queue Server (MSMQ) with the synchronous capabilities of MTS. To accomplish this, our site should write transaction requests to a durable queue using the MSMQ API, which we will examine in the next chapter. Later a component will lift these messages from the queue and process the request. This component should run within the MTS environment so that the lifting of the message from the queue and the processing of the request both occur within a single transaction. If a system failure occurs during the processing of the request, the lifting of the message from the queue will be rolled back because the transaction as a whole did not commit. When the system restarts, it will take that message out of the queue again to process it.

Unfortunately, MTS cannot automatically start MTS components when Windows NT starts up. In this case study, we will build a general-purpose Windows NT service that will do this. The application component must expose an automation method named *Start* that takes one *out* parameter of type long. The application component must also be placed in an MTS package named AutoStart. When Windows NT starts up, the MTSAutoStart service will also automatically start and create all the application components in the AutoStart MTS package. It will then call the *Start* method of all these application components until the service terminates.

The application component will lift a message out of the queue and process a transaction every time the *Start* method is called. (Alternatively, the *Start* method can process a number of messages before it returns.) If the application component sets the *out* parameter at *30*, the MTSAutoStart service will sleep for 30 milliseconds before calling *Start* again. This can lower the CPU utilization of the server.

Eight steps are required to build this application:

Step 1: Create a Generic Windows NT Service

Create a generic Windows NT service called MTSAutoStart using the ATL application wizard that comes with Visual C++ 5.0. Pull up the project settings and select the Debug Multithreaded option for the run-time library within the code generation setting on the C/C++ tab.

Step 2: Modify the *CServiceModule* Definition

Add the following method to the *CServiceModule* class:

```
static unsigned __stdcall MTSThreadProc(void* p);
```

MTSThreadProc is the thread procedure that creates the application components and calls their *Start* method.

Step 3: Add Header Files and Defines to the *CServiceModule* Implementation File

CServiceModule is implemented in a file named MTSAutoStart.cpp. We'll add the following header file (which is required for multithreaded programming), a few defines and typedefs, and a global event handle. We'll also use the *#import* directive to incorporate information from the mtxadmin type library. The *LogEvent* method is used to write errors and warnings to the Windows NT event log.

```
#include <process.h>

#define MAXTHREAD 10000
#import "c:\\winnt\\system32\\mts\\mtxadmin.dll" \
    no_namespace  raw_interfaces_only
HANDLE g_hExitEvent = FALSE;
typedef ICatalog * LPCATALOG;
typedef ICatalogCollection * LPCATALOGCOLLECTION;
typedef ICatalogObject* LPCATALOGOBJECT;
#include <process.h>
void Log_Event(WORD wType, LPCTSTR pszFormat, ...);
```

Step 4: Modify the *CServiceModule* Run Method

The *Run* method spawns threads to start the application components. To allow us to stop these threads gracefully, we will create an event handle called g_hExitEvent as follows:

```
g_hExitEvent = CreateEvent(NULL, TRUE, FALSE, NULL);
HANDLE hMTSThread[MAXTHREAD];
int nthread = 0;
```

When we want to terminate the service, we will inform the threads that they should exit. The following code does this by setting the exit event. It should go at the end of the *Run* method.

```
SetEvent(g_hExitEvent);
WaitForMultipleObjects(nthread, hMTSThread, TRUE, 30000);

for (int j = 0; j < nthread; j++)
    CloseHandle ((HANDLE)hMTSThread[j]);
```

We'll add the following code to *CServiceModule*'s *Run* method to determine the ProgID of the application components that need to be started:

```
LPUNKNOWN pUnk = NULL;
LPCATALOG pCatalog = NULL;
LPCATALOGCOLLECTION pCatCol_Packages = NULL;
LPCATALOGOBJECT pCatObj_Package = NULL;
LPCATALOGCOLLECTION pCatCol_ComponentsInPackage = NULL;
LPCATALOGOBJECT pCatObj_Component = NULL;
LPDISPATCH pdisp1 = NULL;
LPDISPATCH pdisp2 = NULL;
LPDISPATCH pdisp3 = NULL;
LPDISPATCH pdisp4 = NULL;
int i = 0;
long nNumberOfComponents = 0;
BSTR bstrCollName1 = _bstr_t("Packages");

try
{
    CLSID clsid;
    hr = ::CLSIDFromProgID(L"MTSAdmin.Catalog.1", &clsid);
    if (FAILED(hr)) throw "error";

    hr = ::CoCreateInstance(clsid, NULL, CLSCTX_SERVER, IID_IUnknown,
        (void**)&pUnk);
    if (FAILED(hr)) throw "error";

    hr = pUnk->QueryInterface(__uuidof(ICatalog), (void**)&pCatalog);
    if (FAILED(hr)) throw "error";

    hr = pCatalog->GetCollection (bstrCollName1, &pdisp1 );
    if (FAILED(hr)) throw "error";

    hr = pdisp1->QueryInterface(__uuidof(ICatalogCollection),
        (void**)&pCatCol_Packages);
    if (FAILED(hr)) throw "error";

    hr = pCatCol_Packages->Populate();
    if (FAILED(hr)) throw "error";

    long lcount;
    hr = pCatCol_Packages->get_Count(&lcount);
    if (FAILED(hr)) throw "error";

    for (i = 0; i < lcount; i++)
```

(continued)

221

```
{
    hr = pCatCol_Packages->get_Item(i, &pdisp2);
    if (FAILED(hr)) throw "error";

    hr = pdisp2->QueryInterface(__uuidof(ICatalogObject),
        (void**)&pCatObj_Package);
    if (FAILED(hr)) throw "error";

    VARIANT vName;
    BSTR bstrPropName = _bstr_t("Name");
    hr = pCatObj_Package->get_Value (bstrPropName, &vName );
    if (FAILED(hr)) throw "error";

    _bstr_t bstrpackage = _bstr_t("AutoStart");
    if (_bstr_t(vName) ==  bstrpackage)
    {
        VARIANT vkey;
        BSTR bstrPropNameID = _bstr_t("ID");
        hr = pCatObj_Package->get_Value (bstrPropNameID, &vkey );
        if (FAILED(hr)) throw "error";

        BSTR bstrCollName1 = _bstr_t("ComponentsInPackage");
        hr = pCatCol_Packages->GetCollection (bstrCollName1,
            vkey, &pdisp3 );
        if (FAILED(hr)) throw "error";

        hr = pdisp3->QueryInterface(__uuidof(ICatalogCollection),
            (void**)&pCatCol_ComponentsInPackage);
        if (FAILED(hr)) throw "error";

        hr = pCatCol_ComponentsInPackage->Populate();
        if (FAILED(hr)) throw "error";

        hr = pCatCol_ComponentsInPackage->
            get_Count(&nNumberOfComponents);
        if (FAILED(hr)) throw "error";

        for (int k = 0; k < nNumberOfComponents; k++)
        {
            hr = pCatCol_ComponentsInPackage->get_Item(k,
                &pdisp4);
            if (FAILED(hr)) throw "error";
```

```
                  hr = pdisp4->QueryInterface(__uuidof(ICatalogObject),
                      (void**)&pCatObj_Component);
                  if (FAILED(hr)) throw "error";

                  VARIANT vProgID;
                  BSTR bstrPropName3 = _bstr_t("ProgID");
                  hr = pCatObj_Component->get_Value (bstrPropName3,
                      &vProgID );
                  if (FAILED(hr)) throw "error";

                  _bstr_t* pbstrProgID = new _bstr_t(vProgID);
                  if (nthread < MAXTHREAD)
                  {

                      DWORD hThreadID;
                      hMTSThread[nthread] = (HANDLE) _beginthreadex(NULL,
                          0, &MTSThreadProc, (_bstr_t*) pbstrProgID, 0,
                          (UINT*) &hThreadID);
                      nthread++;
                  }
                  throw "error";
                  hr = pdisp4->Release();
                  pdisp4 = NULL;
                  if (FAILED(hr)) throw "error";
                  hr = pCatObj_Component->Release();
                  pCatObj_Component = NULL;
                  if (FAILED(hr)) throw "error";
              }

              hr = pdisp3->Release();
              pdisp3 = NULL;
              if (FAILED(hr)) throw "error";
              hr = pCatCol_ComponentsInPackage->Release();
              pCatCol_ComponentsInPackage = NULL;
              if (FAILED(hr)) throw "error";
          }
          hr = pdisp2->Release();
          pdisp2 = NULL;
          if (FAILED(hr)) throw "error";
          hr = pCatObj_Package->Release();
          pCatObj_Package = NULL;
          if (FAILED(hr)) throw "error";

      }
```

(continued)

```
        hr = pUnk->Release();
        pUnk = NULL;
        hr = pCatalog->Release();
        pCatalog = NULL;
        if (FAILED(hr)) throw "error";
        hr = pdisp1->Release();
        pdisp1 = NULL;
        if (FAILED(hr)) throw "error";
        hr = pCatCol_Packages->Release();
        pCatCol_Packages = NULL;
        if (FAILED(hr)) throw "error";

        if (nNumberOfComponents == 0)
        {
            LogEvent(EVENTLOG_WARNING_TYPE,
                _T("There are no components in AutoStart MTS package"));
        }
    }
    catch(...)
    {

        LogEvent(EVENTLOG_ERROR_TYPE,
            _T("An error occurred when starting the MTSAutoStart Service"));
        if (pUnk) pUnk->Release();
        if (pCatalog) pCatalog->Release();
        if (pCatCol_Packages) pCatCol_Packages->Release();
        if (pCatObj_Package) pCatObj_Package->Release();
        if (pCatCol_ComponentsInPackage)
            pCatCol_ComponentsInPackage->Release();
        if (pCatObj_Component) pCatObj_Component->Release();
        if (pdisp1) pdisp1->Release();
        if (pdisp2) pdisp2->Release();
        if (pdisp3) pdisp3->Release();
        if (pdisp4) pdisp4->Release();
    }
```

The preceding code uses a number of MTS scriptable administration objects to retrieve the ProgIDs of all application components in the AutoStart package. We'll begin by creating the *MTSAdmin Catalog* object to query for the *ICatalog* interface. We'll use its *GetCollection* method to get the *ICatalogCollection* interface for the *Packages* collection. We'll iterate through all the packages until we find the package called AutoStart, using the *ICatalogObject* interface. We'll then use the *ICatalogCollection* and *ICatalogObject* interfaces again to iterate through all the application components in the AutoStart package to identify their ProgIDs. When a ProgID is identified, a new thread is spawned and the ProgID is passed into it.

Automating MTS Administration

The MTS Explorer lets you configure and deploy packages by using a graphical user interface. MTS scriptable administration objects let you do the same thing using code. These objects use the interfaces *ICatalog, ICatalogObject, ICatalogCollection, IPackageUtil, IComponentUtil, IRemoteComponentUtil,* and *IRoleAssociationUtil* to perform tasks such as the following:

- Installing a prebuilt package
- Creating a new package and installing components
- Enumerating through installed packages to update properties
- Enumerating through installed packages to delete a package
- Enumerating through installed components to delete a component
- Accessing a related collection name
- Accessing property information
- Configuring a role
- Exporting a package
- Configuring a client to use remote components

You'll find comprehensive information about the MTS scriptable administration objects in the MTS SDK.

Step 5: Add the Implementation for *CServiceModule*'s *MTSThreadProc* Method

The *MTSThreadProc* thread procedure creates an MTS application component in the AutoStart package as follows:

```
unsigned __stdcall CServiceModule::MTSThreadProc(void* p)
{

    Sleep(3000);
    _bstr_t bstrProgID(*(_bstr_t * )p);
    delete p;
    HRESULT hr = CoInitialize(NULL);
    OLECHAR * FunctionName = L"Start";
    LPDISPATCH pIDispatch = NULL;
    DISPID dispid = NULL;
    try
    {
        if (FAILED(hr)) throw "error";
        CLSID clsid;
        hr = ::CLSIDFromProgID(bstrProgID, &clsid);
        if (FAILED(hr)) throw "error";

        hr = ::CoCreateInstance(clsid, NULL, CLSCTX_SERVER,
            IID_IDispatch, (void**)&pIDispatch);
        if (FAILED(hr)) throw "error";

        hr = pIDispatch->GetIDsOfNames(IID_NULL, &FunctionName,
            1, GetUserDefaultLCID(), &dispid);
        if (FAILED(hr)) throw "error";

        _bstr_t bstrmessage(" has been started.");
        bstrmessage = bstrProgID + bstrmessage;
        Log_Event(EVENTLOG_INFORMATION_TYPE, _T(bstrmessage));

        while (1)
        {
            long lwait;
            VARIANTARG varg[1];
            ::VariantInit(&varg[0]);
            varg[0].vt = VT_BYREF|VT_I4;
            varg[0].plVal = &lwait;
            DISPPARAMS dispparams;
            dispparams.cArgs = 1;
            dispparams.rgvarg = &varg[0];
```

```
            dispparams.cNamedArgs = 0;
            dispparams.rgdispidNamedArgs = NULL;
            EXCEPINFO excepinfo = {0};
            unsigned int nerr = 0;
            hr = pIDispatch->Invoke(dispid, IID_NULL,
                GetUserDefaultLCID(), DISPATCH_METHOD, &dispparams,
                NULL, &excepinfo, &nerr);
            if (FAILED(hr)) throw "error";
            if (WaitForSingleObject(g_hExitEvent, 0) != WAIT_TIMEOUT)
                break;
            Sleep(lwait);
        }

    }
    catch(...)
    {
        _bstr_t bstrmessage("An error occurred using the component :");
        bstrmessage = bstrmessage + bstrProgID;
        Log_Event(EVENTLOG_ERROR_TYPE, _T(bstrmessage));
        if (pIDispatch != NULL) pIDispatch->Release();
        pIDispatch = NULL;
        WaitForSingleObject(g_hExitEvent, INFINITE);

    }

    if (pIDispatch != NULL)
    {
        pIDispatch->Release();
        _bstr_t bstrmessage(" has been stopped.");
        bstrmessage = bstrProgID + bstrmessage;
        Log_Event(EVENTLOG_INFORMATION_TYPE, _T(bstrmessage));

    }

    CoUninitialize();
    _endthreadex(S_OK);

    return 0;
}
```

The ProgID of the application component is passed into the thread procedure and is used to create the component. After the component is created, we query for the *IDispatch* interface and get the DISPID of the *Start* method. The *Start* method of the application component is then invoked and passes in a pointer to a long variable named *lwait* using the DISPPARAMS structure. After the application component processes its task, it can set the value of the *lwait out* parameter, which is returned to the *MTSAutoStart* thread. This value tells the *MTSAutoStart* thread how long it should sleep (in milliseconds) before it calls the *Start* method again. However, the *MTSAutoStart* thread first checks to see whether the exit event has been set and thus determines whether it should terminate instead.

Step 6: Add the Implementation of the *Log_Event* Method

The *Log_Event* method, shown below, is used to log errors, information, or warning messages to the Windows NT event log:

```
void Log_Event(WORD wType, LPCTSTR pFormat, ...)
{
    TCHAR    chMsg[256];
    HANDLE   hEventSource;
    LPTSTR   lpszStrings[1];
    va_list pArg;
    va_start(pArg, pFormat);
    _vstprintf(chMsg, pFormat, pArg);
    va_end(pArg);
    lpszStrings[0] = chMsg;
    hEventSource = RegisterEventSource(NULL, "MTSAutoStart");
    if (hEventSource != NULL)
    {
        ReportEvent(hEventSource, wType, 0, 0, NULL, 1, 0,
            (LPCTSTR*) &lpszStrings[0], NULL);
        DeregisterEventSource(hEventSource);
    }
}
```

Step 7: Create a Resource File for the Event Log

In the Windows NT event log, you will see a message saying that it cannot find a message resource file. Unfortunately, the ATL wizard does not create this for you. To eliminate this message, you must create a resource message file and add it to your project using the MC.EXE program. The input file for this program, MTSAutoStart.mc, is as follows:

```
;// MTSAutoStart Event Messages
MessageID=0
Language=English
%1
```

When you run the input file *C:\>mc MTSAutoStart.mc*, it creates a file named MSG00001.BIN. Add *MSG00001.BIN* to your compile-time directives using the Resource Includes dialog box. The registry is made aware of the location of this file with the following piece of code, which we'll add to the *CServiceModule::RegisterServer* method:

```
// register eventlog message resource
if (bService)
{

    CRegKey keyEventLog;
    lRes = keyEventLog.Create(HKEY_LOCAL_MACHINE,
        _T("SYSTEM\\CurrentControlSet\\Services\\\
EventLog\\Application\\MTSAutoStart"));
    if (lRes != ERROR_SUCCESS)
        return lRes;
    TCHAR szModule[_MAX_PATH];
    GetModuleFileName(_Module.GetModuleInstance(), szModule,
        sizeof(szModule));
    lRes = keyEventLog.SetValue(szModule, _T("EventMessageFile"));
    if (lRes != ERROR_SUCCESS)
        return lRes;
    lRes = keyEventLog.SetValue(EVENTLOG_ERROR_TYPE |
        EVENTLOG_WARNING_TYPE | EVENTLOG_INFORMATION_TYPE,
        _T("TypesSupported"));
    if (lRes != ERROR_SUCCESS)
        return lRes;
}
```

Step 8: Set the Identity of the AutoStart and System Packages

After you register MTSAutoStart as a service with the MTSAutoStart.exe/service command, you can configure it to start automatically when Windows NT starts by using the Services applet in the Control Panel. However, MTS will generate the "server execution failed" error 0x80080005 if the identity of either the System package or the AutoStart package is set to Interactive User because there is no interactive user until someone logs on to Windows NT. To enable the MTSAutoStart service to access the MTS components in the AutoStart package and the *MTxCatEx.CatalogServer* object in the System package before anyone logs on to Windows NT, you must set the identity of these packages to a specific user. You can do this by right-clicking on the package in the MTS Explorer and selecting the Identity tab, which allows you to specify the user.

Following are the code files that we modified using the MTSAutoStart AppWizard–generated project.

STDAFX Header File

```
// stdafx.h : include file for standard system include files,
// or project specific include files that are used frequently,
// but are changed infrequently

#if !defined(\
    AFX_STDAFX_H__48408A59_E169_11D1_9182_0080C7205DC0__INCLUDED_)
#define AFX_STDAFX_H__48408A59_E169_11D1_9182_0080C7205DC0__INCLUDED_

#if _MSC_VER >= 1000
#pragma once
#endif // _MSC_VER >= 1000

#define STRICT

#define _WIN32_WINNT 0x0400
#define _ATL_APARTMENT_THREADED

#include <atlbase.h>
//You can derive a class from CComModule and use it if you want
// to override something, but do not change the name of _Module.

class CServiceModule : public CComModule
{
public:
    HRESULT RegisterServer(BOOL bRegTypeLib, BOOL bService);
    HRESULT UnregisterServer();
    void Init(_ATL_OBJMAP_ENTRY* p, HINSTANCE h, UINT nServiceNameID);
    void Start();
    void ServiceMain(DWORD dwArgc, LPTSTR* lpszArgv);
    void Handler(DWORD dwOpcode);
    void Run();
    BOOL IsInstalled();
    BOOL Install();
    BOOL Uninstall();
    LONG Unlock();
    void LogEvent(LPCTSTR pszFormat, ...);
    void SetServiceStatus(DWORD dwState);
    void SetupAsLocalServer();
```

```
//Implementation
private:
    static void WINAPI _ServiceMain(DWORD dwArgc, LPTSTR* lpszArgv);
    static void WINAPI _Handler(DWORD dwOpcode);

    static unsigned __stdcall MTSThreadProc(void* p);

// data members
public:
    TCHAR m_szServiceName[256];
    SERVICE_STATUS_HANDLE m_hServiceStatus;
    SERVICE_STATUS m_status;
    DWORD dwThreadID;
    BOOL m_bService;
};

extern CServiceModule _Module;
#include <atlcom.h>

//{{AFX_INSERT_LOCATION}}
// Microsoft Developer Studio inserts additional declarations
// immediately before the previous line.

#endif // !defined(\
    AFX_STDAFX_H__48408A59_E169_11D1_9182_0080C7205DC0__INCLUDED)


MTSAutoStart.cpp   Implementation File

// MTSAutoStart.cpp : Implementation of WinMain

// Note: Proxy/Stub Information
//       To build a separate proxy-stub DLL,
//       run nmake -f MTSAutoStartps.mk in the project directory.

#include "stdafx.h"
#include "resource.h"
#include "initguid.h"
#include "MTSAutoStart.h"

#include "MTSAutoStart_i.c"

#include <stdio.h>

#include <process.h>
```

(continued)

```
#define MAXTHREAD 10000
#import "c:\\winnt\\system32\\mts\\mtxadmin.dll" \
    no_namespace  raw_interfaces_only
HANDLE g_hExitEvent = FALSE;
typedef ICatalog * LPCATALOG;
typedef ICatalogCollection * LPCATALOGCOLLECTION;
typedef ICatalogObject* LPCATALOGOBJECT;
#include <process.h>
void Log_Event(WORD wType, LPCTSTR pszFormat, ...);

CServiceModule _Module;

BEGIN_OBJECT_MAP(ObjectMap)
END_OBJECT_MAP()

LPCTSTR FindOneOf(LPCTSTR p1, LPCTSTR p2)
{
    while (*p1 != NULL)
    {
        LPCTSTR p = p2;
        while (*p != NULL)
        {
            if (*p1 == *p++)
                return p1+1;
        }
        p1++;
    }
    return NULL;
}

// Although some of these functions are big, they are
// declared inline because they are used only once.

inline HRESULT CServiceModule::RegisterServer(BOOL bRegTypeLib,
    BOOL bService)
{
    HRESULT hr = CoInitialize(NULL);
    if (FAILED(hr))
        return hr;

    // Remove any previous service since it might point to
    // the incorrect file.
    Uninstall();

    // Add service entries.
    UpdateRegistryFromResource(IDR_MTSAutoStart, TRUE);
```

```
// Adjust the AppID for Local Server or Service.
CRegKey keyAppID;
LONG lRes = keyAppID.Open(HKEY_CLASSES_ROOT, _T("AppID"));
if (lRes != ERROR_SUCCESS)
    return lRes;

CRegKey key;
lRes = key.Open(keyAppID,
    _T("{48408A56-E169-11D1-9182-0080C7205DC0}"));
if (lRes != ERROR_SUCCESS)
    return lRes;
key.DeleteValue(_T("LocalService"));

if (bService)
{
    key.SetValue(_T("MTSAutoStart"), _T("LocalService"));
    key.SetValue(_T("-Service"), _T("ServiceParameters"));
    // Create service.
    Install();
}

// Add object entries
hr = CComModule::RegisterServer(bRegTypeLib);

// Register eventlog message resource.
if (bService)
{

    CRegKey keyEventLog;
    lRes = keyEventLog.Create(HKEY_LOCAL_MACHINE,
    _T("SYSTEM\\CurrentControlSet\\Services\\EventLog\\\
Application\\MTSAutoStart"));
    if (lRes != ERROR_SUCCESS)
        return lRes;
    TCHAR szModule[_MAX_PATH];
    GetModuleFileName(_Module.GetModuleInstance(), szModule,
        sizeof(szModule));
    lRes = keyEventLog.SetValue(szModule, _T("EventMessageFile"));
    if (lRes != ERROR_SUCCESS)
        return lRes;
    lRes = keyEventLog.SetValue(EVENTLOG_ERROR_TYPE |
        EVENTLOG_WARNING_TYPE | EVENTLOG_INFORMATION_TYPE,
        _T("TypesSupported"));
    if (lRes != ERROR_SUCCESS)
        return lRes;
}
```

(continued)

233

```
    CoUninitialize();
    return hr;
}

inline HRESULT CServiceModule::UnregisterServer()
{
    HRESULT hr = CoInitialize(NULL);
    if (FAILED(hr))
        return hr;

    // Remove service entries.
    UpdateRegistryFromResource(IDR_MTSAutoStart, FALSE);
    // Remove service.
    Uninstall();
    // Remove object entries.
    CComModule::UnregisterServer();

    CoUninitialize();
    return S_OK;
}

inline void CServiceModule::Init(_ATL_OBJMAP_ENTRY* p,
    HINSTANCE h, UINT nServiceNameID)
{
    CComModule::Init(p, h);

    m_bService = TRUE;

    LoadString(h, nServiceNameID, m_szServiceName,
        sizeof(m_szServiceName) / sizeof(TCHAR));

    // Set up the initial service status.
    m_hServiceStatus = NULL;
    m_status.dwServiceType = SERVICE_WIN32_OWN_PROCESS;
    m_status.dwCurrentState = SERVICE_STOPPED;
    m_status.dwControlsAccepted = SERVICE_ACCEPT_STOP;
    m_status.dwWin32ExitCode = 0;
    m_status.dwServiceSpecificExitCode = 0;
    m_status.dwCheckPoint = 0;
    m_status.dwWaitHint = 0;
}

LONG CServiceModule::Unlock()
```

```
{
    LONG l = CComModule::Unlock();
    if (l == 0 && !m_bService)
        PostThreadMessage(dwThreadID, WM_QUIT, 0, 0);
    return l;
}

BOOL CServiceModule::IsInstalled()
{
    BOOL bResult = FALSE;

    SC_HANDLE hSCM = ::OpenSCManager(NULL, NULL,
        SC_MANAGER_ALL_ACCESS);

    if (hSCM != NULL)
    {
        SC_HANDLE hService = ::OpenService(hSCM, m_szServiceName,
            SERVICE_QUERY_CONFIG);
        if (hService != NULL)
        {
            bResult = TRUE;
            ::CloseServiceHandle(hService);
        }
        ::CloseServiceHandle(hSCM);
    }
    return bResult;
}

inline BOOL CServiceModule::Install()
{
    if (IsInstalled())
        return TRUE;

    SC_HANDLE hSCM = ::OpenSCManager(NULL, NULL,
        SC_MANAGER_ALL_ACCESS);
    if (hSCM == NULL)
    {
        MessageBox(NULL, _T("Couldn't open service manager"),
            m_szServiceName, MB_OK);
        return FALSE;
    }
```

(continued)

```
    // Get the executable file path.
    TCHAR szFilePath[_MAX_PATH];
    ::GetModuleFileName(NULL, szFilePath, _MAX_PATH);

    SC_HANDLE hService = ::CreateService(
        hSCM, m_szServiceName, m_szServiceName,
        SERVICE_ALL_ACCESS, SERVICE_WIN32_OWN_PROCESS,
        SERVICE_DEMAND_START, SERVICE_ERROR_NORMAL,
        szFilePath, NULL, NULL, _T("RPCSS\0"), NULL, NULL);

    if (hService == NULL)
    {
        ::CloseServiceHandle(hSCM);
        MessageBox(NULL, _T("Couldn't create service"),
            m_szServiceName, MB_OK);
        return FALSE;
    }

    ::CloseServiceHandle(hService);
    ::CloseServiceHandle(hSCM);
    return TRUE;
}

inline BOOL CServiceModule::Uninstall()
{
    if (!IsInstalled())
        return TRUE;

    SC_HANDLE hSCM = ::OpenSCManager(NULL, NULL,
        SC_MANAGER_ALL_ACCESS);

    if (hSCM == NULL)
    {
        MessageBox(NULL, _T("Couldn't open service manager"),
            m_szServiceName, MB_OK);
        return FALSE;
    }

    SC_HANDLE hService = ::OpenService(hSCM, m_szServiceName,
        SERVICE_STOP | DELETE);

    if (hService == NULL)
```

```
    {
        ::CloseServiceHandle(hSCM);
        MessageBox(NULL, _T("Couldn't open service"),
            m_szServiceName, MB_OK);
        return FALSE;
    }
    SERVICE_STATUS status;
    ::ControlService(hService, SERVICE_CONTROL_STOP, &status);

    BOOL bDelete = ::DeleteService(hService);
    ::CloseServiceHandle(hService);
    ::CloseServiceHandle(hSCM);

    if (bDelete)
        return TRUE;

    MessageBox(NULL, _T("Service could not be deleted"),
        m_szServiceName, MB_OK);
    return FALSE;
}


/////////////////////////////////////////////////////////////////////
// Logging functions
void CServiceModule::LogEvent(LPCTSTR pFormat, ...)
{
    TCHAR    chMsg[256];
    HANDLE  hEventSource;
    LPTSTR  lpszStrings[1];
    va_list pArg;

    va_start(pArg, pFormat);
    _vstprintf(chMsg, pFormat, pArg);
    va_end(pArg);

    lpszStrings[0] = chMsg;

    if (m_bService)
    {
        /* Get a handle to use with ReportEvent(). */
        hEventSource = RegisterEventSource(NULL, m_szServiceName);
        if (hEventSource != NULL)
```

(continued)

```
        {
            /* Write to event log. */
            ReportEvent(hEventSource, EVENTLOG_INFORMATION_TYPE,
                0, 0, NULL, 1, 0, (LPCTSTR*) &lpszStrings[0], NULL);
            DeregisterEventSource(hEventSource);
        }
    }
    else
    {
        // Since we are not running as a service, simply
        // write the error to the console.
        _putts(chMsg);
    }
}


//////////////////////////////////////////////////////////////////////
// Service startup and registration
inline void CServiceModule::Start()
{
    SERVICE_TABLE_ENTRY st[] =
    {
        { m_szServiceName, _ServiceMain },
        { NULL, NULL }
    };
    if (m_bService && !::StartServiceCtrlDispatcher(st))
    {
        m_bService = FALSE;
    }
    if (m_bService == FALSE)
        Run();
}

inline void CServiceModule::ServiceMain(DWORD /* dwArgc */,
    LPTSTR* /* lpszArgv */)
{
    // Register the control request handler.
    m_status.dwCurrentState = SERVICE_START_PENDING;
    m_hServiceStatus = RegisterServiceCtrlHandler(m_szServiceName,
        _Handler);
    if (m_hServiceStatus == NULL)
    {
        LogEvent(_T("Handler not installed"));
        return;
    }
```

```
    SetServiceStatus(SERVICE_START_PENDING);

    m_status.dwWin32ExitCode = S_OK;
    m_status.dwCheckPoint = 0;
    m_status.dwWaitHint = 0;

    // When the Run function returns, the service has stopped.
    Run();

    SetServiceStatus(SERVICE_STOPPED);
    LogEvent(_T("Service stopped"));
}

inline void CServiceModule::Handler(DWORD dwOpcode)
{
    switch (dwOpcode)
    {
    case SERVICE_CONTROL_STOP:
        SetServiceStatus(SERVICE_STOP_PENDING);
        PostThreadMessage(dwThreadID, WM_QUIT, 0, 0);
        break;
    case SERVICE_CONTROL_PAUSE:
        break;
    case SERVICE_CONTROL_CONTINUE:
        break;
    case SERVICE_CONTROL_INTERROGATE:
        break;
    case SERVICE_CONTROL_SHUTDOWN:
        break;
    default:
        LogEvent(_T("Bad service request"));
    }
}

void WINAPI CServiceModule::_ServiceMain(DWORD dwArgc,
    LPTSTR* lpszArgv)
{
    _Module.ServiceMain(dwArgc, lpszArgv);
}
void WINAPI CServiceModule::_Handler(DWORD dwOpcode)
{
    _Module.Handler(dwOpcode);
}
```

(continued)

```
void CServiceModule::SetServiceStatus(DWORD dwState)
{
    m_status.dwCurrentState = dwState;
    ::SetServiceStatus(m_hServiceStatus, &m_status);
}

void CServiceModule::Run()
{
    HRESULT hr;

    _Module.dwThreadID = GetCurrentThreadId();

    HRESULT hRes = CoInitialize(NULL);
//  If you are running Windows NT 4.0 or higher, you can use the
//  following call instead to make the EXE free threaded.
//  This means that calls come in on a random RPC thread.
//  HRESULT hRes = CoInitializeEx(NULL, COINIT_MULTITHREADED);

    _ASSERTE(SUCCEEDED(hr));

    // This provides a NULL DACL, which allows access to everyone.
    CSecurityDescriptor sd;
    sd.InitializeFromThreadToken();
    hr = CoInitializeSecurity(sd, -1, NULL, NULL,
        RPC_C_AUTHN_LEVEL_PKT, RPC_C_IMP_LEVEL_IMPERSONATE, NULL,
        EOAC_NONE, NULL);
    _ASSERTE(SUCCEEDED(hr));

    hr = _Module.RegisterClassObjects(CLSCTX_LOCAL_SERVER |
        CLSCTX_REMOTE_SERVER, REGCLS_MULTIPLEUSE);
    _ASSERTE(SUCCEEDED(hr));

    g_hExitEvent = CreateEvent(NULL, TRUE, FALSE, NULL);
    HANDLE hMTSThread[MAXTHREAD];
    int nthread = 0;

    LPUNKNOWN pUnk = NULL;
    LPCATALOG pCatalog = NULL;
    LPCATALOGCOLLECTION pCatCol_Packages = NULL;
    LPCATALOGOBJECT pCatObj_Package = NULL;
    LPCATALOGCOLLECTION pCatCol_ComponentsInPackage = NULL;
    LPCATALOGOBJECT pCatObj_Component = NULL;
    LPDISPATCH pdisp1 = NULL;
    LPDISPATCH pdisp2 = NULL;
```

```
LPDISPATCH pdisp3 = NULL;
LPDISPATCH pdisp4 = NULL;
int i = 0;
long nNumberOfComponents = 0;
BSTR bstrCollName1 = _bstr_t("Packages");

try
{
    CLSID clsid;
    hr = ::CLSIDFromProgID(L"MTSAdmin.Catalog.1", &clsid);
    if (FAILED(hr)) throw "error";

    hr = ::CoCreateInstance(clsid, NULL, CLSCTX_SERVER,
        IID_IUnknown, (void**)&pUnk);
    if (FAILED(hr)) throw "error";

    hr = pUnk->QueryInterface(__uuidof(ICatalog),
        (void**)&pCatalog);
    if (FAILED(hr)) throw "error";

    hr = pCatalog->GetCollection (bstrCollName1, &pdisp1 );
    if (FAILED(hr)) throw "error";

    hr = pdisp1->QueryInterface(__uuidof(ICatalogCollection),
        (void**)&pCatCol_Packages);
    if (FAILED(hr)) throw "error";

    hr = pCatCol_Packages->Populate();
    if (FAILED(hr)) throw "error";

    long lcount;
    hr = pCatCol_Packages->get_Count(&lcount);
    if (FAILED(hr)) throw "error";

    for (i = 0; i < lcount; i++)
    {
        hr = pCatCol_Packages->get_Item(i, &pdisp2);
        if (FAILED(hr)) throw "error";

        hr = pdisp2->QueryInterface(__uuidof(ICatalogObject),
            (void**)&pCatObj_Package);
        if (FAILED(hr)) throw "error";
```

(continued)

241

```
VARIANT vName;
BSTR bstrPropName = _bstr_t("Name");
hr = pCatObj_Package->get_Value (bstrPropName, &vName );
if (FAILED(hr)) throw "error";

_bstr_t bstrpackage = _bstr_t("AutoStart");
if (_bstr_t(vName) ==  bstrpackage)
{
    VARIANT vkey;
    BSTR bstrPropNameID = _bstr_t("ID");
    hr = pCatObj_Package->get_Value (bstrPropNameID,
        &vkey );
    if (FAILED(hr)) throw "error";

    BSTR bstrCollName1 = _bstr_t("ComponentsInPackage");
    hr = pCatCol_Packages->GetCollection (bstrCollName1,
        vkey, &pdisp3 );
    if (FAILED(hr)) throw "error";

    hr = pdisp3->QueryInterface(
        __uuidof(ICatalogCollection),
        (void**)&pCatCol_ComponentsInPackage);
    if (FAILED(hr)) throw "error";

    hr = pCatCol_ComponentsInPackage->Populate();
    if (FAILED(hr)) throw "error";

    hr = pCatCol_ComponentsInPackage->
        get_Count(&nNumberOfComponents);
    if (FAILED(hr)) throw "error";

    for (int k = 0; k < nNumberOfComponents; k++)
    {
        hr = pCatCol_ComponentsInPackage->
            get_Item(k, &pdisp4);
        if (FAILED(hr)) throw "error";

        hr = pdisp4->QueryInterface(
            __uuidof(ICatalogObject),
            (void**)&pCatObj_Component);
        if (FAILED(hr)) throw "error";

        VARIANT vProgID;
        BSTR bstrPropName3 = _bstr_t("ProgID");
```

```
                    hr = pCatObj_Component->
                        get_Value (bstrPropName3, &vProgID );
                    if (FAILED(hr)) throw "error";

                    _bstr_t* pbstrProgID = new _bstr_t(vProgID);
                    if (nthread < MAXTHREAD)
                    {

                        DWORD hThreadID;
                        hMTSThread[nthread] =
                            (HANDLE) _beginthreadex(
                            NULL, 0, &MTSThreadProc,
                            (_bstr_t*) pbstrProgID, 0,
                            (UINT*) &hThreadID);
                        nthread++;
                    }

                    hr = pdisp4->Release();
                    pdisp4 = NULL;
                    if (FAILED(hr)) throw "error";
                    hr = pCatObj_Component->Release();
                    pCatObj_Component = NULL;
                    if (FAILED(hr)) throw "error";
                }

                hr = pdisp3->Release();
                pdisp3 = NULL;
                if (FAILED(hr)) throw "error";
                hr = pCatCol_ComponentsInPackage->Release();
                pCatCol_ComponentsInPackage = NULL;
                if (FAILED(hr)) throw "error";
            }
            hr = pdisp2->Release();
            pdisp2 = NULL;
            if (FAILED(hr)) throw "error";
            hr = pCatObj_Package->Release();
            pCatObj_Package = NULL;
            if (FAILED(hr)) throw "error";

        }

    hr = pUnk->Release();
    pUnk = NULL;
```

(continued)

```
        hr = pCatalog->Release();
        pCatalog = NULL;
        if (FAILED(hr)) throw "error";
        hr = pdisp1->Release();
        pdisp1 = NULL;
        if (FAILED(hr)) throw "error";
        hr = pCatCol_Packages->Release();
        pCatCol_Packages = NULL;
        if (FAILED(hr)) throw "error";

        if (nNumberOfComponents == 0)
        {
            Log_Event(EVENTLOG_WARNING_TYPE,
                _T("There are no components in AutoStart\
MTS package"));
        }
    }
    catch(...)
    {

        Log_Event(EVENTLOG_ERROR_TYPE,
            _T("An error occurred when starting the\
MTSAutoStart Service"));
        if (pUnk) pUnk->Release();
        if (pCatalog) pCatalog->Release();
        if (pCatCol_Packages) pCatCol_Packages->Release();
        if (pCatObj_Package) pCatObj_Package->Release();
        if (pCatCol_ComponentsInPackage)
            pCatCol_ComponentsInPackage->Release();
        if (pCatObj_Component) pCatObj_Component->Release();
        if (pdisp1) pdisp1->Release();
        if (pdisp2) pdisp2->Release();
        if (pdisp3) pdisp3->Release();
        if (pdisp4) pdisp4->Release();
    }

    LogEvent(_T("Service started"));
    SetServiceStatus(SERVICE_RUNNING);

    MSG msg;
    while (GetMessage(&msg, 0, 0, 0))
        DispatchMessage(&msg);

    SetEvent(g_hExitEvent);
    WaitForMultipleObjects(nthread, hMTSThread, TRUE, 30000);
```

```
    for (int j = 0; j < nthread; j++)
        CloseHandle ((HANDLE)hMTSThread[j]);

    _Module.RevokeClassObjects();

    CoUninitialize();
}


//////////////////////////////////////////////////////////////////////
extern "C" int WINAPI _tWinMain(HINSTANCE hInstance,
    HINSTANCE /*hPrevInstance*/, LPTSTR lpCmdLine, int /*nShowCmd*/)
{
    lpCmdLine = GetCommandLine(); //this line necessary for
                                  // _ATL_MIN_CRT
    _Module.Init(ObjectMap, hInstance, IDS_SERVICENAME);
    _Module.m_bService = TRUE;

    TCHAR szTokens[] = _T("-/");

    LPCTSTR lpszToken = FindOneOf(lpCmdLine, szTokens);
    while (lpszToken != NULL)
    {
        if (lstrcmpi(lpszToken, _T("UnregServer"))==0)
            return _Module.UnregisterServer();

        // Register as Local Server.
        if (lstrcmpi(lpszToken, _T("RegServer"))==0)
            return _Module.RegisterServer(TRUE, FALSE);

        // Register as Service.
        if (lstrcmpi(lpszToken, _T("Service"))==0)
            return _Module.RegisterServer(TRUE, TRUE);

        lpszToken = FindOneOf(lpszToken, szTokens);
    }

    // Are we Service or Local Server?
    CRegKey keyAppID;
    LONG lRes = keyAppID.Open(HKEY_CLASSES_ROOT, _T("AppID"));
    if (lRes != ERROR_SUCCESS)
        return lRes;

    CRegKey key;
    lRes = key.Open(keyAppID,
        _T("{48408A56-E169-11D1-9182-0080C7205DC0}"));
```

(continued)

245

```
    if (lRes != ERROR_SUCCESS)
        return lRes;

    TCHAR szValue[_MAX_PATH];
    DWORD dwLen = _MAX_PATH;
    lRes = key.QueryValue(szValue, _T("LocalService"), &dwLen);

    _Module.m_bService = FALSE;
    if (lRes == ERROR_SUCCESS)
        _Module.m_bService = TRUE;

    _Module.Start();

    // When we get here, the service has been stopped.
    return _Module.m_status.dwWin32ExitCode;
}

unsigned __stdcall CServiceModule::MTSThreadProc(void* p)
{

    Sleep(3000);
    _bstr_t bstrProgID(*(_bstr_t * )p);
    delete p;
    HRESULT hr = CoInitialize(NULL);
    OLECHAR * FunctionName = L"Start";
    LPDISPATCH pIDispatch = NULL;
    DISPID dispid = NULL;
    try
    {
        if (FAILED(hr)) throw "error";
        CLSID clsid;
        hr = ::CLSIDFromProgID(bstrProgID, &clsid);
        if (FAILED(hr)) throw "error";

        hr = ::CoCreateInstance(clsid, NULL, CLSCTX_SERVER,
            IID_IDispatch, (void**)&pIDispatch);
        if (FAILED(hr)) throw "error";

        hr = pIDispatch->GetIDsOfNames(IID_NULL, &FunctionName,
            1, GetUserDefaultLCID(), &dispid);
        if (FAILED(hr)) throw "error";

        _bstr_t bstrmessage(" has been started.");
        bstrmessage = bstrProgID + bstrmessage;
        Log_Event(EVENTLOG_INFORMATION_TYPE, _T(bstrmessage));
```

```
        while(1)
        {
            long lwait;
            VARIANTARG varg[1];
            ::VariantInit(&varg[0]);
            varg[0].vt = VT_BYREF|VT_I4;
            varg[0].plVal = &lwait;
            DISPPARAMS dispparams;
            dispparams.cArgs = 1;
            dispparams.rgvarg = &varg[0];
            dispparams.cNamedArgs = 0;
            dispparams.rgdispidNamedArgs = NULL;
            EXCEPINFO excepinfo = {0};
            unsigned int nerr = 0;
            hr = pIDispatch->Invoke(dispid, IID_NULL,
                GetUserDefaultLCID(), DISPATCH_METHOD, &dispparams,
                NULL, &excepinfo, &nerr);
            if (FAILED(hr)) throw "error";
            if (WaitForSingleObject(g_hExitEvent, 0) != WAIT_TIMEOUT)
                break;
            Sleep(lwait);
        }

}
catch(...)
{
    _bstr_t
        bstrmessage("An error occurred using the component :");
    bstrmessage = bstrmessage + bstrProgID;
    Log_Event(EVENTLOG_ERROR_TYPE, _T(bstrmessage));
    if (pIDispatch != NULL) pIDispatch->Release();
    pIDispatch = NULL;
    WaitForSingleObject(g_hExitEvent, INFINITE);
}

if (pIDispatch != NULL)
{
    pIDispatch->Release();
    _bstr_t bstrmessage(" has been stopped.");
    bstrmessage = bstrProgID + bstrmessage;
    Log_Event(EVENTLOG_INFORMATION_TYPE, _T(bstrmessage));

}
```

(continued)

247

```
        CoUninitialize();
        _endthreadex(S_OK);

        return 0;
    }

void Log_Event(WORD wType, LPCTSTR pFormat, ...)
{
    TCHAR    chMsg[256];
    HANDLE   hEventSource;
    LPTSTR   lpszStrings[1];
    va_list  pArg;

    va_start(pArg, pFormat);
    _vstprintf(chMsg, pFormat, pArg);
    va_end(pArg);

    lpszStrings[0] = chMsg;

    /* Get a handle to use with ReportEvent(). */
    hEventSource = RegisterEventSource(NULL, "MTSAutoStart");
    if (hEventSource != NULL)
    {
        /* Write to event log. */
        ReportEvent(hEventSource, wType, 0, 0, NULL, 1, 0,
            (LPCTSTR*) &lpszStrings[0], NULL);
        DeregisterEventSource(hEventSource);
    }

}
```

CHAPTER SEVEN

Microsoft Message Queuing

Microsoft Message Queue Server (MSMQ) is a component within Microsoft Windows NT that provides asynchronous communication services between applications. In this chapter, we'll examine why you need MSMQ and the benefits of asynchronous systems. You'll learn about the components of MSMQ and how they work, and you'll see a practical example of using the C API for MSMQ to build a Microsoft Transaction Server (MTS) resource dispenser for MSMQ.

The Benefits of MSMQ

All of the distributed computing architectures we've discussed so far use synchronous communication. In synchronous systems, the sender of a request must wait for a response from the receiver before executing any other tasks. The sender and the receiver must run simultaneously and be connected through a network if they do not reside on the same computer. COM and DCOM are designed to operate in this way. Asynchronous communication, on the other hand, allows the sender to make a request and then immediately continue processing other tasks without having to wait for a response from the receiver.

COM+ will provide an elegant interface for this kind of capability through the integration of MTS and MSMQ in the Queued Components service. Today you can use the MSMQ API to build these kinds of systems. MSMQ implements asynchronous communication using message queues. This approach offers a number of benefits over other implementations. Message queues prevent messages from being lost in transit due to system or network failures because they can be saved to disk. Messages also automatically continue processing as soon as the system recovers.

Asynchronous systems provide the benefits described in the following sections.

Scalability

Asynchronous systems can provide more scalable solutions than synchronous systems because they allow servers to queue requests during peak hours to reduce processing requirements and avoid overloads. These requests can be processed later when the server is less busy.

Availability

Asynchronous systems allow mobile users to continue to use the system when they are no longer connected. Any requests made by the mobile user are queued in a local MSMQ queue. Requests in the local queue are forwarded to the server for processing when the user reconnects. In addition, this architecture improves fault tolerance because the system can survive network failures. Software and hardware upgrades are also simplified because requests can be queued while different pieces of the system are temporarily off line.

Performance

Asynchronous systems can perform better than synchronous systems in two ways. First, if no response is needed from the server, the sender need not wait for a request to be processed or wait for network round trips over slow Internet connections. Second, if the sender does need a response from the server, the sender can still continue processing other tasks while the receiver is preparing its response.

Load Balancing

You can use MTS or the Microsoft DNS Server to statically load-balance a synchronous system. With this kind of load-balancing, requests are evenly divided among all the servers in a round-robin fashion. No consideration is given to the current use of each server. This means that some servers might be overloaded while others are idle. MSMQ lets you implement a more dynamic load balancing mechanism. All the requests are placed in a queue, and each server lifts a request from the queue when it becomes idle. The load is thus divided among the servers based on their current use, leading to more effective use of your total server capability. This approach also prevents servers from being overloaded because each server determines when it is ready to take a request from the queue.

Prioritized Workloads

MSMQ lets the sender assign different priorities to different requests. Your system can thus prioritize its workload. For example, orders for goods can be given a higher priority than requests for information. You can configure your system to process the higher priority orders first. Or a web site can mark requests from paid subscribers with a higher priority than those from nonsubscribers. Paid subscribers thus experience a faster response time.

Parallelism

Asynchronous systems provide opportunities for parallelism. For example, an order request to buy an item might require the cooperation of three different components that handle billing, inventory, and delivery, respectively. In the synchronous model, the time to complete this transaction is the sum of the time it takes to process each of the three components. In the asynchronous model, these components can simultaneously process the request when it enters the queue. The time needed to complete the transaction is shortened to the time it takes to process the slowest component. In addition, the asynchronous model allows a configuration in which one component can send back a separate response to the client. For example, the delivery component might need a few days to schedule the delivery. It can therefore send a separate response at a later time than the other two components.

Concurrency

Some multiuser applications must be asynchronous in order to function correctly. For example, components that put locks on database tables, which prevent other users from making updates to those tables, can be problematic. If these update requests are made asynchronously and are put in a queue, they can be processed serially at a later time so that no threading or synchronization problems arise.

Logging and Reprocessing

Some mission-critical applications require that every request be logged, audited, and reprocessed in the case of a failure. MSMQ greatly simplifies the implementation of this requirement through its journal and auditing capabilities.

System Bridging

MSMQ can be used to bridge communications between heterogeneous networks, diverse platforms, and legacy systems. For example, you can use Internet Information Server (IIS) and MSMQ to queue requests received over the Web. This allows a legacy mainframe system to be more easily integrated into the architecture to process these requests.

MSMQ Components

MSMQ has the following main components: the MSMQ enterprise, servers, independent clients, dependent clients, queues, messages, the MSMQ Explorer, and the MSMQ ActiveX control.

MSMQ Enterprises

All of the computers that run MSMQ components belong to one MSMQ enterprise. You should not have more than one MSMQ enterprise on your network because this complicates administration and can cause incompatibilities with a later version of Windows NT Server. Different MSMQ enterprises can exchange messages over the Internet using TCP port 1801, which has been registered with the Internet Assigned Numbers Authority (IANA) for this purpose.

An MSMQ enterprise is divided into multiple MSMQ sites, each of which represents a physical collection of computers. The site boundary is usually determined by the actual location of the computers within the enterprise and can span across computers using different network protocols. MSMQ allows fast and inexpensive communication between the computers within the same site. It also allows less efficient communication between computers across different sites by setting up site links. You can have multiple site links across sites to provide a higher level of fault tolerance and load balancing. An administrator can configure a different cost to be associated with each link.

For example, a site link over a telephone line should have a higher cost than a site link over a T1 line. A site link cost can be any number between 0 and 999,999. A site link cost of 0 means that the two sites are not connected. MSMQ's intersite routing takes account of these costs when determining the most efficient path between sites. A site gate is an MSMQ routing server that can be used to reduce the number of sessions between sites. When a site is configured to use a site gate, all MSMQ messages exchanged between the sites will be routed through the site gate. In this way, the number of site-to-site sessions is reduced. If you use site gates, you should have more than one in order to avoid a single point of failure for all intersite communication.

MSMQ sites also contain MSMQ connected networks (CNs). A CN is a label that represents a collection of computers in which any two computers can communicate directly. All computers within a CN must use the same network protocol and be able to establish a session. CNs can span different sites, and a computer can belong to multiple CNs. However, every computer on the same local area network using the same network protocol must be in the same MSMQ connected network. (A site gate must belong to the same CN as a server in the other site. If the other site also uses a site gate, that site gate must belong to the same CN as the site gate in the other site.)

The MSMQ enterprise uses the MSMQ Information Store (MQIS) database to hold information about the enterprise such as its sites, CNs, router configuration, computers, queues, and settings (such as its replication interval, enterprise name, and PEC name). The MQIS is not used to store the MSMQ messages themselves. The current version of MSMQ uses Microsoft SQL Server to manage this database, but a later version will use the Windows NT Active Directory. The MQIS database consists of the following 11 tables: Enterprise, CNs, Machine, MachineCNs, BscAck, MQDeleted, MQPurge, MQUser, Queue, Site, and SiteLink. It has one store procedure to update statistics. The default size of the database is 50 MB for data and 8 MB for logging database transactions. If each computer in your enterprise has two public queues, the default size will give you enough space to manage about 2500 computers.

MSMQ Servers

MSMQ servers are responsible for managing queues, sending and receiving messages, storing messages, routing messages, supporting local clients, and accessing dependent clients. There are four server types:

- Primary enterprise controller (PEC)
- Primary site controller (PSC)
- Backup site controller (BSC)
- Routing server

Every MSMQ enterprise must contain one PEC, but the other server types are optional. The PEC holds the information about the enterprise configuration in the MQIS database. It also stores the certification keys for authenticating messages. The PEC is a PSC for one site, and it is an MSMQ routing server. After you install a PEC, you can also install a PSC for each additional site in your enterprise. The PSC keeps the information about the site's computers and queues in a database. It also acts as an MSMQ routing server. Although a PSC does not require a BSC to function correctly, you should install one or more BSCs to provide load balancing and fault tolerance in case the PSC or PEC fails or is disconnected. The BSC has a copy of the PSC or PEC database and can also function as a MSMQ routing server.

Even though the PEC, PSC, and BSC are MSMQ routing servers, you might want to install additional MSMQ routing servers. The number of additional servers required depends on a combination of factors, including the number of dependent clients, independent clients, sites, CNs, session concentration, network protocols, and message throughput. These servers support dynamic routing of messages and have intermediate store-and-forward message queuing capabilities. All MSMQ computers can support connectivity to computers running other messaging systems. You configure this using foreign computers, queues, and CNs. Note that MSMQ servers are not mobile; you can move them to a different site only by reinstalling them at that site.

MSMQ Independent Clients

MSMQ independent clients allow disconnected or mobile users to create and manage queues and send and receive messages. You can install them on computers running Microsoft Windows 95 and Windows NT 4.0 (Workstation or Server). They differ from MSMQ servers in that they do not store information in the MQIS database, cannot support dependent clients, and do not have the intermediate store-and-forward capability to act as an MSMQ router. If an independent client sends a message to a public queue on an MSMQ server, the message is stored locally on the client if the client is currently disconnected. When the independent client reconnects, these messages are automatically sent to the server.

Unlike MSMQ servers and MSMQ dependent clients, MSMQ independent clients can take advantage of intrasite session concentration to reduce network bandwidth use. For example, if you have a star network topology and your application requires that each computer communicate with every other computer, you can greatly reduce the number of sessions required by configuring each independent client to use up to three dedicated MSMQ In Routing Servers (InRS's) and MSMQ Out Routing Servers (OutRS's). A single server can be both an InRS and an OutRS, but it is better to have more than one InRS and OutRS for fault tolerance purposes. Any outgoing messages sent by the independent clients go through an OutRS. Similarly, any messages received by the independent client come in via an InRS. The PEC, PSCs, BSCs, and MSMQ routing servers can be InRS's and OutRS's. If your star network has 100 computers and the PEC is configured to be both the InRS and OutRS, you reduce the number of sessions required from 5050 to 100. (In the current version of MSMQ, both independent clients and dependent clients are limited to 10 concurrent sessions with other MSMQ clients.)

If independent clients reconnect to the MSMQ enterprise through another site, they do not receive messages that were sent to them while they were disconnected unless the new site was specified before disconnecting. The independent client's InRS and OutRS settings for message routing are also ignored. They become operative again when the client reconnects to the original site.

MSMQ Dependent Clients

Unlike an independent client, a dependent client must always be connected to a PEC, PSC, BSC, or MSMQ routing server to send and receive messages or to create, open, or delete queues. A dependent client does not have to be in the same site as its assigned servers. MSMQ servers can support up to 15 dependent clients, and the communication between the client and server is always synchronous. Dependent clients can be used on computers running Windows 95 and Windows NT 4.0 (Workstation or Server).

Dependent clients are generally used when the client computer cannot support the requirements of an independent client. Dependent clients require less memory or hard disk space because all messages are stored on the server. Dependent clients are also used to simplify administration because there are fewer computers to back up and to monitor for journal or dead letter queues.

While dependent clients can send and receive transactional messages, they cannot transact MSMQ functions with transactional resources on the dependent client computer. Dependent clients also have the limitation of exchanging encrypted messages with the server in an unencrypted format.

MSMQ Queues

MSMQ has public and private queues. Any computer in the enterprise can locate public queues because they are published in the MQIS, which is replicated throughout the enterprise. Private queues are stored in the local Registry and therefore use no MQIS space. These queues can be accessed only by applications that have access to the full pathname or format name of the queue. When you create an MSMQ queue, you must decide whether you want it to be transactional. Transactional messages can be sent only to transactional queues, and nontransactional messages can be sent only to nontransactional queues.

You use transactional queues in five situations:

■ When you include your MSMQ operations in MTS transactions

■ When you include your MSMQ operations in MS Distributed Trans-action Coordinator (DTC) external transactions

■ When you include your MSMQ operations in XA-compliant transactions

■ When you group MSMQ operations into internal MSMQ transactions

■ When you use MSMQ single-message transactions

The integration of MSMQ with MTS avoids sending a message that is part of an aborted transaction. Similarly, MSMQ rolls back the receipt of a message by putting it back in its queue if the receipt operation is part of a transaction that aborts. MSMQ internal transactions are often used for transactions that only send or receive MSMQ messages. Unlike MS DTC external transactions, MSMQ internal transactions do not incur the cost of coordinating between several resource managers. They therefore offer better performance and use fewer resources than external transactions. If you only need to send a message to a transactional queue, you should use the MSMQ single-message send operation for the best performance.

Transactional queues also have the benefit of in-order delivery and exactly-once delivery. With in-order delivery, MSMQ guarantees that all messages sent to a transactional queue arrive in the order in which they were sent within each transaction. "Exactly-once" delivery means that all messages sent to a transactional queue arrive once and only once. MSMQ must take special measures to prevent message duplication or loss, which adversely affects performance. These features are very important for some applications. For example, if you are receiving orders for products over the Internet and messages arrive more than once, you will ship products that your customer did not request. If your application is a service center that deals with customer complaints, messages delivered out of order will cause confusion. Because transactional queues are much slower than nontransactional queues, you might sometimes want to have in-order delivery and exactly-once delivery without using transactional queues. If you configure your enterprise so that the sending and receiving applications are on the same computer and access queues only on that computer, there will be no duplicates or out-of-order messages. You can also prevent out-of-order delivery to queues across computers by using the DIRECT sending method or by configuring MSMQ so that routing always takes place through a specific MSMQ routing server. A future version of MSMQ will let you specify in-order delivery and exactly-once delivery for nontransactional queues.

MSMQ also has other queues, which are listed below. These queues are simply standard MSMQ queues that are used for a specific purpose. You can use the functions in the MSMQ API for all of these queues.

Queue	Queue Type
Message queues	Application
Administration queues	Application
Response queues	Application
Journal queues	System
Dead Letter queues	System
Report queues	System

Following is a description of MSMQ queue types:

- *Message queues* can be public and private and store application-generated messages.

- *Administration queues* are local queues for storing MSMQ-generated positive and negative acknowledgment messages. These messages indicate whether messages have arrived at their target destination, have been retrieved, or have prevented them from being retrieved by an error.

- *Response queues* are used to return application-generated response messages from the application reading the messages in a queue.

- *Journal queues* are used to log or store copies of application-generated messages. The two types of journal queues are machine journal queues and queue journals. A machine journal queue is used to track the messages sent from the computer and MSMQ-generated report messages. This queue is created when MSMQ is installed on the computer. MSMQ creates another queue journal every time a new queue is added. This queue journal is used to track the messages removed from a queue.

■ ***Dead letter queues*** are used to store application-generated messages that cannot be delivered or have expired. There are two types of dead letter queues, one for transaction messages and the other for nontransaction messages. These are created when MSMQ is installed. A message is placed in a dead letter queue if the destination queue is unknown, the message exceeds its maximum number of hops, the message time-to-be-delivered expires, the message time-to-reach-queue expires, or the queue quota is reached. A nontransactional message is put in a dead letter queue when it is sent to a transactional queue and the queue properties cannot be accessed when the message is sent. Similarly, a transaction message is put in a transaction dead letter queue if it is sent to a nontransactional queue or if the transaction fails.

■ ***Report queues*** track the progress of messages as they move through the MSMQ enterprise. Report queues receive MSMQ-generated report messages and can be used to send test messages or to track message routes for specific applications.

Queues and computers can be assigned a *Quota* property value to specify the maximum size (in kilobytes) of all messages stored in a queue or on a computer. Messages can no longer be sent to a queue or a computer if its quota has been reached. Systems queues are not included in the quota for a computer. You can see the following private system queues using the MSMQ Explorer:

■ ***admin_queue$***   Used for storing administrative messages

■ ***msmqadminresp$***   Used for storing administrative response messages

■ ***mqis_queue$***   Used for storing MQPing requests

■ ***notify_queue$***   Used for storing notification messages

■ ***order_queue$***   Used for tracking transactional messages that require in-order delivery

A public queue can be assigned a *BasePriority* property value for use in routing the queue's messages over the network. The queue's base priority has no effect on the order of messages in the queue. Rather, messages are sent with a higher priority to the queues that have the highest *BasePriority* after this value is set.

MSMQ Messages

MSMQ handles the delivery and storage of messages and does not concern itself with the content of those messages. MSMQ messages can contain text or any binary information. Typically, messages are strings, arrays of bytes, or numeric data types. Messages can also be persistent COM objects that support the *IDispatch* and *IPersist* (*IPersistStream* or *IPersistStorage*) interfaces. For example, a message can be a Microsoft Office document or an ADO recordset.

When your MSMQ application sends messages to a queue, it can specify express or recoverable delivery. Express messages are much faster to send and use fewer resources, but they are lost if the server is shut down or fails. Recoverable messages use more resources and are much slower to send because they are persisted to disk. However, they are not lost if any computer is shut down or fails.

Messages are stored in memory-mapped files in the Msmq\Storage directory. These files can be on the hard disk of the sending computer, receiving computer, or intermediate MSMQ routing server. A write operation to disk occurs every time a recoverable message is sent. When messages are sent using express delivery, the memory-mapped files are written to disk only when the computer has insufficient resources to store the file in memory. MSMQ allocates 4 MB of space for each message storage file it creates with the MQ extension. An MSMQ server can store about 2 GB of messages, given enough hard disk space. You can tell what a storage file is used for by looking at the character that it is prefixed with. The character *p* indicates that it is used to store recoverable messages; *r* is for express nonrecoverable messages, *j* is for journal messages, and *i* is for indexes. Messages from a queue can be stored in multiple MQ files, and messages from multiple queues can be stored in one MQ file. A single message cannot be stored in multiple .mq files, so a message cannot be larger than 4 MB. The QMLog file stores a log of all message queue processing and is overwritten when it becomes full. The files MQInSeqs.lg1, MQInSeqs.lg2, MQTrans.lg1, and MQTrans.lg2 store the state of receiving ordered messages and active transactions. The LQ1 and LQ2 are written to in an alternating pattern to prevent the loss of data if either file becomes corrupted in a write operation. MSMQ uses the Msmq\Storage\Lqs directory to store text files that describe the properties of local queues.

MSMQ Explorer

You use the MSMQ Explorer to dynamically configure the MSMQ enterprise. An administrator can configure the MSMQ environment from a single point of control using a simple graphic user interface. The MSMQ Explorer is typically used for adding, deleting, locating, and managing queues and for configuring how messages are routed throughout the enterprise. It is also used to assign access rights and to determine who can send or receive messages from a queue using MSMQ's integration with Windows NT security.

The MSMQ Explorer lets you view and modify the properties of the MSMQ enterprise, sites, CNs, computers, and queues. It displays only computers that are independent clients, MSMQ routing servers, BSCs, PSCs, or the PEC. It also displays MSMQ connector servers such as foreign CNs, foreign computers, and foreign queues. It does not display MSMQ dependent clients. You can also use the MSMQ Explorer to configure the auditing of MSMQ events. Such events include changes to the enterprise properties, the receipt of undeliverable (dead letter) messages and journal messages, the creation of a queue, changes to the queue properties, the deletion of a computer, the display of queue permissions, changes to queue permissions, and changes in computer ownership. MSMQ audited events are recorded in the Windows NT security log; you can view them in the Windows NT Event Viewer.

MSMQ ActiveX Control

MSMQ provides an ActiveX control so that you can easily access MSMQ from IIS ASP scripts, MTS, and the large base of applications that support COM. This control provides a simpler interface to the MSMQ API and consists of the following objects:

- *MSMQQuery*
- *MSMQQueueInfos*
- *MSMQQueueInfo*
- *MSMQQueue*
- *MSMQEvent*
- *MSMQMessage*
- *MSMQCoordinatedTransactionDispenser*
- *MSMQTransaction*
- *MSMQTransactionDispenser*
- *MSMQApplication*

You can use these objects for MSMQ management tasks such as creating, locating, opening, closing, and deleting queues; setting and retrieving queue properties; and configuring security access requirements. MSMQ applications that send messages typically use this control for sending messages that request an acknowledgment or a response, sending private messages, and sending messages within internal and external transactions. MSMQ applications that read messages use this control to read messages synchronously or asynchronously, to read messages using cursors, or to peek at messages.

The MSMQ C API is an alternative to the ActiveX control. It has the following functions, some of which we will use in this chapter's case study:

- *MQCreateQueue*
- *MQOpenQueue*
- *MQReceiveMessage*
- *MQSendMessage*
- *MQCloseQueue*
- *MQDeleteQueue*
- *MQSetQueueProperties*
- *MQGetQueueProperties*
- *MQGetQueueSecurity*
- *MQSetQueueSecurity*
- *MQCloseCursor*
- *MQCreateCursor*

- *MQLocateBegin*
- *MQLocateEnd*
- *MQLocateNext*
- *MQFreeMemory*
- *MQFreeSecurityContext*
- *MQGetMachineProperties*
- *MQGetSecurityContext*
- *MQHandleToFormatName*
- *MQInstanceToFormatName*
- *MQPathNameToFormatName*
- *MQBeginTransaction*

Case Study: MSMQ Resource Dispenser for MTS

Chapter Six explained that resource dispensers manage nondurable state on behalf of MTS application components. You saw that the ODBC resource dispenser manages pools of database connections that can be used by the application components. This greatly speeds up database interaction because the application components can use existing open database connections without having to reestablish them each time. Our case study in this chapter builds an MSMQ resource dispenser for MTS to manage open connections to queues that can be used by MTS application components. The case study in Chapter Six also explained how a web site can use MSMQ to queue transaction requests that can be processed later by MTS. Our case study in this chapter provides a simple interface to MSMQ for this purpose.

This MSMQ resource dispenser manages a pool of open connections to queues that can be handed off to MTS application components. It is typically used by an ASP web page that creates an MTS component to open a queue, send a message to the queue, and then close the queue each time the page is accessed. Using a resource dispenser in this scenario can improve performance considerably. Using a Microsoft Visual Basic test driver, our resource dispenser (shown later in this chapter) increased the rate of message sending from 100 per second to 1666 per second when express delivery was set and from 69 per second to 312 per second when recoverable delivery was set. Our resource dispenser also adds another option for sending messages called expresslog. When you use this option, the messages are sent using express delivery but are also written to a text file. You can thus recover the messages manually if the server fails. The performance of the MTS application component using this option was 1000 per second.

The following Visual Basic code shows how to use this resource dispenser:

```
Dim MSMQRd As Object
Dim lval As Long
Dim ltype As Long
Dim context As ObjectContext
Set context = GetObjectContext()
Set MSMQRd = context.CreateInstance("ResDisp.ResDisp.1")
ltype = 1000
MSMQRd.connect ltype, lval
MSMQRd.SendMsg lval, "this is a test sending a transactional message"
MSMQRd.disconnect lval
context.SetComplete
```

You can see that the MSMQ resource dispenser has three methods: *connect*, *SendMsg*, and *disconnect*. The *connect* method has a long *[in]* parameter to specify a queue type and a long *[out]* parameter that contains the connection number assigned to it. This connection number is passed to the *SendMsg* method along with the text of the message to be sent. The *disconnect* method also passes in the number of the connection and notifies the resource dispenser that it can return the resource back to the pool.

If you pass into the connect method a queue type number less than 1000, you get a queue in which messages are sent with recoverable delivery. For example, 100 creates a queue called rd_recoverableq_100. A number greater than 999 but less than 2000 specifies a transactional queue. In this case, the MTS application that uses the resource dispenser must require a transaction. A number greater than 1999 but less than 3000 specifies a queue in which the messages are sent with express delivery. A number greater than 3000 specifies a queue in which messages are sent with express delivery and are also logged to a text file in the Winnt\System32 directory.

Our resource dispenser communicates with MSMQ using the MSMQ C API. While all the code for the resource dispenser is listed below, we will focus here on the methods to send a message and create, open, and close a queue. These are encapsulated in the methods *CreateQ, OpenQ, CloseQ,* and *WriteQ* of a C++ wrapper class named *CRDMSMQueue.*

Creating a Queue

You create a queue using the API function *MQCreateQueue.* This function creates a queue and registers it in MQIS if it is a public queue or registers it on the local computer if it is a private queue. It is defined as follows:

```
HRESULT APIENTRY MQCreateQueue( PSECURITY_DESCRIPTOR
    pSecurityDescriptor, MQQUEUEPROPS * pQueueProps,
    LPWSTR lpwcsFormatName, LPDWORD lpdwFormatNameLength );
```

The *pSecurityDescriptor* parameter is a pointer to a SECURITY_DESCRIPTOR structure that specifies the security information associated with the queue. A NULL pointer indicates that all default values are used. The *pQueueProps* parameter is a pointer to an MQQUEUEPROPS structure that specifies the created queue's properties. The *lpwcsFormatName* out parameter is a pointer to a buffer that will receive the format name of the queue; its length is specified in the *lpdwFormatNameLength* parameter.

Our C++ wrapper class uses a method called *GetPathName* to get the name of the new queue:

```
HRESULT CRDMSMQueue::CreateQ()
{
    HRESULT hr = E_FAIL;
    try
    {

        MQQUEUEPROPS   qprops;
        MQPROPVARIANT  aPropVar[MAX_VAR];
        QUEUEPROPID    aqPropId[MAX_VAR];
        DWORD          cProps;
        DWORD          dwNumChars;
        WCHAR   wcsFormatQ[MAX_FORMAT];

        cProps = 0;

        USES_CONVERSION;
        aqPropId[cProps]         = PROPID_Q_PATHNAME;
        aPropVar[cProps].vt      = VT_LPWSTR;
        aPropVar[cProps].pwszVal = A2W(GetPathName().c_str());
        cProps++;

        aqPropId[cProps]         = PROPID_Q_TYPE;
        aPropVar[cProps].vt      = VT_CLSID;
        aPropVar[cProps].puuid   = &GetGuidQ();
        cProps++;

        aqPropId[cProps]         = PROPID_Q_LABEL;
        aPropVar[cProps].vt      = VT_LPWSTR;
        aPropVar[cProps].pwszVal = L"Resource Dispenser Queue";
        cProps++;

        // Set Transaction queue if required.
        if (GetTransaction()  != NULL)
        {
            aqPropId[cProps]        = PROPID_Q_TRANSACTION;
            aPropVar[cProps].vt     = VT_UI1;
            aPropVar[cProps].bVal   = MQ_TRANSACTIONAL;
            cProps++;
        }

        qprops.cProp    = cProps;
        qprops.aPropID  = aqPropId;
        qprops.aPropVar = aPropVar;
        qprops.aStatus  = 0;
```

```
                dwNumChars = MAX_FORMAT;
                hr = MQCreateQueue(
                        NULL,
                        &qprops,
                        wcsFormatQ,
                        &dwNumChars);

                if (FAILED(hr))
                {
                    if (hr != MQ_ERROR_QUEUE_EXISTS)
                        throw "Cannot create queue";
                }
                else SetFormatQ(W2A(wcsFormatQ));
                hr = S_OK;
            }
            catch(char* str)
            {
                WriteLog(string(str));
            }
            catch(...)
            {
                WriteLog(string("Error in CreateQ"));
            }
            return hr;
    }
```

Opening a Queue

You open a queue using the API function *MQOpenQueue*. This function opens
a queue for sending messages to the queue or for reading its messages. It is
defined as follows:

```
HRESULT APIENTRY MQOpenQueue( LPCWSTR lpwcsFormatName,
    DWORD dwAccess, DWORD dwShareMode,
    LPQUEUEHANDLE phQueue );
```

The *lpwcsFormatName* parameter is a pointer to the format name string
of the queue you want to open. It can be in a public, private, or direct format.
If you are sending a message to the queue, you might want to use the direct
format name because it instructs MSMQ not to use MQIS (for public queues)
or the local computer (for private queues) to get routing information. Instead,
all routing information is derived from the format name, and MSMQ sends the
messages to the queue in a faster single hop. The *dwAccess* parameter specifies how the application will access the queue (for peeking, sending, or receiving). Its value cannot be changed while the queue is open. The *dwShareMode*

parameter specifies how the queue will be shared. If the access parameter is set for sending messages, the default of MQ_DENY_NONE must be used. This allows everyone to use the queue. The value of MQ_DENY_RECEIVE_SHARE limits those who can receive messages from the queue to the process space of the caller. The *phQueue* out parameter contains the queue handle of the open queue.

Our C++ wrapper class always sets the access type to MQ_SEND_ACCESS because our resource dispenser only sends messages to queues.

```
HRESULT CRDMSMQueue::OpenQ()
{
    HRESULT hr = E_FAIL;
    try
    {
        DWORD        cProps;
        QUEUEPROPID  aqPropId[MAX_VAR];
        MQPROPERTYRESTRICTION aPropRestriction[MAX_VAR];
        MQRESTRICTION Restriction;
        MQCOLUMNSET  Column;
        CLSID guidQ = GetGuidQ();

        cProps = 0;
        aPropRestriction[cProps].rel         = PREQ;
        aPropRestriction[cProps].prop        = PROPID_Q_TYPE;
        aPropRestriction[cProps].prval.vt    = VT_CLSID;
        aPropRestriction[cProps].prval.puuid = &guidQ;
        cProps++;
        Restriction.cRes       = cProps;
        Restriction.paPropRes = aPropRestriction;

        cProps = 0;
        aqPropId[cProps] = PROPID_Q_INSTANCE;
        cProps++;
        Column.cCol = cProps;
        Column.aCol = aqPropId;

        DWORD dwAccess;
        if (GetAccessType() == ACCESS_TYPE_WRITE)
            dwAccess = MQ_SEND_ACCESS;
        else dwAccess = MQ_RECEIVE_ACCESS;
        QUEUEHANDLE qhIn;
        USES_CONVERSION;
        hr = MQOpenQueue(
                A2W(GetFormatQ().c_str()),
                dwAccess,
                0,
                &qhIn);
```

```
        if (FAILED(hr))
            throw "Error in OpenQueue";
        SetQHIn(qhIn);

            hr = S_OK;
    }
    catch(char* str)
    {
        WriteLog(string(str));
    }
    catch(...)
    {
        WriteLog(string("Error in OpenQ"));
    }
    return hr;
}
```

Closing a Queue

You close a queue using the API function *MQCloseQueue,* which is defined as follows:

```
HRESULT APIENTRY MQCloseQueue( QUEUEHANDLE hQueue );
```

The *hQueue* parameter is the handle to the queue you want to close. Any open cursors created for the queue are also closed when this function is called.

Our C++ wrapper class gets the handle of the open queue using a helper function named *GetQH:*

```
HRESULT CRDMSMQueue::CloseQ()
{
    HRESULT hr = E_FAIL;
    try
    {
        hr = MQCloseQueue(GetQH());
        if (FAILED(hr))
            throw "Error in MQCloseQueue";

        hr = S_OK;
    }
    catch(char* str)
    {
        WriteLog(string(str));
    }
    catch(...)
    {
        WriteLog(string("Error in CloseQ"));
    }
    return hr;
}
```

Writing to a Queue

You send messages to a queue using the API function *MQSendMessage*, which is defined as follows:

```
HRESULT APIENTRY MQSendMessage( QUEUEHANDLE hDestinationQueue,
    MQMSGPROPS * pMessageProps, ITransaction * pTransaction );
```

The *hDestinationQueue* parameter is the handle to the queue in which you want to send the message. The *pMessageProps* is a pointer to an MQMSGPROPS structure that describes the message being sent. The *pTransaction* parameter is a pointer to a transaction object, a constant, or a NULL. A NULL indicates that the message is not sent as part of a transaction. A transaction object can be obtained internally from MSMQ by calling the *MQBeginTransaction* API method, or externally from the MS DTC. The constant MQ_NO_TRANSACTION specifies that the call is not part of a transaction. MQ_MTS_TRANSACTION specifies that the current MTS transaction is used to send the message. The constant MQ_SINGLE_MESSAGE is used to send a single message as a transaction to a transaction queue. MQ_XA_TRANSACTION specifies that the call is part of an externally coordinated, XA-compliant transaction.

Our C++ wrapper class checks whether the messages are to be sent with recoverable delivery; if so, it sets this property in the MQMSGPROPS structure. Otherwise, it sends messages with the default of express delivery. The wrapper class also writes the message out to a text file if a queue type of expresslog is used. If a transaction is required, only the MQ_MTS_TRANSACTION value is used:

```
HRESULT CRDMSMQueue::WriteQ(string strData)
{
    HRESULT hr = E_FAIL;
    try
    {

        DWORD           cProps;
        MQMSGPROPS      msgprops;
        MQPROPVARIANT   aPropVar[MAX_VAR];
        MSGPROPID       amPropId[MAX_VAR];
        WCHAR           wcsMsgLabel[MQ_MAX_MSG_LABEL_LEN];

        swprintf(wcsMsgLabel, L"Message from %S",
            GetMachineName().c_str());
        cProps = 0;
        USES_CONVERSION;
        amPropId[cProps]            = PROPID_M_BODY;
        aPropVar[cProps].vt         = VT_UI1 | VT_VECTOR;
        aPropVar[cProps].caub.cElems = strlen(strData.c_str());
```

```
        aPropVar[cProps].caub.pElems =
            (unsigned char*) strData.c_str();
        cProps++;

        amPropId[cProps]            = PROPID_M_LABEL;
        aPropVar[cProps].vt         = VT_LPWSTR;
        aPropVar[cProps].pwszVal    = wcsMsgLabel;
        cProps++;

        if (GetResTypeID() <= MAX_RECOVERABLEQ_RESTYPEID)
        {
            // Set recoverable delivery.
            amPropId[cProps]            = PROPID_M_DELIVERY;
            aPropVar[cProps].vt         = VT_UI1;
            aPropVar[cProps].bVal       = MQMSG_DELIVERY_RECOVERABLE;
            cProps++;
        }
        else if (GetResTypeID() >= MIN_EXPRESSLOGQ_RESTYPEID)
        {
            WriteLog(strData);
        }

        msgprops.cProp    = cProps;
        msgprops.aPropID  = amPropId;
        msgprops.aPropVar = aPropVar;
        msgprops.aStatus  = 0;

        hr = MQSendMessage(
                GetQH(),
                &msgprops,
                GetTransaction());
        if (FAILED(hr))
            throw "Error in sending message";

        hr = S_OK;
    }
    catch(char* str)
    {
        WriteLog(string(str));
    }
    catch(...)
    {
        WriteLog(string("Error in WriteQ"));
    }
    return hr;
}
```

MSMQ Resource Dispenser Code

The code for the MSMQ resource dispenser follows. You must install the MTS SDK to get the required header files and directories.

RDMSMQueue.h

```
#define MAX_VAR        20
#define MAX_FORMAT     100
#define MAX_BUFFER     20500
#define MAX_PATHLEN    1000
#define TIMEOUT     60
#define TIMEOUTLONG    5000
#include <comdef.h>
#include <map>
#include <string>
#include <mq.h>
#include <iostream>

using namespace std ;

#define ACCESS_TYPE_WRITE    1

#define MAX_RECOVERABLEQ_RESTYPEID    999
#define MIN_TRANSACTIONQ_RESTYPEID    1000
#define MAX_TRANSACTIONQ_RESTYPEID    1999
#define MIN_EXPRESSQ_RESTYPEID        2000
#define MAX_EXPRESSQ_RESTYPEID        2999
#define MIN_EXPRESSLOGQ_RESTYPEID     3000

class CRDMSMQueue
{
public:
    CRDMSMQueue(string strComputer, string strQName, int AccessType,
        BOOL bTrans);
    ~CRDMSMQueue();

private:
    CRDMSMQueue& operator=(const CRDMSMQueue&
        CRDMSMQueue); // This has not been implemented.
    CRDMSMQueue(CRDMSMQueue&
        CRDMSMQueue); // This has not been implemented.
    CRDMSMQueue(); // This has not been implemented.
    static CLSID m_guidQ;
    string m_strMachineName;
    string m_strFormatQ;
```

SEVEN: Microsoft Message Queuing

```
        string m_strPathName;
        string m_strFileName;
        QUEUEHANDLE    m_qh;
        int m_nAccessType;
        ITransaction * m_pTransaction;
        long m_lResTypeID;
        HANDLE m_hMutex;

protected:
        CLSID GetGuidQ();
        string GetMachineName();
        string GetFormatQ();
        ITransaction * GetTransaction();
        int GetAccessType();
        QUEUEHANDLE GetQH();

        void SetMachineName(string strMachineName);
        void SetPathName(string strPathName);
        void SetFormatQ(string strFormatQ);
        void SetFileName(string strFileName);
        void SetQHIn(QUEUEHANDLE qhIn);
        void SetTransaction(ITransaction * pTransaction);

public:
        void SetResTypeID(long lResTypeID);
        long GetResTypeID();
        string GetPathName();
        string GetFileName();

        HRESULT WriteLog(string strText);
        HRESULT SetAccessType(int ntype);
        HRESULT DeleteQ();
        HRESULT CreateQ();
        HRESULT CloseQ();
        HRESULT OpenQ();
        HRESULT ReadQ(string* pstrdata);
        HRESULT WriteQ(string strData);
};
```

RDMSMQueue.cpp

```
#include "stdafx.h"
#include "RDMSMQueue.h"
#include <time.h>

CLSID CRDMSMQueue::m_guidQ = { 0x6d737dc0, 0x2538, 0x11d1,
    { 0x9c, 0x94, 0x2a, 0xba, 0xb8, 0x0, 0x0, 0x0 } };
```

(continued)

```
/////////////////////////////////////////////////////////////////////
// CRDMSMQueue

void CRDMSMQueue::SetMachineName(string strMachineName)
{
    if ( strMachineName == "" )
    {
        DWORD dwNumChars = MAX_COMPUTERNAME_LENGTH + 1;
        char chMachineName[MAX_COMPUTERNAME_LENGTH + 1];
        GetComputerName(chMachineName, &dwNumChars);
        m_strMachineName = chMachineName;
    }
    else m_strMachineName = strMachineName;
};

void CRDMSMQueue::SetPathName(string strPathName)
{
    m_strPathName = GetMachineName().c_str() + string("\\") +
        strPathName;
};

void CRDMSMQueue::SetFileName(string strFileName)
{
    m_strFileName = strFileName + string(".txt");
};

void CRDMSMQueue::SetFormatQ(string strFormatQ)
{
    m_strFormatQ = strFormatQ;
};

void CRDMSMQueue::SetQHIn(QUEUEHANDLE qhIn)
{
    m_qh = qhIn;
};

void CRDMSMQueue::SetTransaction(ITransaction * pTransaction)
{
    m_pTransaction = pTransaction;
};

void CRDMSMQueue::SetResTypeID(long lResTypeID)
{
    m_lResTypeID = lResTypeID;
};
```

```
int CRDMSMQueue::GetAccessType()
{
    return m_nAccessType;
}
CLSID CRDMSMQueue::GetGuidQ()
{
    return m_guidQ;
};

long CRDMSMQueue::GetResTypeID()
{
    return m_lResTypeID;
};

QUEUEHANDLE CRDMSMQueue::GetQH()
{
    return m_qh;
};

string CRDMSMQueue::GetMachineName()
{
    return m_strMachineName;
};

string CRDMSMQueue::GetPathName()
{
    return m_strPathName;
};

string CRDMSMQueue::GetFileName()
{
    return m_strFileName;
};


ITransaction * CRDMSMQueue::GetTransaction()
{
    return m_pTransaction;
};

string CRDMSMQueue::GetFormatQ()
{

    HRESULT hr = E_FAIL;
    try
    {
```

(continued)

273

```
            if (m_strFormatQ.length() == 0)
            {
                USES_CONVERSION;
                WCHAR  wcsFormatQ[MAX_FORMAT];
                DWORD dwNumChars = MAX_COMPUTERNAME_LENGTH + 1;
                dwNumChars = MAX_FORMAT;
                hr = MQPathNameToFormatName(
                            A2W(GetPathName().c_str()),
                            wcsFormatQ,
                            &dwNumChars);
                if (FAILED(hr))
                {
                    throw "Cannot retrieve format name";
                }
                else m_strFormatQ = W2A(wcsFormatQ);

            }
            hr = S_OK;
        }
        catch(char* str)
        {
            WriteLog(string(str));
        }
        catch(...)
        {
            WriteLog(string("Error in GetFormatQ"));
        }
        return m_strFormatQ;
};

CRDMSMQueue::CRDMSMQueue(string strComputer, string strQName,
    int AccessType, BOOL bTrans)
{

    SetMachineName(strComputer);
    SetFileName(strQName);
    SetPathName(strQName);
    SetResTypeID(MIN_EXPRESSQ_RESTYPEID);
    SetAccessType(AccessType);
    m_hMutex = CreateMutex(NULL, false, GetFileName().c_str());
    if (bTrans) SetTransaction(MQ_MTS_TRANSACTION);
    else SetTransaction(NULL);
}

CRDMSMQueue::~CRDMSMQueue()
{
    if (m_hMutex)
    CloseHandle(m_hMutex);
}
```

```
HRESULT CRDMSMQueue::SetAccessType(int ntype)
{
    m_nAccessType = ntype;
    return S_OK;
}

HRESULT CRDMSMQueue::WriteQ(string strData)
{
    HRESULT hr = E_FAIL;
    try
    {

        DWORD           cProps;
        MQMSGPROPS      msgprops;
        MQPROPVARIANT   aPropVar[MAX_VAR];
        MSGPROPID       amPropId[MAX_VAR];
        WCHAR           wcsMsgLabel[MQ_MAX_MSG_LABEL_LEN];

        swprintf(wcsMsgLabel, L"Message from %S",
            GetMachineName().c_str());
        cProps = 0;
        USES_CONVERSION;
        amPropId[cProps]            = PROPID_M_BODY;
        aPropVar[cProps].vt         = VT_UI1 | VT_VECTOR;
        aPropVar[cProps].caub.cElems = strlen(strData.c_str());
        aPropVar[cProps].caub.pElems =
            (unsigned char*) strData.c_str();
        cProps++;

        amPropId[cProps]            = PROPID_M_LABEL;
        aPropVar[cProps].vt         = VT_LPWSTR;
        aPropVar[cProps].pwszVal    = wcsMsgLabel;
        cProps++;

        if (GetResTypeID() <= MAX_RECOVERABLEQ_RESTYPEID)
        {
            // Set recoverable delivery.
            amPropId[cProps]            = PROPID_M_DELIVERY;
            aPropVar[cProps].vt         = VT_UI1;
            aPropVar[cProps].bVal       = MQMSG_DELIVERY_RECOVERABLE;
            cProps++;
        }
        else if (GetResTypeID() >= MIN_EXPRESSLOGQ_RESTYPEID)
        {
            WriteLog(strData);
        }

        msgprops.cProp      = cProps;
        msgprops.aPropID    = amPropId;
```

(continued)

```
        msgprops.aPropVar = aPropVar;
        msgprops.aStatus  = 0;

        hr = MQSendMessage(
                 GetQH(),
                 &msgprops,
                 GetTransaction());
       if (FAILED(hr))
           throw "Error in sending message";

        hr = S_OK;
    }
    catch(char* str)
    {
        WriteLog(string(str));
    }
    catch(...)
    {
        WriteLog(string("Error in WriteQ"));
    }
    return hr;
}

HRESULT CRDMSMQueue::ReadQ(string* pstrdata)
{
    HRESULT hr = E_FAIL;
    try
    {
        DWORD           cProps;
        MQMSGPROPS      msgprops;
        MQPROPVARIANT   aPropVar[MAX_VAR];
        MSGPROPID       amPropId[MAX_VAR];
        WCHAR           wcsMsgLabel[MQ_MAX_MSG_LABEL_LEN];
        CHAR            chbuffer[MAX_BUFFER];

        cProps = 0;
        amPropId[cProps]            = PROPID_M_BODY;
        aPropVar[cProps].vt         = VT_UI1 | VT_VECTOR;
        aPropVar[cProps].caub.cElems = sizeof(chbuffer);
        aPropVar[cProps].caub.pElems = (unsigned char *)chbuffer;
        cProps++;

        amPropId[cProps]            = PROPID_M_LABEL;
        aPropVar[cProps].vt         = VT_LPWSTR;
        aPropVar[cProps].pwszVal    = wcsMsgLabel;
        cProps++;

        amPropId[cProps]            = PROPID_M_LABEL_LEN;
        aPropVar[cProps].vt         = VT_UI4;
```

```
            aPropVar[cProps].ulVal    = MQ_MAX_MSG_LABEL_LEN;
            cProps++;

            msgprops.cProp    = cProps;
            msgprops.aPropID  = amPropId;
            msgprops.aPropVar = aPropVar;
            msgprops.aStatus  = 0;

            hr = MQReceiveMessage(
                    GetQH(),
                    INFINITE,
                    MQ_ACTION_RECEIVE,
                    &msgprops,
                    NULL,
                    NULL,
                    NULL,
                    GetTransaction());

            if (!FAILED(hr))
            {
                *pstrdata = string(chbuffer);
            }
            else if (hr != MQ_ERROR_IO_TIMEOUT)
                throw "Error in Receive message";

            hr = S_OK;
        }
        catch(char* str)
        {
            WriteLog(string(str));
        }
        catch(...)
        {
            WriteLog(string("Error in ReadQ"));
        }
        return hr;

}

HRESULT CRDMSMQueue::OpenQ()
{
    HRESULT hr = E_FAIL;
    try
    {
        DWORD          cProps;
        QUEUEPROPID    aqPropId[MAX_VAR];
        MQPROPERTYRESTRICTION aPropRestriction[MAX_VAR];
        MQRESTRICTION Restriction;
```

(continued)

277

```
            MQCOLUMNSET   Column;
            CLSID guidQ = GetGuidQ();

            cProps = 0;
            aPropRestriction[cProps].rel          = PREQ;
            aPropRestriction[cProps].prop         = PROPID_Q_TYPE;
            aPropRestriction[cProps].prval.vt     = VT_CLSID;
            aPropRestriction[cProps].prval.puuid = &guidQ;
            cProps++;
            Restriction.cRes       = cProps;
            Restriction.paPropRes = aPropRestriction;

            cProps = 0;
            aqPropId[cProps] = PROPID_Q_INSTANCE;
            cProps++;
            Column.cCol = cProps;
            Column.aCol = aqPropId;

            DWORD dwAccess;
            if (GetAccessType() == ACCESS_TYPE_WRITE)
                dwAccess = MQ_SEND_ACCESS;
            else dwAccess = MQ_RECEIVE_ACCESS;
            QUEUEHANDLE qhIn;
            USES_CONVERSION;
            hr = MQOpenQueue(
                    A2W(GetFormatQ().c_str()),
                    dwAccess,
                    0,
                    &qhIn);

            if (FAILED(hr))
                throw "Error in OpenQueue";
            SetQHIn(qhIn);

                hr = S_OK;
    }
    catch(char* str)
    {
        WriteLog(string(str));
    }
    catch(...)
    {
        WriteLog(string("Error in OpenQ"));
    }
    return hr;
}
```

```
HRESULT CRDMSMQueue::CloseQ()
{
    HRESULT hr = E_FAIL;
    try
    {
        hr = MQCloseQueue(GetQH());
        if (FAILED(hr))
            throw "Error in MQCloseQueue";

        hr = S_OK;
    }
    catch(char* str)
    {
        WriteLog(string(str));
    }
    catch(...)
    {
        WriteLog(string("Error in CloseQ"));
    }
    return hr;
}

HRESULT CRDMSMQueue::CreateQ()
{
    HRESULT hr = E_FAIL;
    try
    {

        MQQUEUEPROPS    qprops;
        MQPROPVARIANT   aPropVar[MAX_VAR];
        QUEUEPROPID     aqPropId[MAX_VAR];
        DWORD           cProps;
        DWORD           dwNumChars;
        WCHAR   wcsFormatQ[MAX_FORMAT];

        cProps = 0;

        USES_CONVERSION;
        aqPropId[cProps]         = PROPID_Q_PATHNAME;
        aPropVar[cProps].vt      = VT_LPWSTR;
        aPropVar[cProps].pwszVal = A2W(GetPathName().c_str());
        cProps++;

        aqPropId[cProps]         = PROPID_Q_TYPE;
        aPropVar[cProps].vt      = VT_CLSID;
        aPropVar[cProps].puuid   = &GetGuidQ();
        cProps++;
```

(continued)

```
        aqPropId[cProps]        = PROPID_Q_LABEL;
        aPropVar[cProps].vt     = VT_LPWSTR;
        aPropVar[cProps].pwszVal = L"Resource Dispenser Queue";
        cProps++;

        // Set Transaction queue if required.
        if (GetTransaction()  != NULL)
        {
            aqPropId[cProps]        = PROPID_Q_TRANSACTION;
            aPropVar[cProps].vt     = VT_UI1;
            aPropVar[cProps].bVal    = MQ_TRANSACTIONAL;
            cProps++;
        }

        qprops.cProp    = cProps;
        qprops.aPropID  = aqPropId;
        qprops.aPropVar = aPropVar;
        qprops.aStatus  = 0;

        dwNumChars = MAX_FORMAT;
        hr = MQCreateQueue(
                NULL,
                &qprops,
                wcsFormatQ,
                &dwNumChars);

        if (FAILED(hr))
        {
            if (hr != MQ_ERROR_QUEUE_EXISTS)
                throw "Cannot create queue";
        }
        else SetFormatQ(W2A(wcsFormatQ));
        hr = S_OK;
    }
    catch(char* str)
    {
        WriteLog(string(str));
    }
    catch(...)
    {
        WriteLog(string("Error in CreateQ"));
    }
    return hr;
}
```

```
HRESULT CRDMSMQueue::DeleteQ()
{

    HRESULT hr = E_FAIL;
    try
    {

        USES_CONVERSION;
        hr = MQDeleteQueue(A2W(GetFormatQ().c_str()));
        if (FAILED(hr))
            throw "Cannot delete queue";

        hr = S_OK;
    }
    catch(char* str)
    {
        WriteLog(string(str));
    }
    catch(...)
    {
        WriteLog(string("Error in DeleteQ"));
    }
    return hr;
};

HRESULT CRDMSMQueue::WriteLog(string strText)
{

    if (!m_hMutex)
        return E_FAIL;

    HRESULT hr = E_FAIL;
    try
    {

        WaitForSingleObject(m_hMutex, INFINITE);

        DWORD dwBytesWritten;
        HANDLE hFile;
          hFile = CreateFile(GetFileName().c_str(),GENERIC_WRITE,
              FILE_SHARE_READ, NULL,
              OPEN_ALWAYS, FILE_ATTRIBUTE_NORMAL, NULL);

        if (hFile == INVALID_HANDLE_VALUE) throw "Invalid file handle";
```

(continued)

```
            DWORD dw = SetFilePointer(hFile, 0, NULL, FILE_END);
            char szDate[32];
            char szTime[32];
            char szText[128];
            wsprintf(szText, "\r\n %s %s - %d[~]", _strdate(szDate),
                _strtime(szTime), GetCurrentThreadId());
            strText = string(szText) + strText;
            BOOL bResult = WriteFile(hFile, strText.c_str(),
                strlen(strText.c_str()), &dwBytesWritten, NULL);
            if (bResult == FALSE) throw "Error in writing to file";

            bResult = CloseHandle(hFile);
            if (bResult == FALSE) throw "Error in closing file handle";
            hr = S_OK;
        }
    catch(...)
    {
        // handle error
    }
    ReleaseMutex(m_hMutex);
    return hr;
}
```

ResDisp.h

```
// ResDisp.h : Declaration of the CResDisp

#ifndef __RESDISP_H_
#define __RESDISP_H_
#include "mtxdm.h"
#include "txdtc.h"
#include "resource.h"       // main symbols
#include "stdafx.h"
interface IDispenserDriver;

#include <map>
#include <set>
#include <list>
using namespace std;

#define SafeRelease(pUnk) {if (pUnk){pUnk -> Release();pUnk = NULL; }}

typedef set<long> ConnectionSet;
```

```
/////////////////////////////////////////////////////////////////////
// CResDisp
class ATL_NO_VTABLE CResDisp :
    public IDispenserDriver,
    public CComObjectRootEx<CComMultiThreadModel>,
    public CComCoClass<CResDisp, &CLSID_ResDisp>,
    public IDispatchImpl<IResDisp, &IID_IResDisp, &LIBID_RDLib>
{

private:
    IHolder * m_pHolder;
    IDispenserManager * m_pDispMan;

public:
    CResDisp()
    {
        m_bLog = FALSE;
        m_pFreeThreadedMarshaler = NULL;
    }

DECLARE_CLASSFACTORY_SINGLETON(CResDisp);
DECLARE_PROTECT_FINAL_CONSTRUCT();

DECLARE_REGISTRY_RESOURCEID(IDR_RESDISP)
DECLARE_GET_CONTROLLING_UNKNOWN()

BEGIN_COM_MAP(CResDisp)
    COM_INTERFACE_ENTRY(IResDisp)
    COM_INTERFACE_ENTRY(IDispatch)
    COM_INTERFACE_ENTRY(IDispenserDriver)
    COM_INTERFACE_ENTRY_AGGREGATE(IID_IMarshal,
        m_pFreeThreadedMarshaler)
END_COM_MAP()

    HRESULT FinalConstruct();
    HRESULT GetExportObject(long ResId, ITransaction * pTransaction,
        ITransactionExport **ppExport);

    void FinalRelease();

// IDispenserDriver
    STDMETHOD(CreateResource)(/*[in]*/  const RESTYPID ResTypId,
                              /*[out]*/ RESID* pResId,
                              /*[out]*/
                                      TIMEINSECS* pSecsFreeBeforeDestroy);
```

(continued)

```
        STDMETHOD(RateResource)(/*[in]*/   const RESTYPID ResTypId,
                                /*[in]*/   const RESID ResId,
                                /*[in]*/
                                const BOOL fRequiresTransactionEnlistment,
                                /*[out]*/ RESOURCERATING* pRating);

        STDMETHOD(EnlistResource)(/*[in]*/   const RESID ResId,
                                  /*[in]*/   const TRANSID TransId);
        STDMETHOD(ResetResource)(/*[in]*/   const RESID ResId);
        STDMETHOD(DestroyResource)(/*[in]*/
            const RESID ResId); // numeric resource id
        STDMETHOD(DestroyResourceS)(/*[in]*/
            constSRESID ResId); // string resource id

        ConnectionSet m_set;

        IUnknown *  m_pFreeThreadedMarshaler;
        BOOL m_bLog;
        string m_strComputerName;
// IResDisp
public:
        STDMETHOD(SetComputerName)(BSTR bstrComputerName);
        STDMETHOD(Disconnect)(/*[in]*/ long Connection);
        STDMETHOD(Connect)(/*[in]*/ long ResTypId,
                           /*[out]*/ long *hConnection);
        STDMETHOD(SendMsg)(/*[in]*/ long hConnection,
                           /*[in]*/ BSTR bstrMessage);

};

#endif //__RESDISP_H_
```

ResDisp.cpp

```
// ResDisp.cpp : Implementation of CResDisp
#include "stdafx.h"
#include "mtxdm.h"
#include "RD.h"
#include "ResDisp.h"
#include "RDMSMQueue.h"


/////////////////////////////////////////////////////////////////////
// CResDisp

STDMETHODIMP CResDisp::SendMsg(long hConnection, BSTR bstrMessage)
{
    // TODO: Add your implementation code here.
    CRDMSMQueue* pSing = NULL;
    pSing = (CRDMSMQueue*) hConnection;
```

```
        string strdata = string(_bstr_t(bstrMessage));
        pSing->WriteQ(strdata);
        return S_OK;
}

STDMETHODIMP CResDisp::Connect(long ResTypId, long * hConnection)
{
    // TODO: Add your implementation code here.
    if (m_pDispMan)
    {
        if (!m_pHolder)
        {
            _ASSERTE(0);
            return E_INVALIDARG;
        }
    }

    HRESULT hr;
    if (m_pDispMan)
    {
        *hConnection = NULL;
        hr = m_pHolder -> AllocResource((RESID)ResTypId,
            (RESID *)hConnection);
        if (FAILED(hr))
        {
            AtlTrace(_T("AllocResource failed! Error code %x\n"), hr);
        }
    }
    else  // not running under MTS, we must create our own resource
    {
        TIMEINSECS timeout;
        hr = CreateResource((RESID)ResTypId,
            (RESID *)hConnection,&timeout);
    }

    if (m_bLog)
    {
        CRDMSMQueue * pSing = NULL;
        pSing = (CRDMSMQueue *)(*m_set.find((RESID)*hConnection));
        pSing->WriteLog(string("Connect Called"));
    }
    return hr;
}

STDMETHODIMP CResDisp::Disconnect(long Connection)
{
    // TODO: Add your implementation code here.
```

(continued)

285

```
if (m_bLog)
{
    CRDMSMQueue * pSing = NULL;
    pSing = (CRDMSMQueue *)(*m_set.find(Connection));
    pSing->WriteLog(string("Disconnect Called"));
}
if (m_pDispMan)
{
    if (!m_pHolder)
    {
        _ASSERTE(0);
        return E_INVALIDARG;
    }
}

HRESULT hr;
if (m_pDispMan)
{
    hr = m_pHolder -> FreeResource(Connection);
}
else
{
    hr = DestroyResource(Connection);
}

_ASSERTE(hr == S_OK);
return hr;
}


STDMETHODIMP CResDisp::SetComputerName(BSTR bstrComputerName)
{
    // TODO: Add your implementation code here.
    m_strComputerName = string(_bstr_t(bstrComputerName));
    return S_OK;
}
```

RDdispdrv.cpp

```
// RDdispdrv.cpp : implementation of IDispenserDriver

#include "stdafx.h"
#include "RD.h"
#include "txcoord.h"
#include "ResDisp.h"
```

```
#include "txdtc.h"
#include "xolehlp.h"
#include "RDMSMQueue.h"

STDMETHODIMP CResDisp::CreateResource
(
    /*[in]*/  const RESTYPID ResTypId,
    /*[out]*/ RESID* pResId,
    /*[out]*/ TIMEINSECS* pSecsFreeBeforeDestroy
)
{

    ATLTRACE(_T("Creating ResDisp Resource\n"));
    CComBSTR sAppName = L"ResDisp";
    long lHandle;
    CRDMSMQueue * pSing;

    char buf[100];
    _itoa(ResTypId, buf, 10);
    string strQ(buf);

    if (ResTypId <= MAX_RECOVERABLEQ_RESTYPEID)
    {
        strQ = "RD_RecoverableQ_" + strQ;
        pSing = new CRDMSMQueue(m_strComputerName, strQ, 1, FALSE);
    }
    if (ResTypId >= MIN_TRANSACTIONQ_RESTYPEID &&
        ResTypId <= MAX_TRANSACTIONQ_RESTYPEID)
    {
        strQ = "RD_TransactionQ_" + strQ;
        pSing = new CRDMSMQueue(m_strComputerName, strQ, 1, TRUE );
    }
    if (ResTypId >= MIN_EXPRESSQ_RESTYPEID &&
        ResTypId <= MAX_EXPRESSQ_RESTYPEID)
    {
        strQ = "RD_ExpressQ_" + strQ;
        pSing = new CRDMSMQueue(m_strComputerName, strQ, 1, FALSE);
    }
    if (ResTypId >= MIN_EXPRESSLOGQ_RESTYPEID)
    {
        strQ = "RD_ExpressLogQ_" + strQ;
        pSing = new CRDMSMQueue(m_strComputerName, strQ, 1, FALSE);
    }
```

(continued)

```
    pSing->SetResTypeID(ResTypId);
    pSing->CreateQ();
    pSing->OpenQ();

    if (m_bLog) pSing->WriteLog(string("CreateResource Called"));

    lHandle =  (long) pSing;
    *pResId = (RESID)lHandle;

    *pSecsFreeBeforeDestroy = 180;

    m_set.insert(lHandle);
    return S_OK;
}

STDMETHODIMP CResDisp::RateResource
(
    /*[in]*/   const RESTYPID ResTypId,
    /*[in]*/   const RESID ResId,
    /*[in]*/   const BOOL fRequiresTransactionEnlistment,
    /*[out]*/  RESOURCERATING* pRating
)
{
    ATLTRACE(_T("Rating resource\n"));
    CRDMSMQueue * pSing = NULL;
    pSing = (CRDMSMQueue *)(*m_set.find(ResId));

    if (m_bLog) pSing->WriteLog(string("RateResource Called"));

    if (ResTypId == pSing->GetResTypeID())
    {
        if (fRequiresTransactionEnlistment == FALSE)
        {
            *pRating = 100;
        }
        else
        {
            *pRating = 50;
        }
    }
    else *pRating = 0;
    return S_OK;
}
```

```
STDMETHODIMP  CResDisp::EnlistResource
(
    /*[in]*/   const RESID ResId,
    /*[in]*/   const TRANSID TransId
)
{
    if (m_bLog)
    {
        CRDMSMQueue * pSing = NULL;
        pSing = (CRDMSMQueue *)(*m_set.find(ResId));
        char buf[100];
        _itoa(TransId, buf,    10);
        pSing->WriteLog(string("EnlistResource Called - ") +
            string(buf));
    }
    return S_OK;
}


STDMETHODIMP  CResDisp::ResetResource
(
    /*[in]*/   const RESID ResId
)
{
    if (m_bLog)
    {
        CRDMSMQueue * pSing = NULL;
        pSing = (CRDMSMQueue *)(*m_set.find(ResId));
        pSing->WriteLog(string("ResetResource Called"));
    }
    return S_OK;

}


STDMETHODIMP  CResDisp::DestroyResource
(
    /*[in]*/   const RESID ResId
)
{

    ATLTRACE(_T("Destroying a resource\n"));
    CRDMSMQueue * pSing = NULL;
    pSing = (CRDMSMQueue *)(*m_set.find(ResId));
    if (m_bLog) pSing->WriteLog(string("DestroyResource Called"));
    pSing->CloseQ();
```

(continued)

```
    delete pSing;
    HRESULT hr = S_OK;

    m_set.erase(ResId);
    _ASSERTE(hr == S_OK);
    return hr;
}

STDMETHODIMP CResDisp::DestroyResourceS
(
    /*[in]*/  constSRESID ResId
)
{
    return E_NOTIMPL;
}

HRESULT CResDisp::FinalConstruct()
{
    HRESULT hr;

    hr = GetDispenserManager(&m_pDispMan);
    if (SUCCEEDED(hr))
    {
        IDispenserDriver * pDriver;
        hr = GetUnknown()->QueryInterface(IID_IDispenserDriver,
            (void **)&pDriver);
        _ASSERTE(hr == S_OK);
        hr = m_pDispMan -> RegisterDispenser(pDriver,
            L"ResDisp", &m_pHolder);
        _ASSERTE(hr == S_OK);

    }


    hr = CoCreateFreeThreadedMarshaler(GetUnknown(),
        &m_pFreeThreadedMarshaler);
    _ASSERTE(hr == S_OK);

    return hr;
}

void CResDisp::FinalRelease()
{

    ATLTRACE(_T("\nCResDisp::FinalRelease()\n"));
    SafeRelease(m_pDispMan);
    SafeRelease(m_pHolder);
    SafeRelease(m_pFreeThreadedMarshaler);
}
```

```
HRESULT CResDisp::GetExportObject(long ResId,
    ITransaction * pTransaction, ITransactionExport **ppExport)
{
    if (m_bLog)
    {
        CRDMSMQueue * pSing = NULL;
        pSing = (CRDMSMQueue *)(*m_set.find(ResId));
        pSing->WriteLog(string("GetExportObject"));
    }
    return E_NOTIMPL;

}
```

RD.idl

```
// RD.idl : IDL source for RD.dll
//

// This file will be processed by the MIDL tool to
// produce the type library (RD.tlb) and marshaling code.

import "oaidl.idl";
import "ocidl.idl";

    [
        object,
        uuid(B63366AE-B799-11D1-9554-00C04FC26B9D),
        dual,
        helpstring("IResDisp Interface"),
        pointer_default(unique)
    ]
    interface IResDisp : IDispatch
    {
        [id(1), helpstring("method SendMsg")]
            HRESULT SendMsg([in] long hConnection,
            [in] BSTR bstrMessage);
        [id(2), helpstring("method Connect")]
            HRESULT Connect([in] long ResTypId,
            [out] long *hConnection);
        [id(3), helpstring("method Disconnect")]
            HRESULT Disconnect([in] long Connection);
        [id(4), helpstring("method SetComputerName")]
            HRESULT SetComputerName(BSTR bstrComputerName);
    };
[
    uuid(B633669D-B799-11D1-9554-00C04FC26B9D),
    version(1.0),
    helpstring("RD 1.0 Type Library")
]
```

(continued)

```
library RDLib
{
    importlib("stdole32.tlb");
    importlib("stdole2.tlb");

    [
        uuid(B63366AF-B799-11D1-9554-00C04FC26B9D),
        helpstring("ResDisp Class")
    ]
    coclass ResDisp
    {
        [default] interface IResDisp;
    };
};
```

RDdispdrv.cpp

```cpp
// RDdispdrv.cpp : implementation of IDispenserDriver

#include "stdafx.h"
#include "RD.h"
#include "txcoord.h"
#include "ResDisp.h"
#include "txdtc.h"
#include "xolehlp.h"
#include "RDMSMQueue.h"

STDMETHODIMP CResDisp::CreateResource
(
    /*[in]*/  const RESTYPID ResTypId,
    /*[out]*/ RESID* pResId,
    /*[out]*/ TIMEINSECS* pSecsFreeBeforeDestroy
)
{

    ATLTRACE(_T("Creating ResDisp Resource\n"));
    CComBSTR sAppName = L"ResDisp";
    long lHandle;
    CRDMSMQueue * pSing;

    char buf[100];
    _itoa(ResTypId, buf, 10);
    string strQ(buf);

    if (ResTypId <= MAX_RECOVERABLEQ_RESTYPEID)
    {
        strQ = "RD_RecoverableQ_" + strQ;
        pSing = new CRDMSMQueue(m_strComputerName, strQ, 1, FALSE);
    }
```

```
            if (ResTypId >= MIN_TRANSACTIONQ_RESTYPEID &&
                ResTypId <= MAX_TRANSACTIONQ_RESTYPEID)
            {
                strQ = "RD_TransactionQ_" + strQ;
                pSing = new CRDMSMQueue(m_strComputerName, strQ, 1, TRUE );
            }
            if (ResTypId >= MIN_EXPRESSQ_RESTYPEID &&
                ResTypId <= MAX_EXPRESSQ_RESTYPEID)
            {
                strQ = "RD_ExpressQ_" + strQ;
                pSing = new CRDMSMQueue(m_strComputerName, strQ, 1, FALSE);
            }
            if (ResTypId >= MIN_EXPRESSLOGQ_RESTYPEID)
            {
                strQ = "RD_ExpressLogQ_" + strQ;
                pSing = new CRDMSMQueue(m_strComputerName, strQ, 1, FALSE);
            }

            pSing->SetResTypeID(ResTypId);
            pSing->CreateQ();
            pSing->OpenQ();

            if (m_bLog) pSing->WriteLog(string("CreateResource Called"));

            lHandle =  (long) pSing;
            *pResId = (RESID)lHandle;

            *pSecsFreeBeforeDestroy = 180;

            m_set.insert(lHandle);
            return S_OK;
}

STDMETHODIMP CResDisp::RateResource
(
    /*[in]*/  const RESTYPID ResTypId,
    /*[in]*/  const RESID ResId,
    /*[in]*/  const BOOL fRequiresTransactionEnlistment,
    /*[out]*/ RESOURCERATING* pRating
)
{
    ATLTRACE(_T("Rating resource\n"));
    CRDMSMQueue * pSing = NULL;
    pSing = (CRDMSMQueue *)(*m_set.find(ResId));

    if (m_bLog) pSing->WriteLog(string("RateResource Called"));
```

(continued)

```
        if (ResTypId == pSing->GetResTypeID())
        {
            if (fRequiresTransactionEnlistment == FALSE)
            {
                *pRating = 100;
            }
            else
            {
                *pRating = 50;
            }
        }
        else *pRating = 0;
        return S_OK;
}


STDMETHODIMP CResDisp::EnlistResource
(
    /*[in]*/  const RESID ResId,
    /*[in]*/  const TRANSID TransId
)
{
    if (m_bLog)
    {
        CRDMSMQueue * pSing = NULL;
        pSing = (CRDMSMQueue *)(*m_set.find(ResId));
        char buf[100];
        _itoa(TransId, buf,   10);
        pSing->WriteLog(string("EnlistResource Called - ") +
            string(buf));
    }
    return S_OK;
}


STDMETHODIMP CResDisp::ResetResource
(
    /*[in]*/  const RESID ResId
)
{
    if (m_bLog)
    {
        CRDMSMQueue * pSing = NULL;
        pSing = (CRDMSMQueue *)(*m_set.find(ResId));
```

```
        pSing->WriteLog(string("ResetResource Called"));
    }
    return S_OK;

}

STDMETHODIMP CResDisp::DestroyResource
(
    /*[in]*/  const RESID ResId
)
{

    ATLTRACE(_T("Destroying a resource\n"));
    CRDMSMQueue * pSing = NULL;
    pSing = (CRDMSMQueue *)(*m_set.find(ResId));
    if (m_bLog) pSing->WriteLog(string("DestroyResource Called"));
    pSing->CloseQ();
    delete pSing;
    HRESULT hr = S_OK;

    m_set.erase(ResId);
    _ASSERTE(hr == S_OK);
    return hr;
}

STDMETHODIMP CResDisp::DestroyResourceS
(
    /*[in]*/  constSRESID ResId
)
{
    return E_NOTIMPL;
}

HRESULT CResDisp::FinalConstruct()
{
    HRESULT hr;

    hr = GetDispenserManager(&m_pDispMan);
    if (SUCCEEDED(hr))
    {
        IDispenserDriver * pDriver;
        hr = GetUnknown()->QueryInterface(IID_IDispenserDriver,
            (void **
```

(continued)

```
)&pDriver);
        _ASSERTE(hr == S_OK);
        hr = m_pDispMan -> RegisterDispenser(pDriver,
            L"ResDisp", &m_pHolder);
        _ASSERTE(hr == S_OK);
        //
        //      WATCH OUT HERE!!!!!!!!
        //
        // There is a bug in MTS 1.x that was found post
        // ship where the pDriver isn't properly AddRef()'d.
        // In a future version of MTS, we will have a new
        // RegisterDispenser() API (e.g. something like
        // RegisterDispenser2() that will do this correctly.
        // In the meantime, treat this as a "moved" reference,
        // and do not release the pDriver pointer! (All future
        // versions of RegisterDispenser() will behave this way for
        // backward compatibility.)

    }


    //
    // Aggregate in the free-threaded marshaler.
    // This is ABSOLUTELY CRITICAL to do in a resource dispenser!
    // If we take a thread switch because we switched apartments,
    // we will lose the object context, the resource dispenser
    // manager will think that there is no transaction,
    // and EnlistResource() will not be called.
    //
    // NOTE:    You should mark all resource dispensers as "Both" in
    // the Registry (above comments from dispimpl.cpp in MTS SDK).
    //

    hr = CoCreateFreeThreadedMarshaler(GetUnknown(),
        &m_pFreeThreadedMarshaler);
    _ASSERTE(hr == S_OK);

    return hr;
}

void CResDisp::FinalRelease()
{

    ATLTRACE(_T("\nCResDisp::FinalRelease()\n"));
    SafeRelease(m_pDispMan);
```

```
        SafeRelease(m_pHolder);
        SafeRelease(m_pFreeThreadedMarshaler);
}


HRESULT CResDisp::GetExportObject(long ResId,
      ITransaction * pTransaction, ITransactionExport **ppExport)
{
     if (m_bLog)
     {
          CRDMSMQueue * pSing = NULL;
          pSing = (CRDMSMQueue *)(*m_set.find(ResId));
          pSing->WriteLog(string("GetExportObject"));
     }
     return E_NOTIMPL;

}
```

Microsoft Cluster Server

Microsoft Cluster Server (MSCS) is a built-in feature of the Enterprise Edition of Microsoft Windows NT Server. It is one of the most exciting new software technologies and will potentially have a tremendous impact on the way we design and build Internet systems over the next couple of decades. While the first release of MSCS has limited capabilities, it lays a foundation for powerful services that will be available in the future. In this chapter, we will examine the design goals of MSCS and explore why MSCS will be used to build the next generation of highly available and scalable Internet systems. We will also examine the current architecture of MSCS, its components, and its APIs.

Why Do You Need MSCS?

A cluster is two or more systems that are connected together to operate as if they are a single system. You can use clusters to build supercomputers from commodity hardware and software modules. The commodity hardware might be simple PCs or more sophisticated symmetric multiprocessing (SMP) computers developed for Windows NT. A cluster of 16 SMP computers, each having 32 microprocessors, gives you the processing power of 512 CPUs. Cluster software makes these computers appear as a single system to users, administrators, and programmers. Cluster software can also mask component failures within the system to provide greater fault tolerance.

Clusters differ from distributed systems in that members of the cluster tend to be homogeneous, to be configured with the same software, share the same security environment, and run on the same local area network. Every node of a cluster usually has full connectivity and communication with the other nodes in the cluster. This is accomplished through one or more shared SCSI buses for storage, a private network for internal cluster communication, and a public network that can act as a backup for the private network. Typically, each node in the cluster is aware of the resources running on the other nodes and knows when another node joins or leaves the cluster.

Clusters are designed to improve the scalability and availability of systems. They are generally not used for disaster recovery purposes because they do not span across geographically dispersed locations. For example, the use of a SCSI connection limits the distance between the nodes to about 25 meters.

Scalability

You've seen throughout this book that you can build more scalable systems by distributing the system load over multiple servers. This stands to reason because you introduce additional hardware power each time you add a server. However, adding hardware is not sufficient in itself. The system can scale only if the application software is designed to take advantage of this extra hardware. Designing this kind of software can be a complex task. Suppose you want to add 100 servers to an Internet site so that the site can handle peak shopping activity on Valentine's Day. While you can certainly design software that will detect the additional hardware and be able to distribute the system load among all the servers without throttling throughput at any juncture, it isn't easy. The challenge is to do the scaling without incurring huge software development and software management costs.

Clusters eliminate many of the complexities and costs of scaling by plugging additional hardware and software into a system. We are still a long way from the goal of making this transparent to applications. MSCS today supports only two nodes; it will support 16 nodes in a later release. Microsoft Internet Information Server (IIS), Microsoft Transaction Server (MTS), Microsoft Message Queuing (MSMQ), and databases such as SQL Server also must evolve to provide more scalable, cluster-aware services to the applications they support.

COM+ will simplify the building of cluster-aware software components. It will offer cluster-wide group services, expose methods for components to join or leave a cluster, offer a new global component-specific state, and allow a fast component restart if required. While the specifics of how COM+ will be integrated with MSCS are still being worked out, the integration will likely require some kind of routing component that distributes requests to different nodes. This routing component must also be able to analyze the responsiveness of each node to balance the load effectively. Greater fault tolerance will be achieved through the integration of MSCS and MTS. When you use MTS, all system failures can be turned into transaction failures so that partial work is rolled back. A client can be totally unaware that a failure has occurred in the cluster if the MTS application restarts the transaction in the case of a failure.

Availability

Clusters improve the availability of systems. Systems generally become unavailable because they have defects or faults in their hardware or software that eventually cause errors that lead to failures. One approach to achieving greater availability is to try to eliminate faults, but this can never be completely successful. Another approach is to make the system fault tolerant. A system is fault tolerant if it can avoid failures by masking the presence of faults. Such a system has a component that can automatically assume the responsibilities of the failed component. Clusters can use transactions to gracefully handle the first failure of the component and configure the application to retry when an error occurs, ensuring that it uses a different component on the second attempt.

The fault-tolerant approach is especially good for dealing with a transient fault known as a heisenbug. A heisenbug rarely produces an error and is often related to a timing or stress condition. Heisenbugs are difficult to find during the development and testing phase of a project and usually manifest themselves only after the system has been deployed. It is not surprising that they tend to account for many of the failures in production environments.

The availability of a system is determined by its mean time to failure (MTTF) and its mean time to repair (MTTR). It is measured using the following formula:

Availability = MTTF / (MTTF+MTTR)

A cluster provides high availability by reducing a system's MTTR. When an application fails, the cluster causes a fast restart. When a node fails, the cluster passes its responsibilities to another node, which appears externally as an instant reboot of the node. (This process is known as "failing over" responsibility.) The degree of fault tolerance provided by MSCS is, therefore, determined by the speed at which the node can do this. MSCS uses a software "heartbeat" mechanism to detect whether an application or a node has failed. The frequency of the "heartbeats" determines how quickly a failure is detected and consequently affects the MTTR. This takes at least a few seconds. If the failed component is an application, MSCS tries to restart it on the current server before starting it on another server. It usually takes a minute before MSCS can bring the application back into operation. Some real-time systems cannot afford to have an application off line for that long. To achieve maximum availability, these systems require that redundant components be available for instant repair. While this architecture can be expensive, it provides a higher degree of fault tolerance than the MSCS architecture. However, MSCS is much more economical to implement because none of the components is redundant; all components can share the workload.

Protecting system state is a key element of ensuring availability. Cluster applications protect system state by saving their state to disks periodically. Other nodes must have access to these disks in order to successfully take over for the failed node. Clusters can provide this access in three ways—shared disks, mirrored disks, and the "shared nothing" approach—which are listed below:

- **Shared disks**   Every node has access to every disk. A Distributed Lock Manager (DLM) manages situations in which two nodes try to access the disk simultaneously. The disadvantage of this approach is that as you increase the number of nodes, the contention on the DLM increases, leading to a decrease in scalability.

- **Mirrored disks**   Every node has a dedicated disk, and all writes are mirrored to another disk. If a node fails, at least one other node has the required data. With this approach, however, a discrepancy between the disks might occur because the mirroring operation takes a period of time.

- **"Shared nothing"**   Every node has its own disk, which cannot be accessed by any other node. If a node fails, a software mechanism in the cluster transfers ownership of the node's disk to another node. This provides a more scalable solution than the shared disk approach because it does not require a DLM. It also provides more availability than the mirrored disk approach because there can be no discrepancy in the data. The "shared nothing" approach is also the least complicated to implement because cluster applications do not need any special disk access privileges.

The architecture of MSCS is based on the "shared nothing" model. With the exception of registry keys, MSCS does not implement any functionality to save the application's state to disk. Each cluster application must implement this itself. A database application, for example, typically uses transaction logs for this purpose.

MSCS is responsible for the persistence of its own database of cluster configuration information. It uses a quorum resource to maintain access to the database's current state. (A quorum resource either offers a means of persistent arbitration or provides physical storage that can be accessed by other nodes in the cluster.) The quorum resource is usually a SCSI disk, and the node that takes ownership of this resource is the one responsible for initially forming the cluster.

MSCS Components

MSCS uses the following components: the Cluster Service, the Cluster Network Driver, Resource Monitors, and resource DLLs.

Cluster Service

The Cluster Service is the focal point for management of the cluster. It is implemented as a Windows NT Service, and every node runs one instance of it. Its tasks are carried out by nine managers, which are listed here:

- *Checkpoint Manager* Responsible for the persistence of data from the cluster database and system registry files to the quorum resource.

- *Database Manager* Controls access to the cluster database.

- *Event Log Manager* Replicates the Windows NT event log records to all the nodes of a cluster.

- *Fail-over Manager* Transfers groups of resources from one node to another when requested by the Resource Manager.

- *Global Update Manager* Updates the cluster nodes with all changes to the cluster's state and configuration.

- *Log Manager* Writes changes to the recovery log stored on the quorum resource when any of the cluster nodes is down.

- *Membership Manager* Maintains cluster membership and provides membership information to other components in the Cluster Service.

- *Node Manager* Maintains all node and network configuration and state information and controls operation of the Cluster Network Driver.

- *Resource Manager* Manages resource dependencies and initiates transfer of cluster groups to alternate nodes by sending a fail-over request to the Fail-over Manager. For example, if IIS and SQL Server are made dependent on each other, both fail over to another node if either one fails. An administrator can use the MSCS graphical interface to configure which components are dependent on each other.

If a cluster node fails or leaves, the Cluster Service initiates a regrouping operation through the Membership Manager and the Node Manager. This takes the inactive node off line and cancels its membership in the cluster. The Fail-over Managers on the surviving nodes cooperate to redistribute any groups that were hosted by that node. MSCS also supports fail-over of "virtual servers" that simulate a Windows NT node and can represent applications, web sites, print queues, or file shares.

Cluster Network Driver

The Cluster Network Driver provides highly available communication between nodes in the cluster. In addition to providing client systems with access to cluster application services, cluster networks are required for sending heartbeats, replicated state information, cluster commands, application commands, and application data. All internal cluster communication happens via RPC—except for membership heartbeat messages, which happen via UDP. The Cluster Network Driver monitors the status of all network paths to determine which is best for routing messages. By sending out heartbeats to all the nodes in the cluster using all possible network paths, it can determine the status of nodes and network links. If a node fails to respond to a heartbeat message, the Cluster Network Driver notifies the Cluster Service for regrouping and fail-over.

Resource Monitors

A Resource Monitor is a passive intermediary between the Cluster Service and a resource DLL. It transfers requests from the Cluster Service to the appropriate resource DLL. It also transfers any notifications or events from a resource DLL to the Cluster Service. It runs in a separate process space from the Cluster Service to protect the service from any resource failures and to allow the Resource Monitor to take all of the resources and groups on the affected node off line if the service fails. While the Cluster Service starts up only one Resource Monitor by default, you should start separate ones for potentially unstable resource DLLs to minimize the effects of their failure on other resource DLLs.

Resource DLLs

A cluster resource is any component that can be managed by the cluster, moved between nodes, and hosted by only one node at a time, and that can be taken off line and brought on line. Each type of resource is controlled through a resource DLL, which implements the management and monitoring operations. MSCS includes resource DLL support for the following resource types:

■ Physical and logical disk

■ IP address and network name

■ Generic service or application

■ File share

■ Print queue

■ IIS virtual roots

■ Distributed Transaction Coordinator (DTC)

■ MSMQ

■ Time Service

MTS uses the generic application resource DLL, which provides fairly primitive capabilities. If an application process still exists, the generic application resource DLL assumes that it has not failed. It takes a resource off line by terminating its process. You can build a resource DLL for your own application using the Cluster Resource API.

A Failure Scenario

The following failure scenario shows the interaction between the MSCS components. A Resource Monitor monitors a resource DLL to see whether the resource is alive. If it detects a resource failure, it notifies the Resource Manager. The Resource Manager attempts to restart the resource. If it exceeds the resource retry limit, the Resource Manager enumerates all objects in the dependency tree of the failed resource and takes each dependent resource off line. It then notifies the Fail-over Manager that the resource dependency tree is off line and needs to fail over. The Fail-over Manager checks the fail-over window and threshold and determines whether the fail-over conditions are within fail-over constraints. If they are, it performs an arbitration to look for another owner for the resources. If it finds one, it notifies the Fail-over Manager on the other node to bring the resource dependency tree on line. If the resource dependency tree has the first node as a preferred owner, it fails back to it when the first node comes back on line.

MSCS APIs

MSCS provides the Cluster API, the Resource API, and a Cluster Administrator Extension API. We will look briefly at all three and explore how you can program MSCS.

Cluster API

The Cluster API exposes a set of interfaces to the services provided by the Cluster Service. Cluster-aware applications, cluster management applications, resource DLLs, and the Cluster Service use the Cluster API for the following tasks:

- *Network management* To provide access to information about networks that are monitored by the Cluster Service. The Cluster API has functions to open and close a connection to a network, set the network name, return the current state of a network, and enumerate the objects on the network.

- *Network interface management* To manage a network interface. The API has functions to open and close a network interface handle, return the current state of a network interface, and retrieve the name of a node's interface to a network in the cluster.

- *Cluster management* To provide access to event notification, cluster objects, and overall cluster state information. The API has functions to set the name for a cluster, set the quorum resource for a cluster, enumerate the objects in a cluster, create or remove a new resource type in a cluster, retrieve a cluster's name and version, and close a connection to a cluster.

- *Node management* To change a node's state, perform operations, and retrieve information. The API has functions to open and close a node or delete it from the cluster database, retrieve a node's identifier and its current state, and temporarily suspend or resume a node's cluster activity.

- *Group management* To provide access to each group in a cluster for modifying the group's membership or state and to retrieve information. The API has functions to open or close a cluster group, add or remove a group from a cluster, move a group and all of its resources from one node to another, take a group off line or bring it back on line, set the preferred node list for a group, enumerate the resources in a group, enumerate the nodes that are possible owners of a group, and retrieve the current state of a group.

- *Resource management* To perform operations on one or more resources. The API has functions to set the name of a resource, create a dependency relationship between two resources, add a node to the list of possible nodes that a resource can run on, move a resource from one group to another, create a resource in a cluster, remove an offline resource from a cluster, initiate a resource failure, and take a resource off line or bring it back on line.

■ *Cluster database management* To access and update the cluster database. The API has functions to create, delete, set, retrieve, open, and enumerate cluster database keys and values.

Resource API

The Resource API is a set of functions, structures, and macros that allows the Cluster Service to communicate with cluster resources. A Resource Monitor acts as an intermediary in this communication. The Cluster Service initiates its requests with the Resource Monitor, which passes them to the resource DLL. The Resource Monitor also passes back to the Cluster Service all status and event information from the resource DLL.

The Resource API entry point functions that are implemented in a resource DLL to allow a Resource Monitor to manage its resources are as follows:

■ *Arbitrate* Lets a node attempt to regain ownership of a quorum resource

■ *Close* Closes a resource

■ *IsAlive* Determines whether a resource is available for use

■ *LooksAlive* Determines whether a resource appears to be available for use

■ *Offline* Marks a resource as unavailable for use after cleanup processing is completed

■ *Online* Marks a resource as available for use

■ *Open* Opens a resource

■ *Release* Releases a quorum resource from arbitration

■ *ResourceControl* Performs an operation that applies to a resource

■ *ResourceTypeControl* Performs an operation that applies to a resource type

■ *Startup* Loads a resource's resource DLL and returns a structure containing a function table and version number

■ *Terminate* Marks a resource as unavailable for use without waiting for cleanup processing to finish

A resource DLL must in addition implement the *ResourceCallback* function to perform tasks in response to the cluster utility function *ResUtilEnumResources*.

Cluster Administrator Extension API

The Cluster Administrator Extension API is used to create an extension DLL for new resource types. This extension DLL is required so that new resources can be administered with the same consistent MSCS graphical interface as the other resources. The Cluster Service requires that if you implement a resource DLL you also implement a Cluster Administrator Extension DLL to promote this consistency. The Cluster Administrator Extension API consists of a set of COM interfaces. You can create a generic extension DLL that is complete and fully operational using an ATL AppWizard in Microsoft Visual C++.

INDEX

Ronan Sorensen

Ronan Sorensen (MCSD) is an associate technical director at Micro Modeling Associates, where he architects and develops mission-critical Internet and enterprise applications for Fortune 500 companies. As a contributing editor to the *Visual Basic Programmers Journal*, he has published many articles on coding Internet systems with Microsoft Visual C++ and Java. He is also a contributing author of *Official Microsoft Intranet Solutions* (Microsoft Press, 1997). Ronan is vice president of the Association of Windows NT Systems Professionals and is a regular speaker at software industry events, including Tech-Ed, Software Development East, Software Development West, Developers Days, National Association of Broadcasters, Visual C++ Teach, and the Windows NT Intranet Solutions Conference.

The manuscript for this book was prepared and submitted to Microsoft Press in electronic form. Text files were prepared using Microsoft Word 97. Pages were composed by Microsoft Press using Adobe PageMaker 6.5 for Windows, with text in New Baskerville and display type in Helvetica bold. Composed pages were delivered to the printer as electronic prepress files.

Cover Graphic Designer
Tim Girvin Design, Inc.

Cover Illustrator
Glenn Mitsui

Interior Graphic Artist
Michael Victor

Principal Compositors
Barb Runyan
Shanna Brown

Principal Proofreaders/Copy Editors
Devon Musgrave
Teri Kieffer

Indexer
Patti Schiendelman

Microsoft Press has titles to help everyone— from new users to seasoned developers—

Step by Step Series
Self-paced tutorials for classroom instruction or individualized study

Starts Here™ Series
Interactive instruction on CD-ROM that helps students learn by doing

Field Guide Series
Concise, task-oriented A–Z references for quick, easy answers— anywhere

Official Series
Timely books on a wide variety of Internet topics geared for advanced users

All User Training   All User Reference

Quick Course® Series
Fast, to-the-point instruction for new users

At a Glance Series
Quick visual guides for task-oriented instruction

Running Series
A comprehensive curriculum alternative to standard documentation books

start faster and go farther!

The wide selection of books and CD-ROMs published by Microsoft Press contain something for every level of user and every area of interest, from just-in-time online training tools to development tools for professional programmers. Look for them at your bookstore or computer store today!

Professional Select Editions Series
Advanced titles geared for the system administrator or technical support career path

Microsoft® Certified Professional Training
The Microsoft Official Curriculum for certification exams

Best Practices Series
Candid accounts of the new movement in software development

Microsoft Programming Series
The foundations of software development

Professional   Developers

Microsoft Press® Interactive
Integrated multimedia courseware for all levels

Strategic Technology Series
Easy-to-read overviews for decision makers

Microsoft Professional Editions
Technical information straight from the source

Solution Developer Series
Comprehensive titles for intermediate to advanced developers

Microsoft® Press

mspress.microsoft.com

MICROSOFT LICENSE AGREEMENT
(Book Companion CD)

IMPORTANT—READ CAREFULLY: This Microsoft End-User License Agreement ("EULA") is a legal agreement between you (either an individual or an entity) and Microsoft Corporation for the Microsoft product identified above, which includes computer software and may include associated media, printed materials, and "on-line" or electronic documentation ("SOFTWARE PRODUCT"). Any component included within the SOFTWARE PRODUCT that is accompanied by a separate End-User License Agreement shall be governed by such agreement and not the terms set forth below. By installing, copying, or otherwise using the SOFTWARE PRODUCT, you agree to be bound by the terms of this EULA. If you do not agree to the terms of this EULA, you are not authorized to install, copy, or otherwise use the SOFTWARE PRODUCT; you may, however, return the SOFTWARE PRODUCT, along with all printed materials and other items that form a part of the Microsoft product that includes the SOFTWARE PRODUCT, to the place you obtained them for a full refund.

SOFTWARE PRODUCT LICENSE

The SOFTWARE PRODUCT is protected by United States copyright laws and international copyright treaties, as well as other intellectual property laws and treaties. The SOFTWARE PRODUCT is licensed, not sold.

1. **GRANT OF LICENSE.** This EULA grants you the following rights:

   a. **Software Product.** You may install and use one copy of the SOFTWARE PRODUCT on a single computer. The primary user of the computer on which the SOFTWARE PRODUCT is installed may make a second copy for his or her exclusive use on a portable computer.

   b. **Storage/Network Use.** You may also store or install a copy of the SOFTWARE PRODUCT on a storage device, such as a network server, used only to install or run the SOFTWARE PRODUCT on your other computers over an internal network; however, you must acquire and dedicate a license for each separate computer on which the SOFTWARE PRODUCT is installed or run from the storage device. A license for the SOFTWARE PRODUCT may not be shared or used concurrently on different computers.

   c. **License Pak.** If you have acquired this EULA in a Microsoft License Pak, you may make the number of additional copies of the computer software portion of the SOFTWARE PRODUCT authorized on the printed copy of this EULA, and you may use each copy in the manner specified above. You are also entitled to make a corresponding number of secondary copies for portable computer use as specified above.

   d. **Sample Code.** Solely with respect to portions, if any, of the SOFTWARE PRODUCT that are identified within the SOFTWARE PRODUCT as sample code (the "SAMPLE CODE"):

   i. **Use and Modification.** Microsoft grants you the right to use and modify the source code version of the SAMPLE CODE, *provided* you comply with subsection (d)(iii) below. You may not distribute the SAMPLE CODE, or any modified version of the SAMPLE CODE, in source code form.

   ii. **Redistributable Files.** Provided you comply with subsection (d)(iii) below, Microsoft grants you a nonexclusive, royalty-free right to reproduce and distribute the object code version of the SAMPLE CODE and of any modified SAMPLE CODE, other than SAMPLE CODE (or any modified version thereof) designated as not redistributable in the Readme file that forms a part of the SOFTWARE PRODUCT (the "Non-Redistributable Sample Code"). All SAMPLE CODE other than the Non-Redistributable Sample Code is collectively referred to as the "REDISTRIBUTABLES."

   iii. **Redistribution Requirements.** If you redistribute the REDISTRIBUTABLES, you agree to: (i) distribute the REDISTRIBUTABLES in object code form only in conjunction with and as a part of your software application product; (ii) not use Microsoft's name, logo, or trademarks to market your software application product; (iii) include a valid copyright notice on your software application product; (iv) indemnify, hold harmless, and defend Microsoft from and against any claims or lawsuits, including attorney's fees, that arise or result from the use or distribution of your software application product; and (v) not permit further distribution of the REDISTRIBUTABLES by your end user. Contact Microsoft for the applicable royalties due and other licensing terms for all other uses and/or distribution of the REDISTRIBUTABLES.

2. **DESCRIPTION OF OTHER RIGHTS AND LIMITATIONS.**

   · **Limitations on Reverse Engineering, Decompilation, and Disassembly.** You may not reverse engineer, decompile, or disassemble the SOFTWARE PRODUCT, except and only to the extent that such activity is expressly permitted by applicable law notwithstanding this limitation.

   · **Separation of Components.** The SOFTWARE PRODUCT is licensed as a single product. Its component parts may not be separated for use on more than one computer.

   · **Rental.** You may not rent, lease, or lend the SOFTWARE PRODUCT.

   · **Support Services.** Microsoft may, but is not obligated to, provide you with support services related to the SOFTWARE PRODUCT ("Support Services"). Use of Support Services is governed by the Microsoft policies and programs described in the user manual, in "on-line" documentation, and/or in other Microsoft-provided materials. Any supplemental software code provided to you as part of the Support Services shall be considered part of the SOFTWARE PRODUCT and subject to the terms and conditions of this EULA. With respect to technical information you provide to Microsoft as part of the Support Services, Microsoft may use such information for its business purposes, including for product support and development. Microsoft will not utilize such technical information in a form that personally identifies you.

- **Software Transfer.** You may permanently transfer all of your rights under this EULA, provided you retain no copies, you transfer all of the SOFTWARE PRODUCT (including all component parts, the media and printed materials, any upgrades, this EULA, and, if applicable, the Certificate of Authenticity), **and** the recipient agrees to the terms of this EULA.

- **Termination.** Without prejudice to any other rights, Microsoft may terminate this EULA if you fail to comply with the terms and conditions of this EULA. In such event, you must destroy all copies of the SOFTWARE PRODUCT and all of its component parts.

3. **COPYRIGHT.** All title and copyrights in and to the SOFTWARE PRODUCT (including but not limited to any images, photographs, animations, video, audio, music, text, SAMPLE CODE, REDISTRIBUTABLES, and "applets" incorporated into the SOFTWARE PRODUCT) and any copies of the SOFTWARE PRODUCT are owned by Microsoft or its suppliers. The SOFTWARE PRODUCT is protected by copyright laws and international treaty provisions. Therefore, you must treat the SOFTWARE PRODUCT like any other copyrighted material **except** that you may install the SOFTWARE PRODUCT on a single computer provided you keep the original solely for backup or archival purposes. You may not copy the printed materials accompanying the SOFTWARE PRODUCT.

4. **U.S. GOVERNMENT RESTRICTED RIGHTS.** The SOFTWARE PRODUCT and documentation are provided with RESTRICTED RIGHTS. Use, duplication, or disclosure by the Government is subject to restrictions as set forth in subparagraph (c)(1)(ii) of the Rights in Technical Data and Computer Software clause at DFARS 252.227-7013 or subparagraphs (c)(1) and (2) of the Commercial Computer Software—Restricted Rights at 48 CFR 52.227-19, as applicable. Manufacturer is Microsoft Corporation/One Microsoft Way/Redmond, WA 98052-6399.

5. **EXPORT RESTRICTIONS.** You agree that you will not export or re-export the SOFTWARE PRODUCT, any part thereof, or any process or service that is the direct product of the SOFTWARE PRODUCT (the foregoing collectively referred to as the "Restricted Components"), to any country, person, entity, or end user subject to U.S. export restrictions. You specifically agree not to export or re-export any of the Restricted Components (i) to any country to which the U.S. has embargoed or restricted the export of goods or services, which currently include, but are not necessarily limited to, Cuba, Iran, Iraq, Libya, North Korea, Sudan, and Syria, or to any national of any such country, wherever located, who intends to transmit or transport the Restricted Components back to such country; (ii) to any end user who you know or have reason to know will utilize the Restricted Components in the design, development, or production of nuclear, chemical, or biological weapons; or (iii) to any end user who has been prohibited from participating in U.S. export transactions by any federal agency of the U.S. government. You warrant and represent that neither the BXA nor any other U.S. federal agency has suspended, revoked, or denied your export privileges.

6. **NOTE ON JAVA SUPPORT.** THE SOFTWARE PRODUCT MAY CONTAIN SUPPORT FOR PROGRAMS WRITTEN IN JAVA. JAVA TECHNOLOGY IS NOT FAULT TOLERANT AND IS NOT DESIGNED, MANUFACTURED, OR INTENDED FOR USE OR RESALE AS ON-LINE CONTROL EQUIPMENT IN HAZARDOUS ENVIRONMENTS REQUIRING FAIL-SAFE PERFORMANCE, SUCH AS IN THE OPERATION OF NUCLEAR FACILITIES, AIRCRAFT NAVIGATION OR COMMUNICATION SYSTEMS, AIR TRAFFIC CONTROL, DIRECT LIFE SUPPORT MACHINES, OR WEAPONS SYSTEMS, IN WHICH THE FAILURE OF JAVA TECHNOLOGY COULD LEAD DIRECTLY TO DEATH, PERSONAL INJURY, OR SEVERE PHYSICAL OR ENVIRONMENTAL DAMAGE.

DISCLAIMER OF WARRANTY

NO WARRANTIES OR CONDITIONS. MICROSOFT EXPRESSLY DISCLAIMS ANY WARRANTY OR CONDITION FOR THE SOFTWARE PRODUCT. THE SOFTWARE PRODUCT AND ANY RELATED DOCUMENTATION IS PROVIDED "AS IS" WITHOUT WARRANTY OR CONDITION OF ANY KIND, EITHER EXPRESS OR IMPLIED, INCLUDING, WITHOUT LIMITATION, THE IMPLIED WARRANTIES OF MERCHANTABILITY, FITNESS FOR A PARTICULAR PURPOSE, OR NONINFRINGEMENT. THE ENTIRE RISK ARISING OUT OF USE OR PERFORMANCE OF THE SOFTWARE PRODUCT REMAINS WITH YOU.

LIMITATION OF LIABILITY. TO THE MAXIMUM EXTENT PERMITTED BY APPLICABLE LAW, IN NO EVENT SHALL MICROSOFT OR ITS SUPPLIERS BE LIABLE FOR ANY SPECIAL, INCIDENTAL, INDIRECT, OR CONSEQUENTIAL DAMAGES WHATSOEVER (INCLUDING, WITHOUT LIMITATION, DAMAGES FOR LOSS OF BUSINESS PROFITS, BUSINESS INTERRUPTION, LOSS OF BUSINESS INFORMATION, OR ANY OTHER PECUNIARY LOSS) ARISING OUT OF THE USE OF OR INABILITY TO USE THE SOFTWARE PRODUCT OR THE PROVISION OF OR FAILURE TO PROVIDE SUPPORT SERVICES, EVEN IF MICROSOFT HAS BEEN ADVISED OF THE POSSIBILITY OF SUCH DAMAGES. IN ANY CASE, MICROSOFT'S ENTIRE LIABILITY UNDER ANY PROVISION OF THIS EULA SHALL BE LIMITED TO THE GREATER OF THE AMOUNT ACTUALLY PAID BY YOU FOR THE SOFTWARE PRODUCT OR US$5.00; PROVIDED, HOWEVER, IF YOU HAVE ENTERED INTO A MICROSOFT SUPPORT SERVICES AGREEMENT, MICROSOFT'S ENTIRE LIABILITY REGARDING SUPPORT SERVICES SHALL BE GOVERNED BY THE TERMS OF THAT AGREEMENT. BECAUSE SOME STATES AND JURISDICTIONS DO NOT ALLOW THE EXCLUSION OR LIMITATION OF LIABILITY, THE ABOVE LIMITATION MAY NOT APPLY TO YOU.

MISCELLANEOUS

This EULA is governed by the laws of the State of Washington USA, except and only to the extent that applicable law mandates governing law of a different jurisdiction.

Should you have any questions concerning this EULA, or if you desire to contact Microsoft for any reason, please contact the Microsoft subsidiary serving your country, or write: Microsoft Sales Information Center/One Microsoft Way/Redmond, WA 98052-6399.